DEFINING BRITISH CITIZENSHIP

CASS SERIES: BRITISH POLITICS AND SOCIETY
SERIES EDITOR: PETER CATTERALL
ISSN: 1467-1441

Social change impacts not just upon voting behaviour and party identity but also the formulation of policy. But how do social changes and political developments interact? Which shapes which? Reflecting a belief that social and political structures cannot be understood either in isolation from each other or from the historical processes which form them, this series will examine the forces that have shaped British society. Cross-disciplinary approaches will be encouraged. In the process, the series will aim to make a contribution to existing fields, such as politics, sociology and media studies, as well as opening out new and hitherto-neglected fields.

Peter Catterall (ed.), *The Making of Channel 4*

Brock Millman, *Managing Domestic Dissent in First World War Britain*

Peter Catterall, Wolfram Kaiser and Ulrike Walton-Jordan (eds), *Reforming the Constitution: Debates in Twentieth-Century Britain*

Brock Millman, *Pessimism and British War Policy, 1916–1918*

Adrian Smith and Dilwyn Porter (eds), *Amateurs and Professionals in Post-war British Sport*

Archie Hunter, *A Life of Sir John Eldon Gorst: Disraeli's Awkward Disciple*

Harry Defries, *Conservative Party Attitudes to Jews, 1900–1950*

Virginia Berridge and Stuart Blume (eds), *Poor Health: Social Inequality before and after the Black Report*

Stuart Ball and Ian Holliday (eds), *Mass Conservatism: The Conservatives and the Public since the 1880s*

Rieko Karatani, *Defining British Citizenship: Empire, Commonwealth and Modern Britain*

Defining British Citizenship

Empire, Commonwealth and Modern Britain

RIEKO KARATANI

Kyushu University, Japan

Foreword by
Guy S. Goodwin-Gill

FRANK CASS
LONDON • PORTLAND, OR

First published in 2003 in Great Britain by
FRANK CASS PUBLISHERS
Crown House, 47 Chase Side
London N14 5BP

and in the United States of America by
FRANK CASS PUBLISHERS
c/o ISBS, 5824 N.E. Hassalo Street
Portland, Oregon, 97213-3644

Website: www.frankcass.com

British Library Cataloguing in Publication Data
Karatani, Rieko
   Defining British citizenship: empire, commonwealth
   and modern Britain. – (Cass series. British politics
   and society)
   1. Citizenship – Great Britain – History 2. Citizenship
   – Government policy – Great Britain 3. Great
   Britain – Emigration and immigration – Government
   policy – History
   I. Title
   323.6'0941

            ISBN 0-7146-5336-5 (cloth)
            ISBN 0-7146-8298-5 (paper)
            ISSN 1467-1441

Library of Congress Cataloging-in-Publication Data
Karatani, Rieko, 1966–
Defining British citizenship: empire, commonwealth,
and modern Britain / Rieko Karatani.
   p. cm. – (Cass series–British politics and society,
ISSN 1467-1441)
Includes bibliographical references and index.
ISBN 0-7146-5336-5 (cloth)
   1. Citizenship–Great Britain. 2. Emigration and
immigration law–Great Britain. I.
Title. II. Series.
KD4050 .K37 2002
342.41'083–dc21   2002026783

Typeset in 10.5/12.5 Zapf Calligraphic by Frank Cass Publishers Ltd.
Printed in Great Britain by MPG Books Ltd, Victoria Square, Bodmin, Cornwall

Contents

Foreword

Everyone has the right to a nationality, but which one? And what does it mean, in terms of rights and duties, expectations and responsibilities, to *be* the citizen of a State? Even identifying those who are formally members of a particular political community at a particular time and place is rarely as easy as some lawyers and ideologues would like to believe. 'Nationality' is not an absolute, but often relative; not merely a legal tag, but also a factual condition, a matter of social attachment, sentiments, interests and intent.

Given Britain's history of engagements across the globe and the natural persistence of the resulting bonds of culture, language and blood, it is hardly surprising that the concepts of nationality, citizenship of the United Kingdom and Colonies, and British subject, among others, have proved troublesome and complex. For those steeped in the simplicity of a single, simple citizen–State relationship, the manner in which the British Crown and Parliament treated their peoples must have appeared strange, at times even devious and divisive, particularly over the last 40 years or so, when debate and legislation were often driven by crude immigration control arguments and racial considerations.

That was only ever part of the picture, however, and on closer examination the 'truth' of the case proves to be rather more multifaceted – a mix, indeed, of laudable aspects, historical ideals, half-remembered principles, post-colonial debts (not always honoured), and those regrettable tendencies. Dr Karatani's book throws light on that truth, bringing into the open much that had been hidden and much else that was conveniently ignored for the sake of ideological assumptions of one colour or another.

As she points out, the origins of what we are finally beginning to recognize as 'British citizenship' lie not in an idealized conception of the citizen–State relationship, so much as in the essentially personal link between subject and sovereign – the bonds of loyalty and allegiance. It was these bonds, among others, which allowed the

British Empire to include, without regard to place or race, disparate peoples living in territories separated by thousands of miles. The Crown was indivisible and all its subjects 'enjoyed' a common status, so went the theory, and benefited from the protection of the sovereign. This common status (not equality as such, of course) characterized the nineteenth-century British sense of empire, extending even into the mid-twentieth century, so that it could be proclaimed in 1948 and after, without hesitation or doubt, that British subject and Commonwealth citizen had the same meaning.

The reality of a common bond and a common status, with the Crown at the centre, reached its ideological zenith in Victorian times. Like the Crown itself, though, it came to be tested as the self-governing Dominions began to assert their autonomy, and as Australia, Canada and South Africa laid down racially determined immigration laws which included no exceptions for 'fellow' British subjects.

At home, it seems that the British were never very good at institutionalizing citizenship; hence, today's debate about civics and classes in what it is to be British. We seem never to have had much time for 'national days', though more inclined to celebrate (rather for ourselves, perhaps), the sovereign's occasions, such as birth, marriage, accession, death and jubilees.

Perhaps it is not surprising, therefore, that the United Kingdom held out longest against radical change, against the reduction of an imperial and inclusive British subjecthood, and against the fragmentation into mutually exclusive nationalities which accompanied the Crown's increasing divisibility and the Empire's evolution into Commonwealth. Dr Karatani shows how this came about, and how the mixture of ideals, ideology, historical baggage and a felt need, in particular, for control over new Commonwealth immigration combined to produce increasingly complicated relationships among those who, in some way, enjoyed the Crown's protection. She shows, too, the extent to which the debate over immigration policy became a determinant of who 'belongs' to the United Kingdom, whereas most countries take the *a priori* label of citizenship to distinguish between 'them' and 'us'.

To understand British citizenship today requires not just a knowledge of the law, but a sense of history and a feel for the facts. As Dr Karatani shows, this has been a long and often painful process for successive British governments, and a source of understandable confusion for the public. Her work brings those necessary perspectives forward; it provides the reader with an essential corrective to many past assumptions and a solid foundation for present and future debate. For certainly the evolutionary process of British citizenship is far from complete. Some may think it an historically grounded essay working its way slowly towards a final chapter; more likely, there are several sequels to come.

Guy S. Goodwin-Gill
All Souls College, Oxford
September 2002

Series Editor's Preface

All countries in western Europe experienced to varying degrees large-scale immigration after 1945. This was, perhaps, not expected by policy-makers. One facet of population movement, governed by the 1951 UN Convention on Refugees, the seeking of asylum, was certainly not expected to be a problem prolonged after the war. However, immigrants arrived in other ways, not least as outside labour was attracted to work in the booming economies of Western Europe in the 1950s. In a number of instances this process was assisted by deliberate government policy.

Britain also experienced mass immigration in this period, swelling a 'coloured' population estimated at no more than 20–30,000 in 1950. The handling of this process, however, differed in significant ways from elsewhere in Europe. Firstly, with the scrapping in the 1950s of the wartime identity cards, Britain lacked internal controls on its population. Secondly, as is expertly demonstrated in this study, British immigration policy had a very different history. The great value of this book is that, by adopting an entirely different angle of approach, it provides a new way of understanding the unique history of British immigration and citizenship.

Britain had not developed by the twentieth century a national citizenship, with naturalization procedures defining who 'belonged' to Britain and what this meant. Instead, 'belonging' was simply a function of subjecthood, of being born within the allegiance of the Crown. The lack of definition attached to this status was, if anything, seen as a positive good, as one of the few elements common to a somewhat disparate collection of territories loosely held together. Indeed, the idea of a common citizenship derived in this way across the Empire-Commonwealth remained important to British policy-makers into the post-war era, as the 1948 British Nationality Act showed, even though the desire of different parts of that Empire-Commonwealth to enact local citizenship laws was making the practice of this status more variegated. For instance, trade union concerns about immigration from India were met in 1958 by government protests of reluctance to depart from a 'traditional readiness to receive citizens of British status'. Controls on such arrivals were not to be introduced until the 1962 Commonwealth Immigration Act.

The 1962 Act and subsequent legislation did not end the peculiarities of British citizenship law. As Rieko Karatani demonstrates here, Commonwealth citizenship survived. Policy-makers did not choose tightly to define either citizenship, or those who 'belonged' to Britain. Instead, they adopted the politically more expedient line of simply tightening up on who could enter the United Kingdom in order to exercise it. The result was that the different types of citizenship defined here were enjoyed by different groups of people.

Much of the existing literature on this subject has concentrated on the apparent racial orientation of the gradual tightening of immigration controls. It is difficult to deny that there was at least an element of this in the process, for instance in the way the supposedly neutral quotas introduced in 1962 in effect favoured the Old Commonwealth countries. But to concentrate on this element, as is demonstrated by Karatani, is to miss the way in which the policy was also shaped by its historic roots. Insofar as the policy had racist intentions in terms of which groups it was meant to exclude, those intentions were framed to fit existing, historic understandings of Commonwealth citizenship; indeed, that is why the relatively easy and limited target of immigration was addressed. It is also to miss the extent to which access to citizenship was thus controlled by external, rather than internal means, in contrast with certain other countries in western Europe.

The progressive tightening of immigration control in post-war Britain can therefore be characterized as tinkering with the meaning of 'British citizenship', whilst trying to avoid overall redesign of the architecture. This is certainly much in keeping with theories of the incrementalist nature of the British state. And even though concepts such as 'patriality' came to play an increasing role in the legislation this did not, as Karatani shows, amount to a definition of an exclusive British citizenship.

What tightening of immigration controls, both in Britain and more generally across the West, did achieve, however, was a change in the nature of immigration. Refugees, whatever the expectations of post-war policy-makers, did not disappear. Meanwhile, the numbers displaced by political violence or civil war were swollen by those for whom economic factors were perhaps as important. Unable to enter under immigration procedures, the protection of the 1951 Convention was invoked instead by a growing number of 'asylum seekers' in the

1990s. Having tried somewhat ineffectively to discourage such arrivals, in 2002 the British government changed tack and suggested instead a loosening of institutionalized immigration controls with, as a *quid pro quo*, the introduction of formal citizenship training and ceremonies, and some form of internal controls. Immigration controls may thus have enabled the British to retain Commonwealth citizenship whilst tightening entry procedures. But, ironically, the perceived over-efficiency of those controls led policy-makers at the start of the twenty-first century to do what their predecessors had studiously avoided for the previous 50 years – not least because of a continuing attachment to the historical inheritance delineated here – and try to introduce a formal British citizenship.

Peter Catterall
London, February 2002

Acknowledgements

This book is based on my doctoral thesis, which was submitted to Oxford University in 1999. I should like to thank all those who have supported my efforts. My deepest gratitude goes to my supervisors, Dr John Darwin and Dr Andrew Shacknove at Oxford University, and Dr Erica Benner, now at the London School of Economics. All of them gave me much-needed encouragement and invaluable advice, and guided me through countless difficult moments. I am also indebted to my examiners, Dr Martin Ceadel of New College, Oxford, and Professor Robert Holland of the Institute of Commonwealth Studies, University of London, for their excellent comments and suggestions. Professor Rosemary Foot and Professor Adam Roberts in Oxford and Professor Ryuhei Hatsuse and Professor Mitsuo Ogura in Japan have been sources of endless support. During the final stage of writing this book, I have been working in the friendly environment of Kyushu University and am very grateful to all my colleagues there. I have benefited from the advice and expertise of numerous scholars working in areas relevant to my own research but, of course, the responsibility for any errors is mine alone.

In the course of my research I have relied on primary sources from many libraries and archives. I offer thanks to the British Library, the Bodleian Library, the Conservative Party Archives, the Home Office Library, the Labour Party Archives, and the Public Record Office in Kew. Financially, I am grateful to the Swire Centenary Scholarship. Its generous fund made my doctoral study in Oxford possible. My thanks also to an anonymous reader for Frank Cass for his meticulous comments, and to Andrew Humphrys, my editor, for patiently dealing with my long-distance queries from Japan.

I have met many good friends, who helped me bear the burden of my work and generously spared time for me. I owe a great deal to them all. In particular, I should like to thank David Hall-Matthews, Hartmut Mayer and Kayoko Nohara for listening to my never-ending complaints and making me laugh whenever I needed to. A special thanks must go to Shereen Karmali for reading all the drafts and correcting my English.

Sections of Chapters 4 and 5 appeared previously in 'The Making of Commonwealth Citizenship: Britain and the Post-war Commonwealth, 1945–1949', *Journal of International Studies*, 45 (2000), pp. 1–24, and 'The Commonwealth Immigrants Act 1962: the Politics of Membership and the Labour Market', *Journal of International Studies*, 38 (1996), pp. 1–28. I am very much obliged to the publisher of that journal for permission to reproduce these extracts.

Finally, my greatest debt is to my parents, who supported my efforts from start to finish. This book is for my late sister, Yuko. I wish she could have seen it completed.

Abbreviations

AA 1905	Aliens Act 1905
ARA 1914	Aliens Restriction Act 1914
ARA 1919	Aliens Restriction (Amendment) Act 1919
BDTC	British Dependent Territories Citizen
BNA 1948	British Nationality Act 1948
BNA 1964	British Nationality Act 1964
BNA 1981	British Nationality Act 1981
BN & SA act 1914	British Nationality and Status of Aliens Act 1914
BN & SA act 1918	British Nationality and Status of Aliens Act 1918
BN & SA act 1922	British Nationality and Status of Aliens Act 1922
BN & SA act 1943	British Nationality and Status of Aliens Act 1943
BN(O)	British National (Overseas)
BOC	British Overseas Citizen
BPP	British Protected Person
BS	British Subject (in the terms of the BNA 1981)
BSWC	British Subject without Citizenship
CCA 1946	Canadian Citizenship Act 1946
CIA 1910	Canadian Immigration Act 1910
CIA 1962	Commonwealth Immigrants Act 1962
CIA 1968	Commonwealth Immigrants Act 1968
CNA 1921	Canadian Nationals Act 1921
CPA	Conservative Party Archives
CUKC	Citizen of the UK and Colonies
EC	European Community
EU	European Union
EVW	European Volunteer Worker
IA 1971	Immigration Act 1971
IN & CA 1934	Irish Nationality and Citizenship Act 1935
LPA	Labour Party Archives
NCW	New Commonwealth
OCW	Old Commonwealth
PCIJ	Permanent Court of International Justice

PRO	Public Record Office
UN	United Nations
UNFA 1927	Union Nationality and Flags Act 1927

Introduction

'To understand constitutions (or polities), we must inquire into the nature of the state [*polis*]; and to understand that – since the state is a body of citizens [*politai*] – we must examine the nature of citizenship.' (Aristotle)[1]

CENTRAL QUESTIONS AND THE ARGUMENT PUT FORWARD

THE STATUTE book did not contain the term 'British citizenship' until 1981.[2] Before then, there were Citizens of the United Kingdom and Colonies (CUKC), British subjects without citizenship (BSWC), and citizens of Commonwealth countries, all of whom were also known as Commonwealth citizens, but there were no British citizens.[3] Citizenship rights and obligations have historically been granted to all the holders of British subjecthood (later, Commonwealth citizens), whether they were born in London or Kingston, Jamaica.[4] In 1977 the Labour government led by James Callaghan issued a Green Paper in which it admitted that a review of Britain's citizenship policies was long overdue. In describing the aims of the proposed new nationality bill, it said that 'Britain [was] no longer an Imperial power' and that 'the all-embracing concept of nationality with this role' had to be replaced by 'a more meaningful citizenship for those who had close links with the United Kingdom'.[5] Even after the creation of British citizenship by the British Nationality Act 1981 (BNA 1981), the most recent piece of major legislation on citizenship, which replaced the BNA 1948, the right of entry to and abode in the United Kingdom is the only citizenship right that is specifically attached to the status of British citizenship.[6]

Unlike other Western democratic countries, Britain has never completely established a national citizenship, that is, a citizenship based on nationhood, with rights and obligations granted only to its holders. The conception of the nation-state in Europe was closely linked with the historical process of confining citizenship to the territorial-based national unit.[7] It follows in theory that three aspects of citizenship – as a status, a set of rights and obligations, and an identity – which are described in this book as the nominal, the substantive and the functional aspects respectively, complement each other and merge into a national type of citizenship.[8] Under the banner of the principle of national self-determination widely proclaimed since the Second World War, the governments of newly independent countries as well as the former imperial powers claim today, or try to claim, that their citizens are legal as well as national members of a state who are guaranteed full access to rights and duties within its territory.[9] Nonetheless, no government can in reality provide citizenship which completely corresponds with the concept of national citizenship. Moreover, the anomalous cases of national citizenship, such as long-term foreign residents who do not wish to be naturalized in the country of residence (denizens),[10] are increasing in western Europe and North America. Since the 1992 Maastricht treaty established European citizenship, there has also been a heated debate on whether it will eventually replace national citizenship in the EU member states.[11] Some scholars are even exploring a new citizenship model called 'transnational citizenship', trying to find a way to extend citizenship rights to non-citizens or beyond the territorial borders of the state.[12]

In the face of these challenges to national citizenship, there has been a further explosion of interest among academics and politicians in the meaning and role of citizenship. In this context, this book examines two questions which previous research has either taken for granted, or stopped short of answering.[13] Why did it take the British government more than three decades to institute British citizenship by legislation when it had admitted as early as 1949 that Commonwealth citizenship was 'a little more than a fiction'?[14] What were the role and the meaning of immigration and nationality laws in the meantime?

My inquiry into these questions aims to fill a gap in the understanding of the institutional definition and the development of British citizenship. The dominant view in the field concludes that Britain's 'formal membership'[15] and its sense of national identity ('Britishness')[16] are two separate issues, and thus does not pay enough attention to the reciprocal link between the two. Existing work on citizenship in Britain has pointed to the absence of British citizenship from the history of British nationality law, claiming that the institutional definitions of formal membership reveal neither who 'belongs', nor what it means to 'belong', to Britain.[17] One scholar, for example, has stated on the basis of the atypical usages of citizenship in

British legislation that 'there is no such thing [as British citizenship] – not, at least, as citizenship is understood in other countries'.[18] Scholars in the field regard the British case as one of a kind.[19] They have therefore dismissed the analysis of citizenship and its related legislation as 'fruitless' and 'limited'.[20] Yet, given that the definition of Britain's formal membership by law and regulation and that of Britishness by identity and common feelings existed, we need not conclude that each of them developed in a totally isolated context.

This study seeks to analyse the complexities of immigration and citizenship laws in order to understand the meaning and role of citizenship in Britain. It stresses that the unique usage of citizenship in Britain shows the complex relationship which has been developed in Britain between a political unit and its formal membership. After all, citizenship, in combination with immigration laws, constitutes the official expression of who is deemed to be a legitimate member of the political unit and on what terms, and thus offers valuable insight into the thinking of the policy-makers of the time about the political unit and the organization of its population. Citizenship legislation not only creates a legal bond between an individual and a political unit, but, in so doing, regulates the nature of a political unit as an association of citizens. By dismissing citizenship and the related legislation as altogether irrelevant, therefore, existing works have omitted from analysis the following two points. First, Britain as a political unit grew into a 'global institution',[21] whether it was called the British Empire, or the British Commonwealth, or just the Common-wealth, and its formal membership was granted to ethno-linguistically diverse peoples.[22] Second, in consequence, the definition of Britishness (what it means to 'belong' to Britain) could not be the basis of that of its formal membership (who 'belongs' to Britain), but should remain unspecified. The institutional definition of the formal membership could thus be altered in accordance with the constitutional arrangement between the component political units of the global institution.

In other words, this book argues that the 'fuzzy', 'vague' and 'malleable' nature of Britishness, which existing works have also found, resulted from the way in which successive British governments extended the status of Britain's formal membership in order to accept a new group of people in the process of forming the *United* Kingdom and later, the Empire. First, the formal membership came to include 'the Irish, Scottish, Welsh and English, as well as a number of smaller [sub-groups], the Channel Islanders, Manxmen, and Ulster Orange-men'.[23] Second, during Britain's imperial period, British subjects throughout the British Empire were united as 'men bound, not to one another, but to a common superior'.[24] Without a written constitution, the imperial government emphasized the unity of the Empire on the grounds that everybody shared the same title of 'British subject'. Given that Britain's formal membership had to be inclusive of ethno-linguistically diverse peoples in the British Empire, Britishness had to be detached from the institutions of citizenship.[25] Even after the Second World War, when national citizenship became prevalent, the framework of Commonwealth citizenship was maintained. It was thus only through immigration control, whose purpose was to denote who 'belonged' to Britain, that Britishness was gradually taking shape in the 1960s and 1970s. Unlike other developed countries, the dichotomy between citizens and non-citizens, created by immigration and nationality law, was slow to develop in Britain.[26]

In summary, this book clarifies the following three points. First, Britain was not the insulated centre of the Empire and later the Commonwealth, but was the dynamic hub which was interconnected with the rest of the global institution. My account of the institutional definition and development of British citizenship therefore explores the impact of the dynamism within the global institution, focusing on its legislation, regulations and administrative methods. In existing research Britain's post-Second World War immigration policy is studied from the perspective of domestic politics and history or legislation. Previous works asked why immigration restrictions during that period were enacted in such a way as to prevent 'coloured' New Commonwealth (NCW)[27] immigrants from entering Britain.[28] Instead of blaming public attitudes or government intention, a recently published work argues that 'a timid judiciary and an absence of a bill of rights' were the real source of restrictive migration policy in post-war Britain.[29] Taking these works into account, this book tries to shed a different light, drawing from the study of the British Empire and decolonization. It then stresses that Britain's formal membership has always been granted in such a way as to encompass inhabitants of the global institution, that is, the British Empire and the Commonwealth. Significant as this has been with regard to the development and the role of citizenship in Britain, it has barely been explored by previous works, which simply accepted it.[30] Nonetheless, the vast amount of legislative ingenuity and administrative efforts needed to devise and maintain such complex citizenship and immigration rules was simply unnecessary, provided that Britain could ignore the rest of the global institution.

Second, this book also claims the fundamental continuity of Britain's immigration and citizenship policies, both before and after the Second World War. The common elements were an inclusive citizenship policy for the unity of the global institution and an exclusive immigration policy for determining who 'belonged' to each constituent unit of the global institution.

Finally, this book demonstrates that the British government has always tried to maintain an alternative type of citizenship (such as British subjecthood and Commonwealth citizenship) which was conferred upon ethno-linguistically diverse peoples in the global institution. The national citizenship of each colony and of Britain developed through immigration control and alongside British subjecthood and later Commonwealth citizenship. As a result, the British government's efforts to maintain a citizenship structure enabled multiple citizenships to co-exist, leading to the changing meaning and role of citizenship and immigration laws in Britain. The construction of its national citizenship after the Second World War had to wait until 1981, and even today has not been completed.[31]

THE SCOPE OF THIS STUDY

In order to answer the central questions – the reasons for the long delay in attempting to create national citizenship and the role and meaning of immigration and citizenship laws in the meantime – this book extends the arena of debate to cover the British Empire and the Commonwealth instead of concentrating only on Britain. In so doing, it studies the various types of citizenship and citizenship structure which existed in the Empire and continue to exist in the Commonwealth, and Britain's national citizenship in the making. It then attempts to examine the way in which the concepts of Britain's formal membership were defined in response to the need to build and maintain the global institution which consisted of a number of political units with ethnically and linguistically diverse peoples.

Neither British subjecthood nor Commonwealth citizenship – Britain's formal membership in the past – corresponded with the national type of citizenship.[32] Historically, it sometimes happens that two or more political units form a single combined political unit and confer a formal membership on the peoples who live within the boundaries of that combined unit. National citizenship became widespread only after the Second World War, whereas the alternative types of citizenship were prevalent for a much longer period. Alternative types of citizenship, such as British subjecthood, are different from the national type in that they allow their citizens to hold multiple citizenships at the same time. This research introduces the perspective of alternative types of citizenship, and examines the parallel development of national citizenship in the 'Dominions'[33] and in Britain alongside the existing alternative types of citizenship (British subjecthood and, later, Commonwealth citizenship).

My discussion of the global institution is especially relevant in analysing the development of citizenship in Britain, considering the way in which citizenship rights and obligations have been allocated. As will be discussed in the following chapters, the holding of nominal citizenship meant little to the residents of the British Isles (as opposed to those in overseas territories) prior to the twentieth century, except in terms of a few rights such as owning and inheriting land, but only a handful of the privileged could actually enjoy those rights.[34] In contrast, the residents of Britain's overseas territories tried to claim citizenship rights such as that of political representation, which was of concern to everyone, at the same level as those in Britain, on the basis of their holding British subjecthood. As a result, the debates on citizenship in Britain were influenced by social and political events in Britain's overseas territories, possibly more so before the twentieth century, and thus have to be examined in the context of its global institution.

The period of this research goes back to before the twentieth century in order to cover crucial debates in the eighteenth and the nineteenth centuries over the concept of allegiance and the systems of colonial naturalization. It was these debates, which took place in the process of Britain's growing into a global institution, that led to the recommendation for the imperial law of nationality and naturalization in 1901, and later, a statute in 1914.[35] The basis of British subjecthood thereafter was thus formed during those periods. Scholars generally blame Britain's imperial past for the muddled use of nationality and immigration laws. Existing literature, therefore, merely touches upon the 'imperial past' as background information on immigration policy during the post-Second World War period.

This book, in contrast, attempts to analyse the citizenship structure within the British Empire in order to understand how it was transformed from one based on British subjecthood to one based on Commonwealth citizenship. In so doing, it examines the process by which the embryonic form of national citizenship in Britain emerged alongside Commonwealth citizenship, like that of the Dominions, in the shape of immigration control. In other words, in the case of Britain, citizenship legislation was used as a mechanism for including various groups of peoples in a single formal membership of the Empire. Under the framework of British subjecthood, it was immigration control in the Dominions prior to the Second World War that defined who 'belonged' to each of them. Post-war governments in Britain inherited this practice of keeping immigration laws exclusive and citizenship laws inclusive in order both to maintain Commonwealth citizenship and to denote who 'belonged' to Britain.

Finally, my study aims to contribute to a growing body of literature which deals with the state's role in determining who belongs to it and how its definitions come into being and change over time.[36] My work first offers to this debate a detailed historical analysis of the way Britain's formal membership has been defined. In doing so, it challenges the dominant understanding of citizenship, that is, the national type of citizenship, and demonstrates the ways in which a combined political unit which is composed of several political units, such as the British Empire and the Commonwealth, determines its formal membership. Second, unlike the existing research on alternative citizenship, which has concentrated on European citizenship, this study expands the scope of the research to the historical cases of British subjecthood and Commonwealth citizenship.

SOURCES AND THE RANGE OF THE STUDY

This study relies heavily on archival materials, especially cabinet papers, official documents from the relevant ministries, inter-departmental committee papers and parliamentary debates. For the period when, owing to the 30-year rule, primary materials are not available, other sources such as secondary literature and the Conservative and Labour party archives are used extensively.

The main empirical focus is on the period up to 1971 when the Immigration Act 1971 was enacted. A substantial part of this book also covers the formative period of British subjecthood, examining issues such as the *antenati* and *postnati* of settlers in the North American colonies after independence, and colonial naturalization. These events, which took place before the twentieth century, culminated in the recommendation by an inter-departmental committee appointed by the Home Secretary in 1901 that the system of imperial naturalization and nationality be clarified. The 1901 recommendations led to the creation of the common code system in 1914, whereby Dominion and British governments adopted identical citizenship legislation. On the basis of the common code system, Commonwealth citizenship and its citizenship structure were established after the Second World War.

The reasons for dealing with the BNA 1981 in the epilogue are several. First, there is no access to public records after 1971, and thus the analysis of the BNA 1981 cannot be as exhaustive as that of the previous periods. Second, and more importantly, the BNA 1981 implies that British citizenship under the act was in line with the Immigration Act 1971 (IA 1971).[37] Under the IA 1971, immigration control for Commonwealth citizens was integrated with that for aliens into a single system. Since then, from the perspective of immigration control in Britain, Commonwealth citizens and aliens have been treated in the same legal framework. After the IA 1971, furthermore, primary immigration to Britain became virtually impossible, so that the focus of immigration control in the 1970s shifted to dependants and spouses. Additionally, domestic manoeuvres within, and among, political parties, rather than those in the global institution, played a much bigger role in determining the intention and contents of the BNA 1981 than the previous legislation in the field. In contrast with the other chapters, therefore, it is appropriate for my research in the epilogue to focus on party archives. The epilogue also concentrates on the nature of the British citizenship created by the BNA 1981 in the light of the creation of national citizenship in Britain, and what its creation entailed with regard to the subsequent debate on Britishness.

The main purpose of this book is to analyse the changes in the role and meaning of citizenship in Britain and to examine national citizenship in the making in the context of building and maintaining the British Empire and the Commonwealth. It does not therefore cover, except where necessary, such issues as domestic party politics and the economy, the effects of Britain's economic decline after the Second World War, the influence of Enoch Powell on Conservative policy on race and immigration, or Labour's bipartisan policy on immigration in the 1960s.[38] These issues are widely covered in the existing literature. Instead, it is hoped that this book will add another angle to our understanding of the history of citizenship and its development in Britain.

THE STRUCTURE OF THE BOOK

The structure of this study is as follows:

Chapter 1 prepares the ground for the historical analysis of the following chapters. It starts by summarizing the concept of citizenship and presenting an account of the development of national citizenship and the contemporary debate on it. Next, it explores the three alternative types of non-national citizenship which enable a citizenship structure with multiple citizenships to be formed. Finally, it discusses Britain's experience with national citizenship and alternative types of citizenship – British subjecthood and Commonwealth citizenship – and citizenship structures.

Chapter 2 shows how the simple principle of allegiance in return for protection was extended to include various groups of peoples with different cultural and historical backgrounds in accordance with the overseas expansion of the British Empire. It also examines the practice of colonial naturalization and immigration control in the colonies to see the initial stages of the development of their national citizenships.

In Chapter 3, the focus is the construction of the common code system by both the British and Dominion governments before the First World War, and its maintenance by consultation during the inter-war period. It is suggested that the common code system prepared the way for Commonwealth citizenship after the Second World War, and that the emotional bonds between British descendants in the Dominions and the British public became stronger with the common code system, setting the non self-governing colonies further apart from the Dominions.

Chapters 4 and 5 analyse the way in which the Commonwealth citizenship structure with its multiple citizenships was formed and maintained in the era of national citizenship after the Second World War. The focus of Chapter 4 is the construction of Commonwealth citizenship – the composite type of alternative citizenship – on the basis of British subjecthood. In the absence of an understanding of national citizenship, the government of Harold Macmillan in 1962 took the substantive aspects of citizenship away from NCW citizens, but kept the nominal aspect of Commonwealth citizenship intact, thereby maintaining the citizenship structure itself.

In Chapter 5, the focus shifts to the embryonic form of national citizenship which emerged through the imposition of immigration control on the NCW citizens, but still within the framework of Commonwealth citizenship. The chapter follows the process of separating by means of successive immigration acts in 1962, 1968 and 1971 those citizens with nominal citizenship from those with substantive citizenship. When the British government finally decided to create British citizenship in the 1970s, its basis had already been prepared by immigration acts in the 1960s. This was the unintentional, but probably welcome, outcome for most advocates of immigration control in the 1960s.

Finally, British subjecthood might sound dated, as do all the other things which are linked with imperialism. Until very recently

Commonwealth citizenship and its citizenship structure seemed to be forgotten by politicians as well as the public. After the hand-over of Hong Kong in 1997, however, the then Foreign Secretary, Robin Cook, proposed in the following year that residents in the remaining dependent territories (later renamed overseas territories) should be granted full British citizenship.[39] The bill was subsequently introduced and enacted as the British Overseas Territories Act 2002. These moves by the government were intended 'at last [to] lay the Empire to rest', and British subjecthood and Commonwealth citizenship thus now receive little scholarly attention.[40] Nonetheless, as the Epilogue finds, national citizenship is still in the making in Britain even after the enactment of the BNA 1981 with its creation of British citizenship.

In conclusion, the arguments on the alternative types of citizenship which existed in British history are summarized, and on that basis some reflections are offered in the context of the contemporary debate on British citizenship.

NOTES

1. Aristotle, 'The Theory of Citizenship and Constitutions', in *The Politics of Aristotle*, trans. Ernest Barker (Clarendon Press, Oxford, 1948), p. 92.
2. This study defines three aspects of citizenship: nominal, substantive and functional. Nominal citizenship denotes formal membership of a political unit, substantive citizenship consists of citizenship rights and obligations, and the functional aspect of citizenship divides those who are citizens from those who are not. The history and concept of citizenship is discussed in detail in Chapter 1.
3. Rather than creating British citizenship, the British Nationality Act 1948 (BNA 1948) sub-divided British subjects into CUKC and BSWC and citizens of Commonwealth countries. It also officially acknowledged the status of 'British Protected Person' (BPP) and introduced the term 'Commonwealth citizen' as an alternative to 'British subject'. BSWC was created as a transitional status for British subjects of those colonies which were expected to become independent after the enactment of the BNA 1948. This category was therefore expected eventually to disappear, as each newly independent country enacted citizenship laws of its own and conferred citizenship on the BSWC in its territory. The status of BPP was granted to a small group of people who were born in or had a connection with a protectorate, protected state or trust territory. Technically, they fall between subjects and aliens. The BNA 1948 is discussed in detail in Chapter 4.
4. Because the rules and rationale of granting British subjecthood and Commonwealth citizenship are totally different, this book uses the term 'British subject' when discussing the period prior to 1948, and 'Commonwealth citizen' after 1948.
5. *British Nationality Law: Discussion of Possible Changes*, Cmnd. 6795, HMSO, April 1977, pp. 4, 10. Following the recommendations made in the 1977 Green Paper, the Conservative government in 1981 prepared the British Nationality Bill, which later became the British Nationality Act 1981 (BNA 1981).
6. See Appendix IV for details. Details of the BNA 1981 are dealt with in the Epilogue. The Institute for Citizenship Studies, which had pursued a study of the legal rights

and duties of British citizens, concluded in 1998 that 'status [of British citizenship] is not, formally at any rate, necessary for either enjoyment or imposition of most of those rights and duties': J. P. Gardner (ed.), *Citizenship: The White Paper* (British Institute of International and Comparative Law, London, 1998), p. 184.

7. See Reinhard Bendix, *Nation-Building and Citizenship: Studies of Our Changing Social Order* (University of California Press, Berkeley, 1977 [1964]).

8. See Appendix II.

9. The principle of national self-determination is discussed in Chapter 4.

10. Hammar referred to those long-term residents as 'denizens': Tomas Hammar, *Democracy and the Nation State: Aliens, Denizens and Citizens in a World of International Migration* (Avebury, Aldershot, 1990), pp. 12–15.

11. For debates on the development of European citizenship, see, for example, Elizabeth Meehan, *Citizenship and the European Community* (Sage, London, 1993); Jens Magleby Sørensen, *The Exclusive European Citizenship: The Case for Refugees and Immigrants in the European Union* (Avebury, Aldershot, 1996).

12. For example, see Yasemin Nuhoğlu Soysal, *Limits of Citizenship: Migrants and Postnational Membership in Europe* (University of Chicago Press, Chicago and London, 1994). Rainer Bauböck, *Transnational Citizenship: Membership and Rights in International Migration* (Edward Elgar, Aldershot, 1994); Andrew Linklater, *The Transformation of Political Community: Ethical Foundations of the Post-Westphalian Era* (Polity Press, Cambridge, 1998).

13. A recent study of Britain's immigration policy after the Second World War also attempts to go beyond the conventional treatment of the field, i.e., its racially discriminatory features, and examines the way in which post-war society became multi-racial. I am very much obliged to Randall Hansen for letting me read his D.Phil. thesis, which was the basis of his recent book: Randall A. Hansen, *Citizenship and Immigration in Post-War Britain* (Oxford University Press, Oxford, 2000).

14. PRO, CAB 21/1824. Conference of Commonwealth Prime Ministers 1949. The precise nature of Commonwealth citizenship was examined when the Republic of India tried to remain a member of the Commonwealth on the sole basis of Commonwealth citizenship. Chapter 4 discusses this issue in detail.

15. The term 'formal membership' is used in this work in order to indicate membership of the political unit which is legally acknowledged by immigration and nationality laws.

16. In this book, the term 'Britishness' is used to describe a subjective sense of shared national identity which is always in the process of being constructed and re-constructed. As a result, its definition keeps changing and its emphasis differs from one individual to another. For example, some attach Britishness to a territory: those who are born or settled in the British Isles share Britishness; while others attach it to a racial background: non-white people cannot share Britishness.

17. Comparing Britain with France, Favell distinguishes 'Being British "culturally", being a British national (with a right of abode), and being a British citizen (a subject of the sovereign) are distinct forms of "citizenship"'. Adrian Favell, *Philosophies of Integration: Immigration and the Idea of Citizenship in France and Britain* (Macmillan, London, 1998), p. 113.

18. Ann Dummett, 'The Acquisition of British Citizenship: From Imperial Traditions to National Definitions', in Rainer Bauböck (ed.), *From Aliens to Citizens: Redefining the Status of Immigrants in Europe* (Avebury, Aldershot, 1994), p. 75.

19. For example, see a comparative study on immigration and nationality laws by Brubaker: William Rogers Brubaker (ed.), *Immigration and the Politics of Citizenship in Europe and North America* (University Press of America, London, 1989), esp. 'Introduction' and Ch. 5. It is true that the post-Second World War studies on the development of citizenship rights in the United Kingdom and the United States

centred on the influential work first published by T. H. Marshall in 1950, which was based on a British case. Nonetheless, my book stresses again that the status of British citizenship was not legally established until 1981. T. H. Marshall, 'Citizenship and Social Class', in T. H. Marshall and Tom Bottomore, *Citizenship and Social Class* (Pluto Press, London, 1992).

20. Robin Cohen, for example, argues that 'Defining Britishness through citizenship proved particularly fruitless': Robin Cohen, *Frontiers of Identity: The British and the Others*, (Longman, London, 1994), p. 5. Keith Faulks suggests that 'the legal approach to defining citizenship is limited' in the case of Britain: Keith Faulks, *Citizenship in Modern Britain* (Edinburgh University Press, Edinburgh, 1998), p. 3.

21. Denis Judd, *Empire: The British Imperial Experience from 1765 to the Present*, (HarperCollins, London, 1996), p. 8.

22. Prime Minister Clement Attlee in 1946 affirmed that the use of the terms 'Commonwealth', 'British Commonwealth' and 'British Empire' were officially interchangeable. Some scholars, however, argue that the term 'Commonwealth' was often used to refer only to the self-governing colonies of the British Empire before the Second World War, but that after the war it simply replaced the term British Empire. For them, the Commonwealth before the Second World War is, therefore, the 'British Commonwealth' and not the 'Commonwealth'. This book simply uses the term 'Commonwealth' instead of 'British Empire' when discussing the post-Second World War period. See *Parliamentary Debates*, House of Commons, vol. 464, cols 643–4, 2 May 1949; K. C. Wheare, *The Constitutional Structure of the Commonwealth* (Clarendon Press, Oxford, 1960), Ch. 1.

23. Alfred Cobban, *The Nation-State and National Self-Determination* (Collins, London, 1969 [1945]), p. 154.

24. John W. Salmond, 'Citizenship and Allegiance', *Law Quarterly*, 18, 69 (1902), p. 49.

25. Some scholars stress the importance of monarchy, especially after the late Victorian period, as central to Britishness. See David Cannadine, 'The Context, Performance and Meaning of Ritual: The British Monarchy and the "Invention of Tradition", *c.* 1820–1977', in Eric Hobsbawm and Terence Ranger (eds), *The Invention of Tradition* (Cambridge University Press, Cambridge, 1994 [1983]), pp. 101–64. Before the end of the Second World War, however, the common Crown provided unity among the holders of British subjecthood irrespective of their different ethno-cultural backgrounds.

26. Tomas Hammar explains that, typically, immigrants have to go through three gates (those of immigration, domicile and residential status, and naturalization) before becoming citizens of their country of settlement. Britain's immigration and nationality laws do not fit Hammar's model: Hammar, *Democracy*, pp. 15–21.

27. Those colonies which became independent after the Second World War and remained within the Commonwealth are termed the New Commonwealth (NCW), whereas those which had already gained a self-governing status before the war are called the Old Commonwealth (OCW). The NCW immigrants have always been associated with 'coloured' immigrants.

28. Some scholars attribute the tightening of immigration control to popular racism among the British, and claim that successive governments were compelled to introduce immigration acts. See, for example, E. J. B. Rose *et al.*, *Colour and Citizenship* (Oxford University Press for the Institute of Race Relations, London, 1969), Ch. 16. Others consider that policy-makers intentionally stirred racist opinions among the British public. One of the most recent works in this school is Kathleen Paul, *Whitewashing Britain: Race and Citizenship in the Post-war Era* (Cornell University Press, London, 1997). Dummett stresses the importance of civil servants, rather than government ministers: Ann Dummett and Andrew Nicol, *Subjects, Citizens, Aliens and Others: Nationality and Immigration Law* (Weidenfeld & Nicolson,

London, 1990), pp. 177–8. Whichever view scholars take, immigration and nationality laws during that period were always influenced by the idea of 'race'.

29. Hansen, *Citizenship and Immigration in Post-War Britain*, p. 237.

30. Dummett is one of the few scholars who takes into account Britain's imperial history and its influence on immigration and citizenship policies in Britain. See for example Dummett and Nicol, *Subjects, Citizens, Aliens and Others*. My work extends her research by focusing more on the relationship between the development of the global institution and that of the role and meaning of citizenship.

31. This book does not of course intend to claim that the national type of citizenship should be established in Britain. Nor does it imply that it is beneficial to do so. It simply attempts to examine the various types of citizenship which existed in Britain, and in so doing, asks why national citizenship has not been fully created.

32. What some scholars today call 'transnational citizenship' is only one of the three possible alternative types of non-national citizenship which are discussed in Ch. 1. In this book it is termed the cosmopolitan type of citizenship. Unlike the imperial and the composite types, the cosmopolitan type has never previously existed.

33. The capitalized term 'Dominion' indicates the self-governing dominions. At the time of the Statute of Westminster in 1931, the Dominions included Canada, the Commonwealth of Australia, New Zealand, the Union of South Africa, the Irish Free State and Newfoundland. For how the status of Dominions developed see A. Berriedale Keith, *The Constitution Law of the British Dominions* (Macmillan, London, 1933), Ch. 1.

34. The right to vote, for example, was not open to all subjects, but was only conferred upon the male subjects who possessed the relevant qualifications of the time. Female subjects in Britain had to wait until 1918 to achieve the right to vote, and until 1928 for an equal franchise between men and women.

35. *Report of the Inter-Departmental Committee Appointed by the Secretary of State for the Home Department to Consider the Doubts and Difficulties which Have Arisen in Connexion with the Interpretation and Administration of the Acts Relating to Naturalization*, Cd. 723, HMSO, 1901. By the British Nationality and Status of Aliens Act 1914 (BN & SA Act 1914), the status of British subjecthood conferred anywhere in the Empire was recognised both inside and outside the Empire.

36. This type of literature is written by the so-called critical theorists, particularly the social constructivists among them, who claim that 'world politics is socially constructed'. Alexander Wendt, 'Constructing International Politics', *International Security*, 20, 1 (Summer 1995). Among the recent publications by the school of the social constructivism on national identity and citizenship, see, for example, Mathias Albert, David Jacobson and Yosef Lapid (eds), *Identities, Borders, Orders: Rethinking International Relations Theory* (University of Minnesota Press, London, 2001).

37. In a second reading of the 1981 British Nationality Bill which later became the BNA 1981, the Home Secretary, William Whitelaw, claimed that the main aim of the act was to relate citizenship to the right of abode. British citizenship under the BNA 1981 was created in such a way as to correspond to the 'patrial' status under the IA 1971.

38. There are numerous works on these topics; the author learned most from the following. For the impact of Britain's economic decline upon immigrant workers, see M. Castells, 'Immigrant Workers and Class Struggles in Advanced Capitalism: The Western European Experience', *Politics and Society*, 5, 1 (1975), pp. 33–66; for a general overview of the debate on racism and immigration policies in the 1960s and 1970s, see W. L. Miller, 'What was the Profit in Following the Crowd?: Aspects of Conservative and Labour Strategy since 1970', *British Journal of Political Science*, 10 (1980), pp. 15–38; Zig Layton-Henry and Paul Rich, *Race, Government and Politics in Britain* (Macmillan, London, 1986), Chs 1–4; Zig Layton-Henry, *The Politics of*

Immigration: Immigration, 'Race' and 'Race' Relations in Post-War Britain (Blackwell, Oxford, 1992).

39. Robin Cook first revealed his proposal to review the citizenship status of residents in the dependent territories in his speech to the Dependent Territories Association on 4 Feb. 1998. In the following year the White Paper, 'Partnership for Progress and Prosperity', was published and featured Cook's proposal. In June 2001, the British Overseas Territories Bill was finally introduced in the House of Lords. For Cook's speech in 1998, see http://www.fco.gov.uk/news/speechtext.asp?293; *Partnership for Progress and Prosperity: Britain and the Overseas Territories*, Cm. 4264, HMSO, March 1999.

40. *The Times*, 'Better Late than Never', 18 March 1999.

—1—
Understanding Citizenship

WHEN WE fill in an immigration clearance form at an airport, we complete a section on 'nationality' by using terms such as 'British' or 'Canadian'. However, the legal titles for formal membership in Britain and Canada are 'British citizenship' and 'Canadian citizenship'. The indiscriminate use of the terms 'citizenship' and 'nationality' is not merely accidental, but suggestive of the way in which citizenship is understood today. Today it not only describes one's legal status as a formal member of a state, it is also supposed to imply one's national membership however a 'nation' is defined.[1] In the end, 'the state claims to be the state of, and for, a particular, bounded citizenry', asserting its legitimacy on the basis of the will of that citizenry which is grouped by a shared identity and loyalty to the state.[2] Especially after the Second World War, this understanding of citizenship – national citizenship – is the prevalent international mode.

In the history of citizenship, however, it is less common for people to possess a single type of formal membership of a political unit than to have multiple forms of citizenship at the same time. Recently, the national type of citizenship has been facing challenges to its meaning and role, especially in Europe. The European Commission in 1987 declared, for example, that 322 million Europeans had been given a 'new citizenship', European citizenship. Subsequently, it was officially granted by the Maastricht Treaty in 1991 to the citizens of the member countries of the European Union (EU) to supplement, and not supplant, their national citizenship.[3] A citizenship structure with multiple citizenships, such as in Europe today, where people possess two different kinds of citizenship – one of a member state, and the other of the EU itself – has always persisted in Britain. Even today, a child born in London whose parent is a British citizen, for example, automatically acquires both British citizenship and Commonwealth citizenship by birth.[4] In order to examine Britain's experience of citizenship, therefore, we need an analytical framework for understanding the development of a citizenship structure which allows multiple citizenships in one way or another. It is this point that this research emphasizes in carrying out its analysis. Unlike previous works, it provides a study of the development of citizenship structure in Britain by examining the implications and consequences of Britain's effort to build and maintain the global institutions of the Empire and, later, the Commonwealth.

This chapter therefore has two aims. First, it seeks to present a brief account of the concept of citizenship, as a status, as a right and obligation, and as a sense of identity. This account will establish an analytical framework for understanding both national and alternative types of citizenship, which will be applied throughout the book. Second, by using the analytical framework, this chapter re-examines the various types of citizenship in British history, that is, British subjecthood and Commonwealth citizenship, and their citizenship structure, none of which fit into the international mode of national citizenship.

The chapter begins with an analysis of the concept of citizenship by taking into consideration three elements of citizenship, that is, the nominal, the substantive and the functional elements.[5] It then explores the national and the non-national types of citizenship. Among non-national types of citizenship, this study classifies three models of alternative citizenship, referring to them as the imperial, composite and cosmopolitan models.[6] On the basis of a detailed analysis of these models of alternative citizenship, the chapter concludes by discussing Britain's experience of various types of citizenship in order to illustrate how they differ from national citizenship.

THE CONCEPT OF CITIZENSHIP

Subjecthood, citizenship and nationality

In our everyday language, we use the words 'citizen' and 'national' almost interchangeably in order to describe the status of formal membership of a country, saying, for example, that a person is 'a citizen of France'. For some countries, such as Japan, the term 'national' is preferred. Coming from a country which is a monarchy, jurists and politicians in Britain historically preferred the term 'subject' to 'citizen', claiming that 'the law and language of England knows *subjects* only'.[7] Indiscriminate usage of these three terms is typically found in the treaty between the governments of the United Kingdom and the United States in 1870. The treaty was signed in order to 'regulate the *citizenship* of the British *subjects* who have emigrated ... to the United States of America'.[8] It also provided the way in which those *subjects* who had become naturalized within the United States 'shall be at liberty ... to resume their British *nationality*'.⁹ However, since each of the terms originates from a different historical period, their meanings differ from each other, depending on the time and place of their use.

The concept of subjecthood derives from the feudal tradition of vertical links between each individual (subject) and the common ruler of the political unit. Subjects were supposed to owe allegiance to the power or jurisdiction of the political unit in return for the protection which they received.¹⁰ Unlike in some countries, such as the United States, the tradition of subjecthood persisted in Britain well into the twentieth century. In the case of the United States, because of its colonial past, the original concept of formal membership was predominantly influenced by the practice in Britain. However, in the late eighteenth century, the traditional concept of allegiance and subjecthood was dealt a severe blow by the American Revolution and American independence from British rule. As the number of immigrants of non-British origin had increased in the mid-eighteenth century, the basic rule of subjecthood – natural allegiance ('birth within the king's ligeance') – came to be questioned in the 13 American colonies. The colonial government encouraged naturali-zation, which was outside the rule of natural allegiance, so that it could accept newcomers as formal members. Under the system of naturalization, naturalized subjects became formal members purely on the basis of their own will and their consent to the rule of the government. Comparing the mode of ascription by naturalization with that by birth, therefore, those colonists who were not satisfied with the control exercized by the imperial government in London started to question the concept of natural allegiance. They claimed that they had been denied the right to choose loyalty because of the principle of natural allegiance. For them, the status of British subject, and consequently perpetual loyalty towards British rule, was imposed on them at their birth. They were not even allowed to renounce their subjecthood. The American concept of citizenship was inevitably redefined after independence by the idea of 'volitional allegiance', and was based on an act of individual choice.¹¹

British nationality and immigration laws, in the absence of such an interruption as the American Revolution, continued to develop on the basis of allegiance and the common law doctrine of allegiance to the crown.¹² Even in Britain, however, the term 'subject' became obsolete and finally disappeared in 1981. Now, under the British *Nationality* Act 1981, British *citizenship* has become the status of people who are 'closely connected with the United Kingdom' and '"belong" to the United Kingdom for international or other purposes'.¹³ Although both 'citizenship' and 'nationality', as is seen in the BNA 1981, denote formal membership of a political unit, 'citizenship' is said to stress the municipal side of formal membership, and 'nationality', the international.[14] There are cases, as a result, where each term legally indicates a different group of people and is assigned a specific purpose. In the United States, for example, the inhabitants of overseas territories such as the Marianas and American Samoa are 'US nationals', but not 'US citizens'.[15]

Three elements of citizenship[16]

Modern legal usage aside, 'citizenship' is an evolving concept, whose meaning in academic literature changes from time to time and place to place, and in accordance with the focus of each piece of research. As a result, the debates on citizenship tend to begin with a historical survey of the concept.[17] On the basis of existing research, this study considers that there are three elements of citizenship – nominal, substantive and functional – which can be found throughout history.[18] There exist voluminous pieces of research which deal with one or other of the three elements, although some of them have received more scholarly attention than others. First, citizenship denotes formal membership of a political unit. The size or the organization of the political unit, that is, whether it is a city-state, an empire, or an international entity such as the EU, varies. The criteria for qualifying for the status of citizenship also differ from one period to another, such as from being a freeborn male to being willing to become a full member of the political unit. We assume today that citizenship means full membership of a political unit. Yet, in the past citizenship could confer a half-membership, such as *civitas sine suffragio* in the Roman Republic, which did not include the franchise.[19] Nonetheless, the nominal aspect of citizenship – 'citizenship-as-status'[20] – has always been a part of the concept.

Second, formal membership brings with it either a set of rights ('citizenship-as-rights') or duties and obligations ('citizenship-as-desirable-activity'), or both. These constitute the substantive element of citizenship. The issue of citizenship-as-rights has been heatedly debated among academics since the publication of T. H. Marshall's work in 1950.[21] Marshall, taking the British historical experience as an example, classifies citizenship rights into three components – civil, political and social – and argues that each of them was extended to citizens one by one after the eighteenth century. The content of citizenship duties, in contrast, has remained almost the same throughout history. They have mainly consisted of military service and the payment of taxes, as well as the giving of loyalty and support to a political unit. Among the works on 'citizenship-as-desirable-activity' today, however, there are different branches of the argument with respect to what is desirable: whether the emphasis should be placed on economic self-reliance, political participation or civic virtue.[22] It is true that the content of citizenship rights is changing, and the emphasis on the duties and desired behaviour differs in accordance with one's theoretical position. It was also only in the twentieth century that the principle was finally established that all the holders of citizenship should be given an equal set of rights, regardless of gender, wealth, colour or creed. Nonetheless, we cannot dismiss the fact that citizenship-as-status confers certain rights upon, and assigns certain obligations to, its holders.

The third element – the functional – refers to the feature of 'citizenship-as-social-enclosure', which has the functions of both inclusion and exclusion. First, as regards the function of inclusion, the qualifications for citizenship-as-status have historically widened, with slaves, the poor and women now being included as formal members of the political unit. In the face of increasing numbers of immigrants today, some countries, such as Canada and Australia, expect them to apply for formal membership after their entry.[23] They try to incorporate non-citizens into the political unit and demand support and loyalty in return for granting them formal membership and its consequent rights and privileges.

However, owing to the advances of technology and the increasing sophistication of control methods, especially since the Second World War, exclusion has often received more attention than inclusion.[24] Although the degree of the effectiveness of citizenship-as-social-enclosure and the basis on which it is implemented differs from time to time and place to place, citizenship has historically been used as an instrument to divide populations between citizens and non-citizens. As a consequence, intended or not, citizens are expected to share a sense of community with each other. This socio-psychological dimension of citizenship is especially important in the case of national citizenship, and differentiates national citizenship from other types of citizenship.

National citizenship

On the basis of the general analysis of the concept of citizenship (nominal, substantive and functional) above, the term 'national citizenship' is used in this study to refer (i) to the legal status of *state* membership; (ii) to *a whole set* of rights and obligations *equally* conferred on *all* the holders of that status; and (iii) to an instrument for differentiating its holders from non-holders, whose criteria are based on *nationhood*. Some scholars conclude that national citizenship is now, in theory, 'egalitarian, sacred, based on nation-membership, democratic, unique, socially consequential'.[25] In other words, the nominal aspect of citizenship today has to be the legal status of a state, not an empire or a city-state. Neither is it like that of the mediaeval kingdoms in western Europe, where people simultaneously belonged to different and overlapping groups, such as their clan, a kingdom and a religious group. Furthermore, as territorial boundaries were only loosely demarcated in mediaeval Europe, it was often not certain who belonged to which neighbouring kingdoms.[26] National citizenship, in contrast, can only consist of one formal membership.[27] As regards the substantive aspects, the holding of citizenship should warrant citizens all the accompanying rights and obligations in an unqualified manner, and preclude the holding of partial or multiple citizenship. According to the definition of national citizenship, citizens today are supposed to possess a firm loyalty to a state and share a sense of national identity. It is this last aspect of national citizenship that makes citizens of a state different from, and more than, a mere aggregate of populations who legally belong to that state by chance.

In short, we are today entitled, indeed compelled, to become a formal member of one country.[28] When we are abroad we can ask for protection from our country of citizenship on the basis of our citizenship-as-status in order to redress any harm inflicted upon us.[29] Citizenship being not only a status but also the basis for entitlement to rights, tight immigration control based on the holding of citizenship-as-status is a common feature today. The change of citizenship-as-status from that acquired at birth is, to say the least, difficult, because citizenship is also supposed to provide its holders with a sense of identity and belonging to a political unit.[30] As a result, only a few among many non-holders can be allowed, with various conditions as to period of stay and work status, to work and reside outside the country of their citizenship.[31] Without citizenship-as-status, in short, we end up with no political authorities and institutions to guarantee our rights. Some academics therefore conclude that citizenship has become the key to having 'the right to have rights, or the right of every individual to belong to humanity'.[32]

Recently, the number of cases which do not fit into the model of national citizenship, both in theory and practice, is on the increase for every aspect of citizenship. Governments in developed countries have so far maintained tight immigration control and are relatively successful in preventing people from coming in.[33] Once immigrants are legally inside the country, however, they can, even without citizenship-as-status, have access to labour markets and social services.[34] As a result, the number of immigrants who decide not to become naturalized is increasing in some countries, such as Germany, whose naturalization law is rigid and tough.[35] Furthermore, under the mode of national citizenship, EU citizenship cannot and should not exist today; Aron argued in 1971, for example, that 'There are no such animals as "European citizens". There are only French, German, or Italian citizens.'[36] No matter how incomplete the development of EU citizenship is, we cannot deny that there are some aspects of 'new citizenship' emerging today in Europe. For example, some citizenship rights which used to be granted through the holding of national citizenship, such as the right to reside and work in EU countries, are now allocated through EU citizenship. In addition, we cannot explain the long-surviving Commonwealth citizenship under the international model of national citizenship.

NATIONAL CITIZENSHIP AND
ALTERNATIVE TYPES OF CITIZENSHIP

'Transnational citizenship' models and their limits

Various types of citizenship which do not fit into national citizenship existed in the past and are being constructed today. There is, for example, multiple citizenship, such as dual citizenship; multi-layered citizenship, such as that of the EU and of a member state; and partial citizenship, such as what is called 'denizenship'[37] in the developed countries.[38] In the face of these cases, some scholars try to explain these exceptions by treating them as irregularities or by modifying the national citizenship model.[39] Some argue, however, that we need more than just a readjustment of the model of national citizenship, and that it is necessary to establish a completely new theoretical basis for citizenship.[40]

Those scholars whose arguments relate to the limits of national citizenship are all concerned with the discrepancy between the holders of formal membership and the holders of a bundle of rights and obligations. They also point out the possibility of multiple memberships of several different political units. In the face of these issues, some currently advocate the model of 'transnational citizenship' that cuts the nexus between citizenship on the one hand and the territorial boundary of a state and state jurisdiction on the other, as the term 'transnational' implies. As Marshall explains, they argue that citizenship rights were historically extended within the framework of the state as a result of efforts to overcome the social inequalities caused by the modern capitalist economy. In line with Marshall's domestic analogy, they emphasize that the struggle to extend and deepen citizenship rights should now be extended beyond national borders.[41] This does not necessarily mean that 'transnational citizenship' is the same as world citizenship, as there is little possibility of a world government being established in the foreseeable future. The proponents of 'transnational citizenship' also continue to believe that the responsibility for providing the rights falls upon the government of each state. They insist that the entitlement to citizenship rights should not be limited to within, but should become extended beyond, the country of citizenship.

This study agrees that the national citizenship model has its limits, and that it is necessary to overcome its interpretation of citizenship in order to grasp the changing structure and meaning of citizenship today instead of flatly denying that they exist or describing them as exceptions. However, the model of national citizenship is but one way of understanding the concept of citizenship in one historical phase. In looking back over the British history of citizenship, for example, it can be seen that today's model of 'transnational citizenship' has a number of qualities in common with British subjecthood, which existed before the model of national citizenship became the international norm. It was, after all, only in the twentieth century, under the principle of national self-determination, that citizenship became officially linked to a national framework.[42] However, as was typically seen in the case of Britain, national citizenship has never eradicated all the other types of citizenship which tried to co-exist with the emerging concept of national citizenship.

Furthermore, 'transnational citizenship' is supposed to be conferred upon the citizens of those countries which share norms and moral principles. In a sense, advocates of 'transnational citizenship' assume that the concept of 'transnational citizenship' should emerge from below, that is, from among the people.[43] However, it is difficult to measure to what extent the norms and moral principles are shared and with whom. There are also many historical examples whereby governments sign international agreements although the principles and ideas behind them are not accepted by the majority of the population.[44] Instead of the setting of transnational citizenship emerging from below, it has been historically more common for citizenship rights to be handed down to peoples beyond state boundaries by governments from above, on a unilateral or bilateral basis. Federation and confederation are such examples.

This work, therefore, argues that what the theorists now describe as 'transnational citizenship' is only one type of alternative citizenship, which it terms the cosmopolitan type. There are other types of alternative citizenship which can be formed in order to overcome the two problems which national citizenship could not address: the discrepancy between the nominal and the substantive aspects of citizenship, and multiple citizenships of several different political units. All types of alternative citizenship, in short, differ from the model of national citizenship in each of the three elements of citizenship (nominal, substantive and functional). First, alternative types of citizenship are the formal membership of combined political units, thus forming a citizenship structure with multiple citizenships and allowing multiple and partial citizens.[45] Second, their citizenship rights and obligations are conferred on the holders depending on the basis on which the political units are combined. Third, and most important, they are not granted on the basis of nationhood. As a result, the equation of nationality with citizenship under the model of national citizenship is broken in all of the alternative types of citizenship. Nationality, as the legal status of formal membership of a political unit, is not equivalent to citizenship-as-rights. Nationality, as an attribute of cultural groups, is no longer linked to citizenship-as-status. In other words, the division between the holders of alternative types of citizenship and non-holders is not as clear as in the case of national citizens and aliens.

Three alternative types of citizenship[46]

Historically, there are many examples of several political units combining to construct one political unit, leading to a citizenship structure with multiple citizenships. In this book the citizenship of combined political units is classified into three types in accordance with the means by which the combined units are formed, that is, by unilateral means such as settlement, conquest or annexation (the imperial type), by bilateral means such as a contract or an agreement (the composite type) and through shared norms and values (the cosmopolitan type).[47]

The imperial type of citizenship

In the case of the imperial type of citizenship, political units are united on an unequal basis, either economically or militarily or both.[48] Each historical empire employed different methods of ruling its colonies in order to preserve its imperial structure; some relied mainly on military power, others preferred informal influence.[49] As long as an imperial metropole maintains an effective overall control over its subordinates, the former, in theory, does not need to intervene in the latter's local affairs. An imperial type of citizenship is, however, given to all the peoples who are subject to the rule of the imperial government, regardless of whether they are on the peripheries or in the metropole, and regardless of their local identity. This seemingly benevolent attitude is based on the idea of imperial superiority, under which those peoples on the peripheries, who do not belong to the ruling group, are regarded as equal only in a sense that they are all inferior.

The imperial type of citizenship neither requires nor assumes that citizenship-as-status accompanies the cultural identification of its holders. For the imperial metropole, in the end, the existence of different ethnic groups within the same political unit is acceptable, local citizenship and sub-identities in the colonies co-existing with the all-embracing imperial citizenship.[50] In the case of the British Empire, this logic of tolerating various local identities on the basis of imperial superiority was advanced to a greater degree than in other Empires of the time.[51] It was not a problem for Westminster to allow British subjects in Canada to be British subjects, Canadian nationals and also Québécois. In the end, the imperial metropole is supposed to stand, with equal neutrality, above peoples on the peripheries, who all live within combined political units and are subject to its rule.

In other words, the imperial government can, in theory, agree that colonial citizens possess multi-layered identities. Apart from in an emergency such as a war, it is up to individual citizens to decide which identity they value most in a private setting, given that they respect and comply with the fact that in the public sphere they are colonial citizens. Colonial citizenship, after all, remains a way of expressing the identity of the people in the colonies, which was often not recognized in the international arena. With regard to the substantive aspects of citizenship, both citizenship-as-rights and citizenship-as-desirable-activity are attached to the imperial citizenship itself. Since constituent political units are not necessarily deemed to have equal status, the universal status of imperial citizenship does not necessarily guarantee all its holders the same set of rights or obligations. Colonial peoples were sometimes prevented from enjoying their citizenship rights, but they might also be released from some of the citizenship obligations on the basis of being colonial citizens.[52]

The composite type of citizenship
In contrast to the imperial type of citizenship, which is often achieved unilaterally, several political units have deliberately established a

combined political unit on the basis of consultation or treaty, as if they form a 'composite state'.[53] According to international lawyers, two or more internationally recognized political units can form a composite state in two different categories. In the first case, each constituent political unit remains internationally recognized, while the composite state does not become so.[54] In the second, the composite state itself, and not each constituent unit, becomes one internationally recognized political unit. In short, according to the first pattern, even if constituent political units form, by a recognized treaty, a union with organs of its own, each of them is still individually represented in an international organization and treaty. Personal unions, such as that between Great Britain and Hanover from 1714 to 1837, and confederated states, such as the United States from 1778 to 1787, fall into this category. In both cases, constituent units are theoretically capable of making war against each other, even after forming a composite state. Composite states in the second pattern are represented by real unions and federal states. A real union is formed under the same monarch, as in the case of Sweden–Norway from 1814 to 1905. At present, there are no real unions in the world. A federal state, such as the United States today, is established on the basis of a treaty between each constituent unit and the duly constituted federal state.

The way in which the composite type of citizenship is conferred, and the rights and obligations granted to its holders, are all determined by agreement between the participating political units. They therefore differ in each case. As is seen in the imperial type of citizenship, cultural identification among the holders of the composite type of citizenship is not a requirement. The residents of each constituent political unit might be forced to integrate into the ruling group of that unit, yet the power of the dominant culture of each unit does not go beyond its territorial boundaries. (Nobody, for example, thought it a problem to establish the Common Market in 1957, even though people in Rome did not, and do not, speak the same language as those in Bonn.) Thus two political units with completely different political systems, languages and moral norms can form a composite state, the formal members of each constituent unit being provided with the composite type of citizenship.

This book argues that this type of alternative citizenship, the composite type, is most capable of forming a citizenship structure which is 'multi-layered', and which allows multiple and partial citizenship to exist even in an age of national citizenship.[55] Although scholars have debated 'multi-layered citizenship' for some time, they tend to concentrate on an emerging EU citizenship as the best example of a 'multi-layered citizenship' and analyse its current citizenship structure, predicting the birth of a new type of citizenship.[56] This book relies on the previous pieces of work on a multi-layered citizenship structure, and bases its argument upon their findings. Unlike them, however, this study distinguishes EU citizenship from 'transnational citizenship', and treats them separately. EU citizenship today is granted on the basis of citizenship of the member states, and thus should only be treated as the composite type of citizenship, however advanced it might be in comparison with the other historical cases.[57] This book also disagrees with other scholars who treat today's EU citizenship as a novel phenomenon exemplifying a multi-layered citizenship structure.[58]

The cosmopolitan type of citizenship
Unlike with the imperial and composite types of citizenship, hardly any constitutional link is required among constituent political units in order to achieve the cosmopolitan type of citizenship. The combined political unit does not need to possess a set of legislative, administrative and juridical institutions of its own. Instead, each constituent unit, rather than the combined political unit, is responsible for implementing citizenship rights and obligations. Formed by 'like-minded'[59] political units, the cosmopolitan type of citizenship is a multi-level citizenship structure under which the possibility of extending rights is infinite, whether or not one is a citizen of a member country.

So far, we have never actually experienced a cosmopolitan type of citizenship, although the idea has existed throughout human history. For example, Linklater describes three different possible frameworks (pluralist, solidarist and post-Westphalian) for inter-state relationships within which states co-operate with each other to promote shared principles such as peace and human rights.[60] A pluralist framework can even be achieved by states with dissimilar political and economic systems and differences of culture and morality, since it is formed simply on the basis of respect for the freedom and equality of independent political units. A solidarist framework is, however, grounded on an agreement about a range of moral principles by the constituent political units, whereby they are at least willing to work together on issues of common concern. In contrast to the two previous examples, participating units of the post-Westphalian framework are prepared to relinquish many of their sovereign powers in order to promote their shared norms and moral principles. Even the EU is still working towards the solidarist stage. Some scholars, therefore, criticize the cosmopolitan type as being unrealistic, or worse, a 'purely senti-mental, and slightly absurd, notion'.[61]

Comparison between national and alternative types of citizenship

In sum, this work has argued so far that the current attempts to overcome the limits of national citizenship, as represented by the theories on 'transnational citizenship', are often too hypothetical and idealistic to be realized in practice. They also do not seem to take into account various alternative types of citizenship which have existed in the past. There have been cases where, as a result of colonization or federation, citizenship has been deliberately conferred upon peoples beyond state boundaries. This has created, from above (via sovereigns or governments), a citizenship structure with multiple citizenships such as the imperial and the composite type.

This research indicates that the anomalous cases of national citizenship derive from the rigidity of the relationship between three aspects of citizenship. Under the premise of national citizenship, once the nominal aspect of citizenship is conferred upon a group of people on the basis of nationhood, it is the holding of this citizenship-as-status which assigns each individual to a country and through which citizenship rights and obligations are granted to the holders. National citizenship therefore does not allow any partial and multiple citizens, and, if there are any, this situation should soon be corrected. Furthermore, since citizenship-as-social-enclosure is defined by nationhood, however it is understood at the time, it is expected that all holders of citizenship-as-status identify with a collective consciousness embodied by nationhood. Expressions of difference by the holders, whether they are on matters of culture, language or religion, therefore become unacceptable. In the end, national citizenship, as a source of status as well as feeling, is intertwined with and defined by an inner, subjective sense of shared national identity. With the sophisticated administrative methods available today, it has become possible to pursue exclusive-ness towards non-citizens and inclusiveness towards citizens to a far greater extent than in previous periods.

The difference between each type of alternative citizenship can be summarized as follows.[62] In contrast to the model of national citizenship, all of the three alternative types of citizenship accept both multiple and partial members, and their citizenship rights and obligations differ from citizen to citizen, depending on their position in terms of citizenship-as-social-enclosure. In the case of an imperial type of citizenship, for example, the nature of the citizenship rights and obligations assigned to its holders in colonies is decided by the rules (or orders) of the metropole. The composite type of citizenship, on the other hand, bases its citizenship-as-social-enclosure upon citizenship of a constituent political unit, so that the distribution of citizenship rights and obligations is determined by the agreement or the contract on which a combined political unit is founded. The model of the cosmopolitan type of citizenship, compared with the other two, is least clear and even patchy on this point. Unlike the imperial, composite and national types, the cosmopolitan type is relieved of any territorial boundaries, and can therefore be most inclusive towards the increasing number of immigrants who live outside their country of citizenship. However, it is prone to re-create the exclusiveness of national citizenship on a wider geographical scale, being rigorous about the norms and moral principles on which it is based and being insensitive towards those people who do not share them.

A framework for examining both national and alternative types of citizenship having been outlined, the final section of this chapter applies it to the diverse types of citizenship found in Britain in the past and at the present day. The historical details of how and why each type of citizenship was formed and reformed are covered in the subsequent chapters of the book.

CITIZENSHIP IN BRITISH HISTORY

Under the Conservative government of the late 1980s, citizenship was added to the political agenda as one of the most debated topics. It was considered at that time that the introduction of the notion of 'active citizenship' was the key to re-establishing a sense of self-help and responsibility.[63] In so doing, the government thought to overcome the 'dependency culture' which it claimed had been nurtured by the welfare state. Subsequently, in 1991, each of the three main political parties published a plan for promoting citizenship. Although they all talked about 'citizens', it was not clear whom they meant by 'citizen' and whose responsibility as a 'citizen' they wished to promote. It was even possible that they were talking about different groups of people while using the same term, 'citizens'.

At that time, the status of British citizenship had already been established by the BNA 1981. However, the right to enter and reside freely in the United Kingdom is specifically attached only to the status of British citizenship, while all the other citizenship rights and obligations continue to be conferred on the holding of Common-wealth citizenship.[64] Furthermore, in the 1980 White Paper which laid the basis for the BNA 1981, it was stated that the main reason for creating the status of British citizenship was to [equate] that right [to enter and remain in the country without restriction] with citizenship, and so ending the confusion which has existed on this score since it first became necessary in 1962 to limit the right of entry of certain Commonwealth citizens and Citizens of the United Kingdom and Colonies.[65]

Although it also claimed that British citizenship would be 'the status of people closely connected with the United Kingdom',[66] its definition of 'people closely connected with the UK' was based on immigration status under the Immigration Act 1971 (IA 1971), with no definition of Britishness being specifically linked to British citizenship. As a result, the programmes of 'active citizenship' could be interpreted, for example, to include those citizens of the Commonwealth countries who were exempted from immigration control, such as Australian citizens born prior to 1983 with a parent of British descent. British citizenship today, therefore, still does not fully match the national model of citizenship: its citizenship-as-social-enclosure is based on other legislation, immigration acts, and its citizenship-as-rights only includes the rights of free entrance and residence in the United Kingdom.

In other words, not a single citizenship-as-status has yet been constructed in Britain which carries with it a full set of citizenship-as-rights and citizenship-as-desirable-activity, and also functions as citizenship-as-social-enclosure.[67] As is examined in the Epilogue, therefore, the three aspects of citizenship are still divorced from one another. To be able to discuss the different types of citizenship which existed in British history, namely British subjecthood in the colonies (till 1948) and under the common code system in Britain and the Dominions (between 1914 and 1946),[68] and Commonwealth citizenship (1948 onwards), we therefore need to bring into the discussion the alternative types of citizenship.[69] How and on what points does each of them differ from the national model of citizenship with regard to the three aspects of citizenship?

First, subjecthood is granted to people on their basis of allegiance. People could therefore become subjects as long as they were born under the protection of the Crown.[70] Under the principle of allegiance, groups of peoples within the Empire with different cultural backgrounds and languages were included as British subjects. The lack of a guiding rule in nationality laws for the colonies and England (later, Britain) prior to the enactment of the BN & SA act 1914 created the situation where, on the one hand, everyone possessed the same title of 'British subject' before the imperial government. On the other hand the access to the rights and obligations attached to that status were controlled by colonial immigration laws which in practice decided who could enter each territory.[71] This way of dealing with the nominal and substantive aspects of citizenship in overseas territories persisted till the end of the Second World War, and also influenced the development of nationality and immigration laws in post-Second World War Britain.

Second, in contrast to the previous period, the status of British subjecthood during the period between the enactment of the BN & SA act 1914 and the Canadian Citizenship Act 1946 was sustained by two different methods. In the colonies it was granted unilaterally on the basis of an age-long principle of common law and the BN & SA act 1914, whereas in the Dominions and Britain it was by the so-called common code (a set of statutory provisions defining who was a British subject and in what circumstances British subjecthood was acquired and lost) based on mutual agreement and consultation.[72] During this period, furthermore, the granting of local citizenship by the Dominions was officially approved by the imperial conference of 1930.[73] As a result, the common code system succeeded in forming, in terms of the nominal aspect of citizenship, a citizenship structure with multiple citizenships: British subjecthood and citizenship of a Dominion.[74]

From the perspective of the substantive aspects of citizenship, however, it was still the status of British subjecthood which granted citizenship rights and obligations, local citizenship being enacted only in relation to immigration control. British subjects under the common code system did not necessarily possess citizenship rights and obligations throughout the Empire, because of the existence of immigration control in each colony and Dominion. Unlike British governments, which had not established immigration control for British subjects (later, Commonwealth citizens) in any form before 1962, the Dominion and colonial governments had always imposed immigration control upon those holders of British subjecthood who came from outside their territories.

In terms of a multi-level structure of identity, it was not clear either to what extent a sense of identity and belonging, separate from that of Britishness, existed among the rank and file in the Dominions. As was proved during the two world wars, a number of peoples in the Dominions were, by and large, proud of being 'British subjects' and supported Britain. After all, local citizenship during this period was used to differentiate between British subjects in each overseas territory, rather than between those in overseas territories and the mother country itself. The division between the Dominions and the rest of the empire was consolidated through the system of the common code. This division subsequently became that between the OCW and the NCW.

The third type of citizenship which existed in Britain is Commonwealth citizenship. Just like British subjecthood, it is the common status which is shared by all the formal members of Commonwealth countries. In contrast to British subjecthood, however, Commonwealth citizenship is granted to citizens of Commonwealth countries on the basis of their holding the citizenship of each member country, instead of allegiance to the Crown or the common legislation established among them.[75] As a result, citizenship of each member country has become the main citizenship status through which citizenship rights and obligations are granted, Commonwealth citizenship being an additional status.

Commonwealth citizenship is again a form of multiple citizenships only in terms of citizenship-as-status, not citizenship-as-rights and as-desirable-activity. Even in Britain, where citizenship rights and obligations continued to be granted to all the holders of Commonwealth citizenship, the status of Commonwealth citizen has practically lost its element of citizenship-as-rights since the enactment of the Commonwealth Immigrants Act (CIA) 1962.[76]

In sum, before the BNA 1948 British subjecthood, whether in the colonies or the Dominions, had a number of features in common with the imperial type of citizenship. Through local naturalization and immigration control, each colonial government could, to a certain extent, differentiate from others those British subjects who belonged to them. A Dominion government was even entitled to form a citizenship of its own. Nonetheless, neither colonial nor Dominion governments introduced local naturalization and immigration control with the specific intention of creating a national citizenship of their own. The Dominion governments also accepted, either actively or passively, the common status of British subjecthood. They were satisfied as long as they participated in discussions with regard to the common status – British subjecthood – under the common code system, and had the right to depart from that system by creating citizenships of their own, if they wished. Nonetheless, through local legislation on immigration and nationality, their local identity gradually became clarified.

Commonwealth citizenship after BNA 1948, on the other hand, is closer to the composite type. A citizenship structure with multiple citizenships, however, remained an embryonic form of the multi-layered model. In terms of the nominal aspect of citizenship, a citizenship structure based on Commonwealth citizenship is clearly multi-layered. Yet, in both cases, the substantive aspects of citizenship are granted to the holders of the status only through one level:

citizenship of the member country. They are therefore not multi-layered. From the perspective of the functional aspect of citizenship, it is also difficult to claim that it established a multi-layered structure, as the sense of Commonwealth citizenship is merely symbolic in comparison with that of citizenship of Commonwealth countries.

The following chapters examine how the concepts of British subjecthood and Commonwealth citizenship were reconstructed in order to allow that of national citizenship to evolve alongside them, first in the self-governing colonies and later within Britain itself. The historical survey begins in the next chapter by examining how Britain's imperial citizenship was constructed in accordance with its overseas expansion.

NOTES

1. It is well known that there is no agreement among scholars on the definition of a nation. For example, some of them argue that the nation is a modern phenomenon, and others see it as something natural or at least with roots that long pre-date the modern era of centralized states and industrialization. For the former, see, for example, E. Gellner, *Nations and Nationalism* (Basil Blackwell, Oxford, 1994 [1983]); E. J. Hobsbawm, *Nations and Nationalism since 1780: Programme, Myth, Reality* (Cambridge University Press, Cambridge, 1995 [1990]). For the latter see Edward Shills, 'Primordial, Personal, Sacred and Civil Ties', *British Journal of Sociology*, 7 (1951), pp. 113–45; and Anthony D. Smith, *The Ethnic Origins of Nations* (Basil Blackwell, Oxford, 1986).
2. Rogers Brubaker, *Citizenship and Nationhood in France and Germany* (Harvard University Press, London, 1994), p. 21.
3. European Commission, 'New Rights for the Citizens of Europe', *European File*, 11 (1987). See also Consolidated Version of the Treaty Establishing the European Community (as amended by the Treaty of Amsterdam), article 17.
4. BNA 1981, section 37. Under section 1, British citizenship is conferred upon children provided that at least one of their parents is either a British citizen or settled in the United Kingdom.
5. The nominal element of citizenship implies citizenship as a status; the substantive, as a right and obligation; and the functional, as a sense of identity. Details of the three elements are discussed in the next section. As the main purpose of this chapter is to prepare the analytical framework for the rest of the book, the survey here is biased towards developments and definitions of citizenship in the West, especially western Europe.
6. This work points out that the cosmopolitan type of citizenship, which some theorists call 'transnational citizenship', is a hypothetical type of citizenship. Unlike the cosmopolitan type, the imperial and composite types of citizenship have existed in both the past and the present. For 'transnational citizenship', see, for example, Bauböck, *Transnational Citizenship*; Linklater, *Transformation of Political Community*. Soysal refers to 'postnational citizenship', yet, according to her definition, 'postnational citizenship' is identical to what others call 'transnational citizenship': Soysal, *Limits of Citizenship*.
7. Salmond, 'Citizenship and Allegiance', p. 49 (emphasis added).

8. *British and Foreign State Papers (1869–70)*, LX, 1876 (emphasis added). Convention between Great Britain and the United States of America, relative to Naturalization – signed in London, 13 May 1870, section 2. Richard Plender, *International Migration Law*, 2nd rev. edn (Martinus Nijhoff Publishers, London, 1988), pp. 9–10.

9. Convention between Great Britain and the United States of America, relative to Naturalization (emphasis added).

10. Allegiance is the feudal system of personal loyalty, which can be classified as four different types: natural, acquired, local or legal. For a detailed account see Salmond, 'Citizenship and Allegiance', pp. 49–50, and Clive Parry, *Nationality and Citizenship Laws of the Commonwealth and of the Republic of Ireland* (Stevens & Sons Ltd., London, 1957), pp. 41–2.

11. Kettner elegantly explains how the Americans constructed their concept of citizenship, first cutting their ties with Britain, and later, extending the status of citizenship to native Indians and slaves: James H. Kettner, *The Development of American Citizenship 1608–1870* (University of North Carolina Press, Chapel Hill, NC, 1978), Ch. 7. Until the late nineteenth century, however, there existed disagreement between the judiciary and the executive regarding to what extent the idea of volitional allegiance should be reflected in the practice of naturalization and the consequent renunciation of the original citizenship. Details of naturalization practice in the United States in the nineteenth century are discussed in Ch. 2. According to Koessler, it is in the Federal Constitution (1787) that the term citizens is first used exclusively, the use of 'subject' as a synonym being completely dropped: Maximilian Koessler, '"Subject," "Citizen," "National," and "Permanent Allegiance"', *Yale Law Journal*, 56 (1946–7), pp. 58–60.

12. Laurie Fransman, *Fransman's British Nationality Law* (Fourmat Publishing, London, 1989), p. 24.

13. *British Nationality Law: Outline of Proposed Legislation*, Cmnd 7987 (HMSO, July 1980), p. 7.

14. Paul Weis, *Nationality and Statelessness in International Law* (Sijthoff & Noordhoff, Alphen aan den Rijn, 1979 [1956]), pp. 4–5. L. F. L. Oppenheim, and H. Lauterpacht, *International Law*, I (Longman, Green, London, 1955 [1905]), pp. 644–5.

15. In the United States, since the beginning of the twentieth century citizenship rights have gradually been extended to non-citizen nationals in overseas territories. Today, as a result, the distinction between citizens and non-citizen nationals is insignificant. Charles Gordon *et al.*, *Immigration Law and Procedure*, VII (Matthew Bender, New York, 1998), §91. 01[3][b].

16. See Appendix I.

17. For example, see Dawn Oliver and Derek Heater, *The Foundation of Citizenship* (Harvester Wheatsheaf, London, 1994), Ch. 1.

18. Here, this section has developed Sørensen's argument on the history of the concept of citizenship. Sørensen, *Exclusive European Citizenship*, pp. 23–4.

19. Derek Heater, *Citizenship: The Civic Ideal in World History, Politics and Education* (Longman, London, 1990), p. 16.

20. This and the following two terms – 'citizenship-as-rights' and 'citizenship-as-desirable-activity' – are borrowed from Will Kymlicka and Wayne Norman, 'Return of the Citizen: A Survey of Recent Work on Citizenship Theory', in Ronald Beiner (ed.), *Theorizing Citizenship* (State University of New York Press, Albany, 1995), pp. 284–5. According to Brubaker, *Citizenship and Nationhood*, pp. 21–2, political sociology tends to overlook the aspect of citizenship-as-status, concentrating on that of citizenship-as-rights.

21. Marshall, 'Citizenship and Social Class'. There are a number of works which both support and criticize Marshall's argument. For those critical of Marshall, see, for

example, Anthony Giddens, *The Nation-State and Violence* (Polity Press, Cambridge, 1985), Ch. 8. Michael Mann, 'Ruling Class Strategies and Citizenship', *Sociology*, 21, 3 (1987), pp. 339–54. Bryan S. Turner, 'Outline of a Theory of Citizenship', *Sociology*, 24, 2 (1990), pp. 189–217.

22. The argument on self-reliance was triggered by the rise to power of the New Right and neoconservatism in Britain and the United States in the 1980s. See Maurice Roche, *Rethinking Citizenship: Welfare, Ideology and Change in Modern Society* (Polity Press, Cambridge, 1992). Lawrence Mead, *Beyond Entitlement: The Social Obligations of Citizenship* (Free Press, New York, 1986). Although scholars today agree that political participation should be encouraged as one of the most important citizenship obligations, some go even further and emphasize the intrinsic value of participation for the participants. Adrian Oldfield, *Citizenship and Community: Civic Republicanism and the Modern World* (Routledge, London, 1990). Michael Walzer, 'The Civil Society Argument', in Chantal Mouffe (ed.), *Dimensions of Radical Democracy: Pluralism, Citizenship, Community* (Verso, London, 1992), Ch. 4.

23. For recent changes of immigration and nationality laws in western Europe and north America, see Dilek Çinar, 'From Aliens to Citizens. A Comparative Analysis of Rules of Transition', in Rainer Bauböck (ed.), *From Aliens to Citizens: Redefining the Status of Immigrants in Europe* (Avebury, Aldershot, 1994), pp. 64–5. Randall Hansen and Patrick Weil (eds), *Towards a European Nationality: Citizenship, Immigration and Nationality Law in the EU* (Palgrave, Houndmills, 2001).

24. Governments today have established sophisticated mechanisms for preventing non-citizens from entering their territories. See, for example, Alan Dowty, *Closed Borders* (Yale University Press, New Haven, CT, 1987), Chs 3–6; John Torpey, *The Invention of the Passport: Surveillance, Citizenship and the State* (Cambridge University Press, Cambridge, 2000).

25. William Rogers Brubaker, 'Introduction', in Brubaker (ed.), *Immigration and the Politics of Citizenship in Europe and North America* (University Press of America, London, 1989), pp. 2–3.

26. Susan Reynolds, *Kingdoms and Communities in Western Europe 900–1300* (Clarendon Press, Oxford, 1984).

27. While it is true that dual nationality is more tolerated today in some countries, it is still an anomaly which is accepted at the discretion of government.

28. Universal Declaration of Human Rights 1948, article 15. Convention Relating to the Status of Stateless Persons, 1954.

29. This is termed diplomatic protection, and is accepted as the right of a state to intervene on behalf of its own citizens in order to obtain redress, if their rights are violated by another state.

30. Rules of naturalization therefore require applicants to meet residential requirements prior to application and to show intention to stay in that country, in order to check the extent of their commitment for an indefinite future.

31. Normally, non-citizens have to go through three 'gates' before acquiring full citizenship status. The first gate regulates immigration in order to grant work and residence permits for short periods, and is usually based on immigration acts. The second gate controls permanent work and residence permits and confers quasi-citizenship without full political rights. The third gate is usually referred to as naturalization. Hammar, *Democracy*, pp. 16–25. He points out that a large number of people intentionally decide not to go through all three gates to become full citizens.

32. Arendt argues that the stateless, having failed to obtain citizenship, do not even have a right to have rights. Hannah Arendt, *The Origins of Totalitarianism* (Harcourt Brace, London, 1973 [1948]), p. 298.

33. Gary P. Freeman, 'Can Liberal States Control Unwanted Migration?', *The Annals of*

the American Academy of Political and Social Science, 534 (July 1994), pp. 17–30. For recent developments in the mechanisms of immigration control in European countries, see, for example, Grete Brochmann and Tomas Hammar (eds), *Mechanisms of Immigration Control: A Comparative Analysis of European Regulation Policies* (Berg, Oxford, 1999).

34. See, for example, William Rogers Brubaker, 'Membership without Citizenship: The Economic and Social Rights of Noncitizens', in Brubaker (ed.), *Immigration and the Politics of Citizenship*, Ch. 7.

35. See William Rogers Brubaker, 'Citizenship and Naturalization', ibid., pp. 99–127.

36. Raymond Aron, 'Is Multinational Citizenship Possible?', *Social Research*, 41, 4 (1971), pp. 638–56.

37. Long-term foreign residents in developed countries today enjoy almost all the citizenship rights; these quasi-citizens are termed 'denizens'. Hammar, *Democracy*, pp. 12–15.

38. Heater explains the history of multi-layered citizenship, beginning with Roman citizenship. Heater, *Civic Ideal*, pp. 320–30. Recent works on a multi-layered citizenship concentrate on the development of European citizenship. Close presents a model to clarify the way in which citizenship rights are granted in the case of European citizenship, while Roche's model of European citizenship focuses on the development of a multi-layered identity. Paul Close, *Citizenship, Europe and Change* (Macmillan, London, 1995), Ch. 6. Roche, *Rethinking Citizenship*, pp. 218–19. This work does not use the term 'multi-layered citizenship', but instead uses multiple citizenships to include both the horizontal (that is, dual citizenship) and the vertical cases (that is, European citizenship).

39. For example, Joppke insists that denizenship and other forms of citizenship which do not match national citizenship should be considered as irregularities subject to correction. Christian Joppke, 'Immigration Challenges the Nation-State', in Christian Joppke (ed.), *Challenge to the Nation-State: Immigration in Western Europe and the United States* (Oxford University Press, Oxford, 1998), p. 24.

40. Scholars tend to term this new type of citizenship 'transnational citizenship' or 'postnational citizenship'. Yet the definition of 'postnational citizenship' implies the same type of citizenship that others call 'transnational citizenship'. Soysal, *Limits of Citizenship*.

41. For example, see Linklater, *Transformation of Political Community*, Chs 5 and 6. He writes that 'the moral capital which has accumulated in the struggle to extend and deepen the rights of citizens is a resource that can be used to envisage a new conception of community and citizenship which is freed from the constraints of national sovereignty' (p. 178).

42. This study is not saying that the state is or should be populated by one nation. Yet state officials often use the principle of national self-determination as the basis of their legitimacy to govern the people in its territory. The impact of the principle of national self-determination upon the concept of citizenship after the Second World War is discussed in Ch. 4.

43. Turner, in attempting to improve a theory of citizenship established by Marshall, argues that citizenship can be developed either from above (via the state) or from below (in terms of more local participatory institutions, such as trade unions). Turner, 'Outline of a Theory', pp. 189–217. His argument is based on the development of citizenship within national boundaries. By analogy, however, advocates of 'transnational citizenship' seem to expect that the norms and moral principles are shared by peoples across state boundaries, which provides the basis for 'transnational citizenship' to be created.

44. For example, the North Korean government has signed both the International

Covenant on Economic, Social, and Cultural Rights and on Civil and Political Rights. Yet it is doubtful to what extent the government of, and people in, North Korea understand and honour the principles behind the two covenants.

45. It is a combined political unit only from the perspective of the formal membership. It therefore does not need to form a state with its own judicial, administrative and legislative organs. Nor does it need to be considered as one political unit in an international society. In that sense, dual citizenship can be included in a category of alternative citizenship, although a dual citizen is usually prevented, through an agreement between the two governments, from benefiting simultaneously from the citizenship rights and privileges of both citizenships. In practice, therefore, one citizenship is treated as if it is dormant, leaving only one national citizenship at work. This study considers that denizenship is a way of expanding the national citizenship model by bringing in the idea of 'residence'. Denizenship thus aims to complement, rather than take over, the national citizenship model.

46. See Appendix II for a comparison of three types of alternative citizenship.

47. It must be stressed that these three types have theoretical limits when they are used to examine historical cases of alternative citizenship. As is always true with ideal-types, they are not identical to the various alternative citizenships that have actually existed, and neither do they cover them all. However, they are not intended to do so; by presenting the three ideal-types of alternative citizenship, this book hopes to argue that there are several possible types of alternative citizenship being formed, and examines the way in which one type is transformed into another.

48. According to Doyle, empire is defined by 'effective control, whether formal or informal, of a subordinated society by an imperial society'. Michael W. Doyle, *Empires* (Cornell University Press, London, 1986), p. 30.

49. For an account of the different colonial structures of historical empires, see, for example, D. K. Fieldhouse, *The Colonial Empires: A Comparative Survey from the Eighteenth Century* (Macmillan, London, 1982 [1966]).

50. As Arendt explains, the purpose of imperialists was 'expansion of political power without the foundation of a body politic'. Arendt, *Totalitarianism*, p. 135.

51. See Doyle, *Empire*, Ch. 12. Most notably, the Japanese Empire, the only active non-Western imperial power before the Second World War, imposed cultural assimilationism on its colonies, which often resulted in conscious attempts at cultural homogenization. Wan-yao Chou, 'The Kominka Movement in Taiwan and Korea: Comparison and Interpretation', in Peter Duus, Raymon H. Myers and Mark Peattie (eds), *The Japanese Wartime Empire, 1931–1945* (Princeton University Press, Princeton, NJ, 1996), pp. 40–68.

52. For example, the Japanese imperial government did not enforce conscription on Japanese nationals of Korean origin and those of Formosan origin until 1938 and 1942 respectively. The official reason for their exemption was that the Japanese imperial army had secured enough personnel. In truth, because of persistent resistance movements in these two colonies, the government thought it impossible to be certain of the loyalty of the colonial peoples. Hiroshi Tanaka, 'Nihon no Taiwan, Chosen Shihai to Kokuseki Mondai (Japanese Imperial Rule over Formosa and Korea and the Issue of Nationality)', *Horitsu Jiho*, 47, 4 (1975), pp. 86–7.

53. The idea of a 'composite state' is borrowed from Weis, *Nationality*, pp. 13–15.

54. See Oppenheim and Lauterpacht, *International Law*, pp. 169–76.

55. For a multi-layered citizenship see, for example, Heater, *Civic Ideal*, pp. 320–30.

56. See, for example, Linklater, *Transformation of Political Community*, and Soysal, *Limits of Citizenship*.

57. In addition to the right to reside and work in EU countries, for example, citizens of

the EU member states have the right to petition the European Parliament directly. Consolidated Version of the Treaty Establishing the European Community (as amended by the Treaty of Amsterdam), article 21. Nonetheless, the Amsterdam Treaty made it clear that EU citizenship is granted through citizenship of a member state and thus it should not be treated as the cosmopolitan type (article 17 of the EC Treaty).

58. Today, two groups of scholars with different focuses are now attempting to establish models for a multi-layered citizenship structure in relation to EU citizenship. The first group emphasizes multi-layered identities, and the second multi-layered rights and obligations. See, for example, Roche, *Rethinking Citizenship*, for multi-layered identities, and Close, *Citizenship, Europe and Change*, for multi-layered citizenship rights.

59. Linklater, *Transformation of Political Community*, p. 167.

60. Ibid., pp. 166–7.

61. Richard Falk, 'The Making of Global Citizenship', in Bart van Steenbergen (ed.), *The Condition of Citizenship* (Sage, London, 1994), p. 139.

62. See Appendix II for details.

63. The notion of 'active citizenship' was first introduced in 1988 by the then Home Secretary, Douglas Hurd. His idea of 'active citizenship' was given official endorsement at the 1988 Conservative Party conference by the then Prime Minister Margaret Thatcher. The Thatcher government's attempt to promote 'active citizenship' and that of her successor, the government of John Major, through the Citizen's Charter, are explained in detail in Faulks, *Citizenship in Modern Britain*, Ch. 7.

64. See Appendix IV. Meticulous research on the legal rights and duties of British citizens undertaken by the British Institute of International and Comparative Law with the Institute for Citizenship Studies, and concluded that 'In virtually all the hallmarks, the enjoyment or imposition of a right or duty is not exclusive to British citizens, but is shared with other categories of person by virtue of a status other than that of British citizen': Gardner, *White Paper*, p. 184.

65. *British Nationality Law*, Cmnd. 7987, p. 7.

66. Ibid.

67. In an elaborate work by Low with regard to the development of the concept of citizenship in twentieth-century Britain, she argued that the idea of active citizenship at the beginning of the 1990s was based on a commercial-market ethos and was unrelated to any sense of political activity. She points out that protagonists of the current constitutional reform movement therefore call for a clear legal definition of citizenship as a way of promoting social unity, and in consequence, active political participation. Eugenia Low, 'The Concept of Citizenship in Twentieth-Century Britain: Analysing Contexts of Development', in Peter Catterall, Wolfram Kaiser and Ulrike Walton-Jordan (eds), *Reforming the Constitution: Debates in Twentieth-Century Britain* (Frank Cass, London, 2000), Ch. 7.

68. During the period between the enactment of the BN & SA act 1914 and the BNA 1948, the status of British subjecthood was maintained by the Dominions and the United Kingdom through discussion and agreement at imperial conferences. Unlike the Dominion governments, however, colonial governments simply had to follow the decisions that were made. Details of the common code system are discussed in Ch. 3.

69. Again, it is not the purpose of this book to build comprehensive and all-inclusive models of alternative types of citizenship. Models are introduced to demonstrate the limits of national citizenship and 'transnational citizenship' and to discuss a citizenship structure with multiple citizenships in Britain.

70. Salmond, 'Citizenship and Allegiance', p. 49.

71. The historical developments of British subjecthood prior to 1914 are analysed in detail in Ch. 2.
72. The colonial conference (later, imperial conferences) provided the opportunity for the prime ministers and leading ministers of the self-governing colonies (or Dominions) and Britain to discuss matters of mutual interest. For details of their early development, see John Edward Kendle, *The Colonial and Imperial Conferences: A Study in Imperial Organization* (Longman, London, 1967).
73. *Imperial Conference 1930: Summary of Proceedings*, Cmd. 3717, HMSO, November, 1930, 'Inter-Imperial Relations'. It concluded that 'it is for each Member of the Commonwealth to define for itself its own nationals, but that, so far as possible, those nationals should be persons possessing the common status'.
74. Details of the local citizenship which was established in the Dominions during the period of the common code system are discussed in Ch. 3.
75. The development and role of Commonwealth citizenship is discussed in Ch. 4.
76. Under the CIA 1962, Commonwealth citizens outside the United Kingdom lost the automatic right to enter Britain and were thus denied access to their citizenship rights in the United Kingdom. Citizens of the Republic of Ireland, however, continued to be exempt from immigration control in the United Kingdom. Details of the CIA 1962 are discussed in Ch. 4.

—2—
The Development of British Subjecthood before the Twentieth Century

THE UNION of Great Britain and Ireland was finally achieved by the Act of Union in 1800, which claimed to 'promote and secure the essential interests of Great Britain and Ireland, and to consolidate the strength, power and resources of the British Empire'.[1] By the time the three kingdoms – England, Scotland and Ireland – and the principality of Wales in the British Isles were unified, Britain had won and lost the 13 colonies in North America. In the following period up to the Second World War, however, it expanded to form the biggest empire of the time, covering, at its peak, nearly a quarter of the earth's land surface and embracing a similar proportion of its population, over 500 million in all.[2]

In the course of its expansion, the British Empire grew into a 'global institution' in the true sense, including large areas with non-European inhabitants and few British residents.[3] In order to cope with this development, a more elaborate colonial structure than before was evolved, in which each colony was granted a different degree of autonomy from the imperial government in London.[4] For all the growing complexities of ruling an empire with a much greater range of constitutions, there was still only one status for 'formal members' under the nationality law throughout the Empire: British subject. No one was a subject of England or of Newfoundland; they were either *British* subjects or they were aliens.

The issues of the status of British subjecthood prior to the twentieth century are usually dealt with in the research which examines the way English (later, British) laws applied to the colonies.[5] These studies, as a part of legal studies, concentrate on the legal character of British subjecthood without explaining its development. Little attention was paid, therefore, to the link between the development of the concept of British subjecthood and of the British Empire, whose formal members came to include, for example, Cantonese-speaking factory workers in Hong Kong as well as Muslim peasants in the Straits Settlements.[6] Yet, as was discussed earlier in the book, the nature of a political unit and of its formal membership are interrelated and cannot be divorced. In this chapter, therefore, the main focus is on the way in which the concept of British subjecthood was developed in response to territorial expansion and the diversified needs of each part of the vast Empire. Unlike the other works which barely touch upon the pre-Second World War period, this chapter argues that the characteristics of Britain's immigration and citizenship policies today – exclusive immigration control and an inclusive definition of formal membership (British subjecthood and later, Commonwealth citizenship) as well as a separation between the nominal, substantive and formal aspects of citizenship – were all evolved prior to the twentieth century.

This chapter is divided into three sections. First, it examines the basis of British subjecthood – the common law doctrine of allegiance – and the way in which the statutory rules of conferring British subjecthood were established to supplement it. The status of British subjecthood was extended in the course of forming the United Kingdom and the overseas Empire, whereas a way of terminating its status was also accepted, rather reluctantly, as a direct consequence of the loss of the American colonies. Second, it focuses on the development of colonial naturalization in the colonies, separate from imperial naturalization, in order to meet the different needs in each colony. The system of colonial naturalization unintentionally prepared the means by which an embryonic form of local identity in the colonies, especially the self-governing colonies, gradually emerged. The final part of this chapter examines the complex relationship between the concepts of British subjecthood and Britishness (a shared sense of British national identity). As the sole status of formal membership in the ethno-culturally diversified Empire, that of British subjecthood had to be granted not only to those who shared the concept of Britishness but also to those who should not.

ALLEGIANCE: THE BASIS OF BRITISH SUBJECTHOOD

The extension of British subjecthood

Allegiance and the common law doctrine of allegiance to the Crown are said to be the forerunners of modern nationality laws in England (later, in Britain). Scholars who are interested in those issues usually begin their debate by introducing Calvin's case in 1608.[7] In this case, the main point of contention was whether Calvin, a Scotsman who was born after the accession of James I (a *postnatus*), was an English subject or not. The question of his English subjecthood was crucial, as at that time only subjects were allowed to inherit lands in England. It was ruled that 'as the subject oweth to the King his true and faithful ligeance and obedience, so the Sovereign is to govern and protect his subjects'.[8] Given that allegiance was owed to the king, his ability to protect subjects derived from his kingship. Therefore, while those Scots who were born before the accession (the *antenati*) were subjects of James I, they could not be considered English subjects. The *postnati*, such as Calvin, were on the other hand acknowledged as his subjects in England. As was discussed earlier in the book, Britain did not experience the radical changes in its political institutions and forms of rule that happened, for example, in France in the aftermath of the Revolution, so that this political heritage of allegiance persisted well into the twentieth century. Furthermore, in line with this principle of granting formal membership in return for allegiance, peoples in the new colonies, whether acquired by conquest, settlement or treaty, were all accepted as British subjects, regardless of their ethno-cultural and linguistic differences.

Alongside this common law principle of allegiance, a body of laws had developed, for example, with regard to the inheritance of subjecthood by birth, and the acquisition of subjecthood by colonization and also by legislation (naturalization and denization).[9] The complexity of citizenship statuses in Britain today results from this piecemeal development of immigration and nationality laws, which were established to supplement the common law principle. One of the first rules was in relation to the inheritance of subjecthood by birth. Descent of subjecthood to foreign-born children whose parents were subjects themselves had been explicitly acknowledged since as early as the fourteenth century by the statute *De natis ultra mare* (1351).[10] Its unclear contents, however, caused confusion with regard to the number of generations through which subjecthood could be passed and from which parent. It was finally solved four centuries later by the Act of 13 Geo. III., c. 21 (1773), which decided that the right of subjecthood was conferred up to the second generation born abroad. The case of *De Geer* v. *Stone* also confirmed that the third generation born abroad was not a subject.[11] The question of whether both parents had to be natural-born was clarified by the Act of 4 Geo. II., c. 21, sec. 1 (1731), which established that the transmission of subjecthood was only through the male line.

By the mid-eighteenth century in Britain, therefore, the rules of acquisition of British subjecthood at birth had been settled in the following ways. First, it was confirmed that subjecthood was granted to 'all men born within the king's dominions immediately upon their birth',[12] on the grounds that they owed natural allegiance in return for the king's protection. Natural allegiance could not be 'forfeited, cancelled, or altered, by any change of time, place, or circumstance, nor by anything but the united concurrence of the legislature';[13] thus English subjects would have the same allegiance all through their lives wherever they might be. Second, it was confirmed that the children of natural-born subjects could still become British subjects by descent for up to two generations through the male line. Those who could not acquire subjecthood at birth were only admitted to it by a strict system of legislation, either naturalization or denization.

In the course of expanding the British Empire, the concept of a single uniform 'British subjecthood' became fundamental to the British Empire, just as it had been to the *United* Kingdom, in order to include peoples in overseas territories. The focus of debate thus moved to how to extend the common law principle of granting British subjecthood in order to include new peoples as formal members. This debate again has its origin in Calvin's case in 1608. It was explicitly elucidated then by Sir Edward Coke that the way in which the territory had been acquired, either by settlement, or by conquest or cession from other countries, decided the subject status of its inhabitants.[14] Comparing Scotland with Ireland, he argued that, unlike the case of Scotland and England whose crowns coincidentally settled upon the same person through two independent laws of succession, Ireland was acquired by conquest.[15] By virtue of the victory, the conqueror would have an absolute authority over the conquered.[16] Regardless of their date of birth, therefore, all the inhabitants (both the *antenati* and the *postnati*) of Ireland were considered as English subjects. Yet, because Ireland was a Christian kingdom, its ancient laws remained until the conqueror decided to alter them. In contrast with Coke's view on the automatic transfer of subjecthood to the conquered population, Francis Bacon inclined to the view that the conqueror needed expressly to confer subjecthood on the people either by treaty or statute.[17] It was Bacon's view in the end that prevailed in the eighteenth century. The French inhabitants in Canada, for example, became British subjects only through the Treaty of Paris of 1763.[18]

In addition to those two methods – by personal union and conquest – of expanding the empire, there were other ways of doing so. Most of the 13 colonies of North America, for example, were acquired by settlement.[19] It was generally understood that their inhabitants were English subjects on the assumption that English settlers did not lose their allegiance when they left England, and their descendants born there were of necessity natural-born subjects.[20] Going to a territory which had no organized system of law of its own, the settlers carried with them the common law and the statute laws obtaining in England at that time. Those laws were applied in consideration of the colony's locality and the circumstances of the settlers. Although the allegiance of the colonists would eventually become debatable, with the increase in the number of non-British immigrants, it remained true in British law that the inhabitants of the settled colonies were British subjects.[21] It was therefore inevitable that Westminster's understanding of allegiance – that it was natural – and that of the American colonists – that it was more contractual – diverged in the course of time.[22] The differences were finally resolved only by the Revolution and the subsequent independence of American colonies from the British Empire.

Finally, a territory could be annexed by treaty. In the case of annexation, the residents were supposed to be given a certain period of time in which to choose whether to retain their own nationality. If they chose to do so, they would have to leave the territory during that period.[23] Once it was accepted, either actively or passively, that all the inhabitants in colonies were subjects permanently, as a corollary they were, in theory, treated as subjects in Britain itself. They were then entitled to receive rights and required to undertake obligations as British subjects.

As is clear by now, the statutory rules for conferring the status of British subjecthood had a long history of development. However, they had always been regarded as a technical issue which was best left in jurists' hands, and thus did not receive, in Britain, much public attention until the nineteenth century. It was true that through the holding of British subjecthood peoples in the colonies tried to increase their citizenship rights to the same level as their counterparts in Britain.[24] The British settlers in particular claimed that they were British subjects and thus should be secured the same rights as those in Britain, such as that to representative government. In contrast, as long as one was resident in Britain, the status of British subjecthood did not mean much in everyday life. Before the twentieth century the acquisition of British subjecthood either by birth or by naturalization conferred only a few rights, such as the right to own land or to sit in Parliament, upon only a select group, such as those with property.[25] In the area of political rights, for example, the campaign for electoral reform to extend the franchise to working men only started in the mid-nineteenth century. The government also offered very few social services until the late nineteenth and early twentieth centuries, as they were considered until that time to be the responsibility of families, churches and private charities.[26] Furthermore, the number of emigrants from Britain to the colonies, especially to the settled colonies, far outnumbered those of immigrants to Britain prior to the twentieth century.[27] As a result, extension of the status of British subjecthood to peoples in the newly acquired colonies, and consequently that of the rights attached to this status, remained largely a theoretical matter for the British government and was not of interest to residents in Britain.[28]

Challenge to indelible allegiance

At the end of the eighteenth century, the long-held principle of indelible allegiance was called into question after the British loss of the American colonies in 1783. It was inevitable that such major changes in the nature of a political unit as the loss of 13 colonies accompanied changes in the nature and rule of formal membership of the political unit. After the American Revolution, therefore, the concepts of British subjecthood and the way in which it was granted led to public debate in and outside Parliament.[29] A difference of opinion between governments in the United States and the United Kingdom persisted throughout the nineteenth century regarding the allegiance of the inhabitants of the newly independent country.

Signs of changes can be found in the Declaration of Independence of 1776, which proclaimed that:

> Governments are instituted among Men, *deriving their just powers from the consent of the governed*, That whenever any Form of Government becomes destructive of these ends, it is *the Right of the People to alter or to abolish it, and to institute new Government*, laying its foundation on such principles and organizing its powers in such forms, as to them shall seem most likely to effect their Safety and Happiness. (Emphasis added)

Behind the Declaration lay the colonists' challenge to the principle of natural and indelible allegiance and their claim to the right to break it, if they found it intolerable.[30] The common law principle of allegiance, until then, only needed to provide unity within the British Empire by connecting peoples in overseas territories and Britain alike under the universal status of British subjecthood. American independence, however, posed a series of questions about the subject status of the *ante-* and *postnati* in the United States. Did those who were born before the secession of the 13 colonies remain British subjects? Could they cast off British subjecthood? What was the test for the decision, and could the *postnati* be granted British subjecthood by descent? In answering these questions, the very foundation of British subjecthood – the concept of allegiance – was once again examined, nearly two centuries after Calvin's Case.

At the time of the American Revolution, British subjects who moved, for example, to France or to China, could not remove their allegiance, but continued to owe 'the same allegiance to the king of England there as at home, and twenty years hence as well as now'.[31] It had been acknowledged, at least in Britain, as 'a principle of universal law' that natural-born subjects could not give up their natural allegiance by any act of their own such as swearing allegiance to another sovereign. For natural allegiance was understood as 'intrinsic, and primitive, and antecedent to the other [type of allegiance]'.[32] The only way to discharge natural allegiance was by 'the concurrent act of that prince to whom [natural allegiance] was due'.[33] Following this line of understanding, the British government continued to regard a large number of American citizens of British origin and descent as its subjects even after independence.

As a result, the British government was theoretically providing protection to them in return for their allegiance, although they were sometimes hostile to Britain.[34] The issue was not whether the British government could practically provide protection for them. Nor did it matter whether they actually owed allegiance to the British government and the British Empire. Given that the acquisition of subjecthood by descent was to be allowed, moreover, the number of British subjects in the United States of America was substantial, and even growing.[35] In the absence of a clear declaration from the British government regarding the status of American citizens of British birth, the argument centred on whether the Treaty of Peace of 1783 was 'the united concurrence of the legislature'.[36] The US government obviously thought so, whereas its British counterpart did not. This difference of views caused further friction between the two governments over the press-ganging of seamen during the Napoleonic Wars and the right of expatriation (whether or not naturalized American citizens of British origin would remain British subjects) until 1870.[37]

From the perspective of the pro-Revolutionary American thinkers, the Revolution broke up the Empire, and each resident in the 13 colonies was given the chance to choose whether to stay a British subject or to become a citizen of the United States. As for the *antenati*, however, even the British government originally accepted that those who made a commitment to Britain remained British subjects and those who did not became US citizens. When the two countries signed the Jay Treaty on commerce and navigation in 1794, for example, the residents in the United States were given a year to declare their intention to remain British subjects, at least in terms of commerce and trade.[38] Those who failed to do so, according to the treaty, would be considered as 'having elected to become citizens of the United States'.[39]

Shortly afterwards, however, the debate on the subjecthood of the *antenati* was revived by an English legal historian, John Reeves, and a Scottish-born lawyer, George Chalmers.[40] Basing his argument on Calvin's Case, Reeves concluded that the American *antenati* only owed local allegiance to America and their rights as subjects could revive as soon as they moved to Britain. Chalmers, on the other hand, emphasized that people owed allegiance in return for protection, thereby those *antenati* Americans who remained in the United States became aliens in Britain after 1783. The argument was finally resolved in the case of *Doe* v. *Acklam* in 1824, when the issue was to determine if a child, Frances Mary, born in the United States after the recognition of independence of parents born there before that time, could inherit lands in Britain.[41] It was decided that her father ceased to be a subject because of his continued residence before her birth, thus she was also an alien and incapable of inheriting land in England. The statement concluded that 'by continued residence in [America]', a British subject 'manifestly became a citizen of [America]' in order to avoid the inconvenient situation where a large number of people become 'at once citizens and subjects of two distinct and independent States'. In the end, a decade-long controversy as to the status of the *antenati* ended by basing the decision on the inconvenience of dual citizenship. This led the focus of argument to another cause of dual citizenship: the naturalized citizens of British origin in the United States.

During the early days of independence, it was only necessary to decide who would remain British subjects and who would not. In the course of time, the number of British immigrants into the United States increased and, consequently, so did the number of naturalizations. Naturally, the focus of debate shifted to the further question of whether naturalization was a way to cast off the old allegiance. The original controversy between Britain and the United States – on whether or not Britain would give up the doctrine of perpetual allegiance – therefore developed into the issue of whether or not people possessed the right of expatriation (the divestment of allegiance).

Given the history of the Revolution and America's active naturalization policy, it would be logical to assume that American concepts of allegiance were contractual and volitional, and therefore consistent with the right of expatriation and the right of people to renounce their old allegiance and acquire new loyalties. Contrary to that assumption, however, opinions in the United States were not always unanimously supportive of the right of expatriation. The courts of the United States, for example, often made inconsistent decisions, sometimes ruling for the right of expatriation and sometimes against.[42] Furthermore, there was no legislation in the United States on the right of expatriation until 1868. The judicial tribunals therefore concluded that 'as there is no existing legislative regulation on the case [of renouncing allegiance], the rule of the English common law [of indelible allegiance] remains unaltered'.[43] The judiciary's conclusion against the right of expatriation angered the committee in the House of Representatives, and it criticized the judiciary for being 'often governed less by reason than by precedents'.[44] However, delay in legislating the right of expatriation could also be attributed to some members of Congress who worried that such legislation by the national government would be an attempt to increase its power over the states.[45] This contradiction between the judiciary on the one hand, and the executive branch in the United States on the other, provided a convenient excuse for the British government to continue to deny the existence of the right of expatriation.[46]

In contrast to the ambivalent attitude of the United States, the British government had always been in favour of the principle of indelible allegiance and consequently against the right of expatriation. It insisted on maintaining the doctrine of perpetual allegiance to the sovereign of the country where the subject was born. This position was typically presented by the proclamation of King George III in November 1807, when he tried to justify the right to search the merchant ships of neutral countries on the high seas for British seamen.[47] Since 1792 successive governments in the United States had incessantly criticized the British practice of searching American ships and impressing any seamen of British origin who were aboard on the grounds of treason. George III, in the face of complaints from the US government, pronounced then that 'no such letters of naturalization, or certificates of citizenship, do, or can, in any manner, divest our natural-born subjects of the allegiance, or in any degree alter the duty which they owe to us, their lawful Sovereign'.[48]

This dispute between the two countries was finally settled by the Naturalization Convention in 1870. It was enacted in consequence of disturbances in Ireland in 1848 and 1866, which were triggered by Irish demands for independence.[49] The British government was informed in 1848 that a plot had been organized in the United States for the purpose of sending men to assist the malcontents in Ireland. In response, the British government issued an order to arrest every American or returned emigrant landing in Ireland.[50] The arrest and detention of two men, an American and an Irishman naturalized in America, immediately followed. The US government protested against this action, only to be told by its British counterpart that 'natural-born subjects of Great Britain, who may become naturalized in a foreign country, but who return to the United Kingdom, are as amenable as any other of Her Majesty's subjects to any laws which may be in force, either of a permanent or of a temporary nature'.[51] Just before the conflict of opinion became overheated, the two arrested men were released on condition that they left the United Kingdom.

After a short interval the issue of naturalized Americans of British origin was again brought to general attention when in 1866 Habeas Corpus was suspended in Ireland. The controversy this time was greater than in 1848, because naturalized Americans of Irish origin were again arrested and some were sentenced to death when in the same year the Fenian raid on Canada took place.[52] A number of resolutions were presented to Congress in the following years in order to secure the rights of naturalized Americans abroad, while the British government fought back by pointing out the conflict of doctrine on this issue between the executive and the judiciary in the United States.[53] President Andrew Johnson finally clarified the position of the government in a message in 1868, which stated that 'naturalization in conformity with the constitution and laws of the United States absolves the recipient from his native allegiance'.[54] After further debate in Congress, a conclusion was finally reached in the same year that the right of expatriation was 'a natural and inherent right of all people, indispensable to the enjoyment of the right of life, liberty, and the pursuit of happiness'.[55] It also pronounced 'any declaration, instruction, opinion, order, or decision of any officers of this government which denies, restricts, impairs, or questions the right of expatriation,' to be 'inconsistent with the fundamental principles of this government'.[56]

By then diplomatic negotiations had been proceeding between the two countries for a long time, and they were accelerated after the act of 25 July 1868 was passed in Congress. In the meantime, the US government had successfully completed a treaty with the North German Confederation in 1868 to enable citizens of both countries to renounce their original citizenship by naturalization. This treaty was followed by similar treaties with countries such as Baden, Bavaria, Hesse, Mexico, Sweden and Norway. Signing a treaty with Britain had proved more difficult than with other countries, in view of the large number of the naturalizations involved and the history of imperial rule and subjection between the two countries. The successes with the other countries nonetheless strengthened the commitment of the US government, which repeatedly insisted that it would not discuss with its British counterpart any other issues until the matter of naturalization was resolved.[57] In addition to the determination of the US side, the British government was well aware that it was not practically possible to provide protection to all British emigrants abroad, which was what its doctrine of indefeasible allegiance would have entailed. As one MP pointed out, the British government gave up protecting naturalized American citizens of British origin during the course of the American civil war, so that the US government had conscripted them into the war.[58] The British government, therefore, had by then accepted in principle the need to sign a treaty with the US government. Thus when asked in Parliament about the possibility of a treaty, the Attorney General, Sir J. B. Karslake, simply pointed out that legal details had to be worked out, 'however willing [the British government] might be to enter into such an arrangement [of naturalization]'.[59] Although he ruled out the chances of signing a treaty immediately, he frankly admitted that his government was ready to do so as soon as it could.

Succumbing to the pressure from the United States and accepting the impossibility of the doctrine of indelible allegiance, the Gladstone government signed a protocol in 1868, and promised to introduce legislation in order to realise the principles of the protocol.[60] The following year the Report of the Royal Commissioners with regard to the laws of naturalization and allegiance explicitly acknowledged that this doctrine of common law was 'neither reasonable nor convenient'.[61] It continued:

[the doctrine of indelible allegiance] is at variance with those principles on which the rights and duties of a subject should be deemed to rest; it conflicts with that freedom of action which is now recognized as most conducive to the general good as well as to individual happiness and prosperity; and it is especially inconsistent with the practice of a State which allows to its subjects absolute freedom of emigration. It is inexpedient that British law should maintain in theory, or should by foreign nations be supposed to maintain in practice, any obligations which it cannot enforce and ought not to enforce if it could; and it is unfit that a country should remain subject to claims for protection on the part of persons who, so far as in them lies, have severed their connexion with it.[62]

It accepted that a British subject, by voluntarily becoming naturalized in another country, thereupon lost the status of British subjecthood and became an alien. It even allowed British subjects who had dual citizenship at birth to make a declaration of alienage renouncing their British subjecthood.

In recommending that the doctrine of indelible allegiance be abolished, furthermore, the 1869 Royal Commissioners required a number of British subjects to lose their status of British subjecthood. Consequently, its accompanying rights and privileges, such as the right to hold and inherit land in Britain, had to be taken away also. By then, aliens were able to hold land in many European countries and even in quite a few colonies within the British Empire, such as British Columbia, Queensland and Victoria.[63] The commissioners thus advised that these disabilities which had been imposed on aliens should also be abrogated in Britain. The Naturalization Act (33 & 34 Vict., c. 14) 1870 gave effect to all these recommendations. In the end, it not only abolished the doctrine of indelible allegiance, which was said to have originated from feudal society, but also swept away restrictions upon the holding of land by aliens in Britain and greatly increased the status of aliens in Britain.[64]

DIVERSIFICATION WITHIN BRITISH SUBJECTHOOD: COLONIAL AND IMPERIAL NATURALIZATION

The emergence of various naturalization systems

Naturalization or denization was another exception to the main rule of acquiring subjecthood: 'birth within the king's ligeance'.[65] The practice of denization or naturalization was historically pursued in particular by wealthy people, because before 1870 it was only by these methods that the prohibition on owning or inheriting real estate could be removed. As was discussed in the previous chapter, egalitarian and democratic citizenship has been acknowledged as the international norm only since the Second World War.[66] Until then, it was common for the holders of citizenship to be granted different citizenship rights and obligation from each other, some citizenship rights, such as that to vote, being dependent upon income level or social background. Neither was immigration control in Britain based on the holding of citizenship (at that time, British subjecthood) until the First World War, as the main aim of control in the nineteenth century was to keep out revolutionary individuals from the Continent.[67]

The difference between naturalization and denization was that denizens, on the one hand, could purchase and own land, but only children born after denization could inherit it. On the other hand, naturalized subjects and their children could inherit as well as purchase and own the land. Unlike denization, naturalization could operate retrospectively. Some people, however, preferred denization as it was obtainable without taking any oaths, thereby allowing Jews and Roman Catholics to apply for denization. Because denization was based on the discretion of the Crown, its condition and operation could be flexibly applied to each individual case.[68]

Neither naturalization nor denization, however, conferred the same rights on the naturalized as upon natural-born subjects. The disadvantageous position of naturalized or endenized subjects had been engraved in legislation at the beginning of the eighteenth century due to the partiality, or fear of it, displayed by William III towards his Dutch officers and their dependants. First, the Act of 12 & 13 Will. III., c. 2 (1700) prohibited naturalized subjects from becoming members of the Privy Council or of either House of Parliament, or holding a public office, or receiving grant of crown lands (s. 3). After the Act of 1 Geo. I., c. 4 (1714), all the bills of naturalization had to include a clause containing the disqualifications laid down in the 1700 act. Governments sometimes passed special legislation in order to encourage the naturalization of a certain group of people, for example, those who had a special skill.[69] Naturalization outside these special acts was, however, a costly and cumbersome procedure, and so was rarely practised. The report by the select committee on the laws affecting aliens in 1843, for example, attributed the small number of applications for naturalization (less than an average of eight a year) to the cost (above £100) and the time required for naturalization.[70] In spite of successive recommendations by parliamentary committees, the disadvantages imposed on naturalized subjects remained on the statute book till the enactment of the BN & SA act 1914.[71]

In addition to the division between natural-born and naturalized subjects, there were further sub-divisions within the category of naturalized subjects as a result of two factors: the existence of several different structures of naturalization and the difference in the extra-territorial effect of each structure. For example, unlike the English Parliament, the Irish Parliament naturalized those Scots who were born before the accession of James I as well as those born after.[72] The situation became more complicated when it was decided in *Craw* v. *Ramsey* in 1669 that legislation by the Irish Parliament had no effect in England, whereas English laws were valid in Ireland, because Ireland was conquered by England and thus subordinate to England.[73] Those subjects naturalized in England were, therefore, treated as subjects in Ireland, but those naturalized in Ireland remained aliens in England. As a result, until the union between England and Ireland in 1800, there existed a common nationality law which was enacted at Westminster, and two distinctive naturalization laws under English (later, British) and Irish law within the British Isles.

Outside the British Isles, systems of colonial naturalization also developed, and were diverse in form and extent. Since their early days in the seventeenth century, the north American and West Indian colonies had experienced an urgent and consistent need to increase their populations.[74] It was necessary for them, therefore, to enact naturalization laws for local inhabitants and aliens and to entice them to stay there by enabling them to own land.[75] Although nobody was certain, at that time, on what legal authority colonial governments could confer subjecthood upon foreigners, the practice of colonial naturalization continued without interference from London.[76] The imperial government simply thought it impossible to control a local matter such as naturalization in a colony so far away from Britain. In contrast to the stringent conditions of naturalization in Britain, which persisted at least until the mid-nineteenth century, colonial governments granted subjecthood under extremely generous conditions.[77] For example, one scholar points out 'the virtual carte blanche to foreign Protestants, the absence of the performance of any religious rite, the limited but deliberate welcome to foreign Jews, the willingness at times to incorporate Roman Catholic aliens'.[78] In addition to religious requirements, the high fee for applying for naturalization was often attenuated in the colonies.[79]

Not only the colonial laws but also the laws of Britain were passed specifically to simplify the naturalization procedure in the colonies for the purpose of encouraging settlement there. The precedent was the Act of 13 Geo. II., c. 7 (1740). Under this act, all the foreign Protestants living in any of His Majesty's colonies in America for seven years without a period of absence longer than two months at any one time were allowed to be naturalized without having to seek a special act in London. Furthermore, those who became British subjects under the 1740 act were also able to enforce their rights not only in a particular colony but also throughout the Empire. Unlike naturalization in other colonies, whose extraterritorial validity was always uncertain outside the specific territory, the 1740 act guaranteed the validity of the naturalization across the Empire.[80] In short, when the British and Irish naturalization laws were unified in 1800 by the Act of Union, there were four different sub-categories within the single category of British subject: natural-born, naturalized with imperial effect, naturalized with local effect and denizens. All of them, although belonging to the single category of British subject, owned different rights and privileges.

Other works on British immigration policy overlook this point, but this study stresses that to have formal members (British subjects prior to the Second World War and Commonwealth citizens, afterwards) divided into sub-categories, of whom some were allowed to enjoy more rights than others, was not a novel post-Second World War phenomenon. It is true that the criteria for dividing formal members differ depending on the period: imperial versus colonial prior to the BN & SA act 1914, and the OCW versus the NCW after the Second World War.[81] However, as is seen in the case of naturalization up to 1914, holding the same citizenship-as-status did not necessarily guarantee its holders the same citizenship-as rights and as-desirable-activity. Also, holding the same citizenship-as-status did not mean that the holders belonged to the same ethno-cultural group. Nor did it imply that they shared a sense of attachment. It was not expected by the imperial government that farm workers in Jamaica should identify themselves with bankers in London. Nor did it matter to Westminster if they did not.[82]

The separate development of the imperial and colonial naturalization systems

Before the eighteenth century the confusing state of the law on subjecthood status in relation to naturalization and nationality was caused mainly by the inheritance of subjecthood by descent. After it was resolved, the lack of a guiding judicial principle on naturalization became the main cause for confusion about the status of British subjecthood within the empire.[83] As the British empire expanded geographically, so the laws of naturalization developed according to what suited each colony. They thereby increasingly lost any overall coherence.

In the early nineteenth century the focus of immigration policy moved, for a while, from naturalization to control of the admission of aliens and, if necessary, their expulsion.[84] This happened in the context of, first, political turbulence after the French Revolution and, second, the Napoleonic Wars.[85] Several acts, namely, the Aliens Acts of 1793, 1826 and 1848, were enacted to regulate immigration flows by authorizing the collection of the list of foreign passengers on board an arriving ship, enabling their expulsion when this was deemed necessary.[86] Control over the entry of immigrants into Britain had, however, remained an emergency measure which could be justified only in extraordinary circumstances.[87] As soon as peace returned to the Continent in the mid-nineteenth century, therefore, fairly liberal policies were again adopted towards aliens and their immigration to Britain. As the government began to place a stronger emphasis on overseas trade and economic expansion under the banner of free trade, so immigration came to be judged in the context of what would be to Britain's economic advantage.[88] In that context, the immigration and settlement of foreigners were supported by a number of policy-makers on the basis of the immigrants bringing new skills and technologies to Britain. In contrast to the previous long history of stringent controls on naturalization in Britain, successive governments during this period changed their policy and tried to encourage naturalization by providing easier admissions and more rights for naturalized subjects than before.

Efforts to simplify the naturalization process and extend the rights of the naturalized in Britain were highlighted by motions made several times by a Liberal MP, W. Hutt in 1843, in which he aimed to introduce a general naturalization scheme for foreigners.[89] The main purpose of his motions was to 'confer on the Crown the power of granting to foreigners all the privileges of British subjects, including the right to sit in Parliament, and to sit at the Privy Council'.[90] Hutt emphasized that, in order to compete with foreign rivals, the British government needed to promote a ready movement of the inhabitants of different countries. As a stout believer in the principle of free trade, he compared the movements of peoples to those of goods, and justified his support for an easier naturalization procedure and the improvement of the status of aliens as a means to encourage highly skilled artisans and manufacturers to come to Britain. He reminded Parliament that highly skilled artisans used to flee continental countries such as France and the Netherlands because of religious persecution and take refuge in Britain, thereby benefiting Britain.[91] Nowadays, he lamented, stringent naturalization laws and the disadvantages imposed on aliens forced them to go elsewhere. As a solution to reviving the immigration of skilled workers, he stressed the need to provide 'the appointed means by which new arts, new discoveries, and new additions to the comforts and conveniences of life' would be introduced to Britain.[92]

The issues of naturalization were left to the Select Committee on the Laws Affecting Aliens, which was established later in the same year. The report which it prepared suggested a further advance of the free trade movement.[93] Claiming economic benefits to the country, the committee recommended the easier admission by law of foreign residents 'to whatever rights the legislature may think fit to invest them with, and that such rights should include the capacity to fill certain offices of trust, and employments civil and military'.[94] The high cost and long delay of the naturalization process were criticized for lessening the extent of the practical benefits which might accrue from the migration of skilful and industrious foreigners to Britain. As a country which was 'so deeply interested in trade and manufactures', the report found it undesirable 'to maintain laws which deter from settling here foreigners who may be better acquainted than [British] people with processes, inventions, and discoveries important to the pursuits of industry'.[95] It completely agreed with the line of argument of free-traders such as Hutt, claiming that naturalization in Britain should not 'create inducements to foreigners to carry away and disburse in other countries the wealth they have accumulated'.[96] As a response to the report, in the end the Act of 7 & 8 Vict., c. 66 was passed and on 6 August 1844 received the royal assent.[97]

The 1844 act rendered the practice of granting letters of denization or special acts of Parliament unnecessary except in some special cases, and introduced a simple, administrative form of naturalization.[98] On the basis of a 'memorial' (similar to the character reference in the private bill procedure) the Secretary of State could issue a certificate of naturalization to a person who wished to settle and was willing to take an oath of allegiance. As a result, naturalization became a matter of administrative discretion, with no lengthy process being required. The provision of the 1714 act requiring the disqualifying clause to be inserted into all the private bills of naturalization was also repealed by the 1844 act (s. 2). However, section 6 of the 1844 act still prohibited naturalized subjects from becoming members of the Privy Council or of either House of Parliament and made them subject to such further restrictions as might be imposed by the certificate of naturalization. Once imposed, restrictions could only be removed by grant. Thus, after 1844, foreigners were naturalized, as one specialist on nationality and immigration laws described it, 'either, *under* an Act of Parliament, which retained two of the disqualifications; or, *by* an Act of Parliament which could confer upon them the maximum rights of a natural-born subject'.[99] Supported by the mood of the time, which increasingly encouraged a free-trade policy, the 1844 act, in the end, established, and confirmed, the generous system of naturalization in Britain.[100] By reducing the restrictions imposed upon naturalized subjects, their status in terms of rights and obligations became closer to that of natural-born subjects, further consolidating the status of British subjecthood into one. In so doing, in my view, this act brought the status of British subjecthood a step closer to the modern-day notion of formal membership: dividing the world's population into members and non-members.

While the way to earn the status of British subjecthood was further systematised by the 1844 act, doubts arose soon after its enactment as to whether it extended to the colonies. Until then, each colony had been left relatively free from the control of London and developed naturalization and immigration policies of its own. For example, even in a colony such as Trinidad, where there was no 'responsible government' and the entire control of the colony's affairs was reserved to Britain, the colony had its own naturalization system.[101] There, an alien became entitled within the limits of the colony to all the privileges of a natural-born subject after having taken the oath of allegiance before the governor.[102] The practice of colonial naturalization developed in parallel with colonial policy in the nineteenth century under which the autonomy of colonial governments over local matters was extended, especially in settled colonies. As has been argued in this work, the nature of the political unit influences, and is exemplified by, the definition of formal membership. Although the degree of autonomy differed from one colony to another, each was able to decide to some extent its own rule for ascribing subjecthood within its territory.

The Act of 10 & 11 Vict., c. 83 (1847), passed without any parliamentary debate, stated that the 1844 act did not apply to the colonies. In this way, it officially ensured, for the first time, the power of the colonial government to enact naturalization laws, statutes, or ordinances of their own 'within the respective limits of such colonies or possessions respectively' (s. 1). As a result of the territorial limit of colonial naturalization thereby confirmed, a Frenchman naturalized in New Zealand was a British subject there, but a Frenchman in England. Those who were naturalized in Victoria became British subjects, while on crossing the border into New South Wales they found themselves to be aliens. A locally naturalized subject in Victoria, however, was, as a subject of the Queen, entitled to the protection of the British government outside the British Empire, except in his or her country of birth.[103]

The 1870 act, which was enacted to approve the right of expatriation by way of naturalization, also reconfirmed in its section 16 that colonial legislation could confer the rights of a naturalized British subject only within the limits of the colony.[104] Parry thus claimed that the system of colonial naturalization, which was officially confirmed by the 1847 and 1870 acts, exemplified colonial policy in the nineteenth century: 'that of devolution to both the executive and legislative branches of colonial governments of an ever-increasing responsibility for local affairs'.[105] Adding to Parry's observation, this study again stresses that these two acts provided colonial governments with the power to determine who, among the holders of British subjecthood, were entitled to receive citizenship rights and obligations within their territories. In other words, the 1847 and 1870 acts not only confirmed the validity of local naturalization, but they also ended up encouraging colonial governments to strengthen colonial immigration policies of their own. Citizenship, immigration and naturalization laws are related to each other, immigration and naturalization laws determining potential, and nationality laws, innate, citizens. They are thus implemented in a co-ordinated manner. The governments of self-governing colonies (later called the 'White Dominions') established immigration policies in combination with colonial naturalization acts in order to prevent people of Asian origin from entering their territories. For example, the New South Wales Act 4 of 1888 linked immigration control with naturalization. It prohibited any Chinese from being naturalized on any ground whatsoever and, moreover, all Chinese residents leaving New South Wales, except those who had been naturalized therein, would on returning be subject to immigration control.[106] With exclusive immigration and naturalization laws combined, colonial governments were better equipped to exclude peoples whom they did not wish to include.

As a result, the immigration policy of each colony was developed and strengthened in parallel with the practice of colonial naturalization. Together they provided the basis for establishing local citizenship in the Dominions in the first half of the twentieth century, and then a citizenship structure with multiple citizenships after the Second World War. It is true, however, that colonial naturalization originated from the need of each colony to increase its population, and was not intended to consolidate a local identity, whatever that was. By the mid-nineteenth century some colonies, such as those in Australia, Canada and New Zealand, began actively to use immigration control and linked it to colonial naturalization laws. Nonetheless, the definition was arrived at by excluding a certain group of people – those of Asian origin – rather than by requiring conformity to positive obligations such as being loyal to the political community. Those legislators and politicians in Britain who were involved in the debate on naturalization were, furthermore, unaware at that time that the practices of colonial naturalization and immigration control would eventually lead to the creation of local citizenship alongside the vague notion of British subjecthood. They surely did not imagine then that the citizenship structure based on British subjecthood would be destroyed by local demand in Canada for a citizenship law of its own in 1946. There was simply no debate on the concept of British subjecthood in relation to colonial naturalization, nor did anyone express then the fear that the creation of local citizenship might conflict with the notion of British subjecthood. The 1844 act, for example, aimed mainly to encourage naturalization as a part of free-trade policy, and the 1847 act was passed without any debates in Parliament. Without a guiding principle in the framing of naturalization laws, successive governments simply responded to the immediate demands of the time, such as labour shortages in the colonies and the free-trade policy in Britain itself.

The very foundations of the empire in which all subjects shared the single status of 'British subject' and were tied to a common superior were also preserved and never questioned during the period under discussion. In comparison with imperial naturalization, colonial naturalization had always been strictly limited to its own territory. It is true that this practice subsequently produced a hierarchy within the category of 'British subject' in terms of the rights and obligations which each British subject enjoyed. Yet because colonial naturalization had only limited effects, the British government paid little attention to it and could continue to maintain an inclusive concept of British subjecthood. The diversified needs of each part of the vast Empire were, at the same time, catered for by colonial naturalization. To the extent that the system of local naturalization was not directly destructive of the unity of British subjecthood, it was allowed to develop.

We cannot ignore, however, the fact that the system of colonial naturalization ended up, however unintentionally, by providing a basis for each colony to develop an identity of its own, separate from the imperial one.[107] In order to define who among the British subjects throughout the Empire belonged to them, some of the Dominions in the twentieth century increasingly used immigration, and to a lesser degree naturalization, laws which had been developed during this period. The naturalization system which had been established by the 1870 act continued until 1914, when the status in the colonies of a naturalized British subject became recognized for the whole empire.[108] In sum, the diversified nature of each colony, and consequently that of its peoples, was accommodated within the unity of the British Empire and British subjecthood, the needs of individual colonies being fulfilled by colonial naturalization laws with a limited territorial effect.

BRITISH SUBJECTHOOD AND BRITISHNESS

It was clear from the debate on the definition and making of national citizenship set out in Chapter 1 that British subjecthood developed in a different way from national citizenship. Unlike national citizenship,

British subjecthood, and the common law principle of allegiance which provided the basis of British subjecthood, had to confer a single citizenship-as-status upon ethno-culturally diversified populations who might share little loyalty or affection with those in Britain. Since formal membership was not based on nationhood, there was room for local identities to emerge alongside the imperial status of British subjecthood.

Before the turn of the twentieth century, the citizenship structure based on the principle of allegiance was almost complete, each detail being added as necessary to solve the problems of the time, such as the treatment of the naturalized subjects in the newly independent United States or the complicated development of naturalization systems in the colonies. As a unifying force among the diversified people who lived in the British Empire, however, the status of British subjecthood had always been shared equally by all of them. In the mid-nineteenth century, for example, this unity of citizenship-as-status was used by Lord Palmerston, with regard to the so-called Don Pacifico Affair, to justify his imperialistic policy. David Pacifico, who had become a British subject as a consequence of his birth in Gibraltar, had his house in Athens mobbed in 1847. In response to his appeal to the British government to secure compensation from the Greek government, Palmerston sent a fleet to Greece to blockade Piraeus three years after the actual incident had taken place. For those who criticized his gunboat action, he proudly stated in the House of Commons in 1850 that

> as the Roman, in days of old, held himself free from indignity, when he could say *Civis Romanus sum*; so also a British subject, in whatever land he may be, shall feel confident that the watchful eye and the strong arm of England, will protect him against injustice and wrong.[109]

Comparing a British subject's rights anywhere in the world ('*Civis Britannicus sum*') to those claimed by a citizen of ancient Rome, Palmerston defended his policy on the grounds that the British government had an obligation to provide protection to its subjects all over the world.[110]

Whereas an all-embracing status of British subjecthood led to Palmerston's claim of '*Civis Britannicus sum*' as its corollary, David Pacifico was a Spanish Jew who was normally resident in Portugal and had hardly any substantial contacts with Britain. It is therefore highly questionable whether he shared with British subjects in Britain any sense of belonging. Colley, in her work on the period between 1707 and 1837, illustrates the way that Britain's shared sense of national identity (Britishness) was superimposed on an array of 'much older allegiances' of Welshness, Scottishness and Englishness, and continued to develop in response to contact (or conflict) with the 'others' in the shape of militant Catholicism, a hostile continental European power or an exotic overseas empire.[111] Those people who were portrayed as the 'others', such as the Catholic Irish and the colonial people, were, nonetheless, simultaneously included among the holders of British subjecthood under the principle of allegiance. Here, we find the roots of the characteristics of citizenship in Britain: the decoupling of each aspect of citizenship and the separation between Britishness and Britain's formal membership. It is therefore essential to look at the period before the twentieth century, although most of the existing works on nationality and immigration policy in Britain have hardly done so.

By presenting a survey of the origin and development of British subjecthood, this chapter has argued that, for the then policy-makers, the concept of Britishness, however it was defined, could never be the condition for granting British subjecthood. In addition, they allowed, to a certain extent, each colonial government to pass colonial naturalization and immigration laws and confer British subjecthood within its territory. Ultimately, among the holders of the all-embracing status of British subjecthood there developed two groupings of people: those who were regarded as British subjects throughout the world and the others who were British subjects only within a particular colony. For the latter group, unlike the former, their status of British subjecthood had an imperial name, but only a local effect.

More specifically, the system of colonial naturalization indicated that the imperial government in Westminster accepted, along with the clearer division between British subjects and aliens, the internal division of British subjects between those in the metropole and those on the peripheries of the British Empire in terms of the status and the identity of formal membership. Although all British subjects, whether they were from London or Hong Kong, were regarded equally as British subjects once they were outside the Empire, villagers in Hong Kong, for example, did not need to identify with the Londoners. The colonial government in Hong Kong at the same time could enact its naturalization and immigration laws which were based on its own needs and interests. With the abolition of indelible allegiance in 1870, the significance of allegiance as the main basis for British subjecthood was also weakened, while an element of volition and contract was introduced.

It is, however, important to keep in mind the following two points in order to avoid over-emphasizing the development of the local identities which began to emerge through colonial naturalization and immigration laws prior to the twentieth century. First, the local identity in each colony was still very much at an embryonic stage, even in those self-governing colonies where it was most developed. All the rights and obligations were also attached to the holding of British subjecthood. The emergence of what was to become local citizenship in the twentieth century was only seen in relation to immigration and naturalization laws. Furthermore, immigration and naturalization laws during the period under discussion were most actively implemented in the self-governing colonies mainly to prevent British subjects of Asian origin from entering their territories, rather than to preserve whatever nationhood they held at the time.[112]

Unlike the relationship between peoples in Britain and the non-self-governing colonies, furthermore, there existed a strong mutual sentiment between those in Britain and the self-governing colonies (later, the Dominions). This sentiment, which was supported and promoted through flows of immigrants from Britain to those areas, is the second point which we have to remember when we discuss the emergence of local identity in the colonies. While British subjects of Asian origin were prevented from entering Canada, for instance, the promotion of emigration to Canada continued in the British Isles in order to secure a flow of immigrants from the mother country and to keep the British component of Canada's population high.[113] In the face of this strong mutual sentiment, for the majority of the population in Britain the colonial Empire remained a remote entity. In so far as they thought about the Empire at all, their attention was more likely to concentrate on the 'White Dominions' to which relatives or friends might have emigrated. Both policy-makers and the public in Britain maintained an affection towards people in Australia, Canada, New Zealand and, to a lesser extent, South Africa, and vice versa. As a result, people in some Dominions, especially Australia and New Zealand, were proud of being British subjects and their governments consequently opted not to enact local citizenship laws until the end of the Second World War.

This does not mean that people in non-self-governing colonies were unaware of, or totally denied, their link with Britain. On the contrary, those in the Caribbean colonies, for example, often felt strongly about being British subjects.[114] As one scholar stresses, people there 'took their British [subjecthood] seriously, and many regarded themselves not as strangers, but as kinds of Englishmen'.[115] Their affection for their fellow subjects in the mother country was, however, largely unreciprocated. This was demonstrated when colonial subjects started immigrating into the United Kingdom after the Second World War. Inside the mother country, they met with prejudice from the host population, who treated them as *immigrants*, rather than as *British subjects*.[116]

After all, the psychological link between peoples in Britain and the Dominions was much stronger than that between peoples in Britain and the colonies. The division between Britain and the Dominions on the one hand and the colonies on the other became sharpened and institutionalized by the creation of the common code system in 1914. Under the common code system, the imperial type of citizenship, British subjecthood, was maintained through agreement and consultation between the governments of Britain and the Dominions, while it continued to be granted by the imperial act to peoples in the colonies. The embryonic form of local identity in the Dominions which began to emerge prior to the twentieth century was further strengthened during the period of the common code system. This common code system is the subject of Chapter 3.

NOTES

1. 40 Geo. III., c. 67 (1800), the preamble. The Act of Union came into force in 1801. The union of Great Britain and Ireland, which had covered the whole of the British Isles, broke up when the southern 26 counties of Ireland formed the Irish Free State in 1921.
2. Fieldhouse, *Colonial Empires*, p. 242.
3. New Zealand, Australia and British Columbia as well as much of southern Africa and central Canada were all to be settled by British colonists in the nineteenth century. Some areas, however, had a significant non-British population when they became parts of the British Empire; others came to receive increasing numbers of non-British immigrants in the course of time. A. F. Madden, 'Constitution-Making and Nationhood: The British Experience – An Overview', *Journal of Commonwealth and Comparative Politics*, 26, 2 (July 1988), pp. 128–31.
4. Minty classifies colonies into four groups in accordance with their constitutional status and degree of autonomy. They are: self-governing dominions, those with responsible government subject to the reservation of certain matters for the legislation of the imperial government, British India and the Crown colonies. Leonard Le Marchant Minty, *Constitutional Laws of the British Empire* (Sweet & Maxwell, London, 1928), pp. 1–2.
5. For example, see Sir Charles James Tarring, *Chapters on the Law Relating to the Colonies to which are Appended Topical Indexes of Cases Decided in the Privy Council on Appeal from the Colonies, Channel Islands and the Isle of Man and of Cases Relating to the Colonies Decided in the English Courts otherwise than on Appeal therefrom* (Stevens & Haynes, London, 1913 [1893]), Ch. 1.
6. Dummett and Nicol's is one of the few existing works which covers nationality and immigration laws during this period and attempts to analyse their development in

relation to the historical background. Unlike their work, this chapter aims to put more emphasis on the development and changing character of the British Empire and its impact on the immigration and nationality laws of the time. Dummett and Nicol, *Subjects, Citizens, Aliens and Others*.

7. Calvin's Case, 7 Co. Rep. I (1608). Constitutional historians regard Calvin's Case as the origin of the principle of allegiance. The common law rule of conferring subjecthood on the basis of place of birth was established in the mid-fourteenth century, and reconfirmed in Calvin's Case. D. H. Wilson, 'King James and Anglo-Scottish Unity', in W. A. Aiken and B. D. Henning (eds), *Conflict in Stuart England* (Jonathan Cape, London, 1960), pp. 43–55. J. M. Ross, 'English Nationality Law: *Soli* or *Sanguinis?*', *Grotian Society Papers* (Martinus Nijhoff, The Hague, 1972), p. 6.

8. Calvin's Case.

9. The first case of naturalization is commonly considered to be that of 1295. Clive Parry, *Nationality and Citizenship Laws of the Commonwealth and of the Republic of Ireland* (Stevens & Sons, London, 1957), pp. 34–40. 'Endenization' was quasi-subjecthood which was obtainable by the king's letter patent under his prerogative.

10. All children of the king himself or of fathers on the king's service were allowed to inherit the status of British subjecthood, even if they were born abroad. Dummett and Nicol, *Subjects, Citizens, Aliens and Others*, pp. 35–7.

11. *De Geer* v. *Stone*, 22 Ch.D. 243 (1882) . It was argued in this case whether De Geer could inherit property from a testator whose great-grandfather had been born in Britain but whose grandfather and father had been born in Holland. For details of this case, see Fransman, *Fransman's British Nationality Law*, pp. 26–7.

12. William Blackstone, *Commentaries on the Laws of England, A Facsimile of the First Edition of 1765–1769: of the Rights of Persons Published in 1765*, ed. Stanley N. Katz (University of Chicago Press, London, 1979), p. 357.

13. Ibid.

14. As for the extent to which the laws of England (later, Britain) applied to each type of colony, see for example, Minty, *Constitutional Laws*, pp. 25–43.

15. Calvin's Case. Since the king inherited the kingdom under the laws of that kingdom, he could not change those laws without the consent of Parliament. Scotland and England, therefore, could maintain their own legal systems. Even after Calvin's Case, Scotsmen were not treated as English subjects, for example, in the field of colonial trade. The Act of 7 & 8 Will. III., c. 22 (1696) only allowed ships built either in England, Ireland or the colonies or plantations, and wholly owned by the people thereof, to participate in the colonial trade. Ambiguity with regard to their subject status disappeared after the Act of Union (1707).

16. It was confirmed in the case of *Campbell* v. *Hall* (1774) that the Crown had the power and right to introduce the common law into a conquered or ceded colony, and that the conquered inhabitants, both the *antenati* and the *postnati*, became subjects under the Crown's protection. *Campbell* v. *Hall*, 1 Cowp. 204.

17. For details see Parry, *Nationality and Citizenship Laws*, pp. 72–3.

18. George Chalmers, *Opinion of Eminent Lawyers on Various Points of English Jurisprudence* (Reed & Hunter, London, 1814), pp. 364–6. Although it became more and more common for the status of the inhabitants to be decided by treaty in the case of the territorial transfer, Coke's view was still cited in the nineteenth century. *Mayor of Lyons* v. *East India Company* (1836), 1 Moo. P. C. 175.

19. New York, formerly known as New Amsterdam, was captured by the English from the Dutch in 1664.

20. W. A. Shaw, *Letter of Denization and Acts of Naturalization for Aliens in England and Ireland*, The Publications of the Huguenot Society of London, 18 (1911), p. xxvii. Whether the native Indians were British subjects or not was dealt with separately

from other settlers. For details see Kettner, *Development of American Citizenship*, Ch. 10 and Epilogue.

21. For example, according to the Navigation Acts, colonial-built ships were allowed to conduct colonial trades.

22. Kettner brilliantly examines the development of concepts of citizenship in America during the period between 1608 and 1870, and the way in which they came to clash with those in Britain prior to the Revolution. Kettner, *Development of American Citizenship*.

23. *Jephson v. Riera* (1835), 3 Knapp 130.

24. Even at the turn of the twentieth century, for example, Naoroji, trying to attract public support in Britain, famously demanded that the Indian people should achieve perfect equality with their British counterparts as 'fellow-subjects', and criticized the political system in India as 'un-British'. Dadabhai Naoroji, *Poverty and Un-British Rule in India* (Ministry of Information and Broadcasting, Government of India, 1962 [1901]).

25. Differences in the entitlement to rights between natural-born and naturalized subjects were set out in the Act of Settlement (1700). Although some of the disadvantages imposed on naturalized subjects were repealed by the act of 1844 and 1870, they remained on the statute book until the enactment of the BN & SA act 1914. This process is discussed in detail later in this chapter.

26. According to Harris, the view still strongly persisted in the nineteenth century that governments should not interfere in the private domain but should focus instead on limited functions such as ensuring law, liberty and sound finance. José Harris, *Private Lives, Public Spirit: Britain 1870–1914* (Penguin, London, 1994), Ch. 7. In the area of social provision before the twentieth century, Finlayson also summarized its features as being the minimal state in the form of the poor law and its close co-operation with the concept of voluntarism in various sections. Geoffrey Finlayson, *Citizen, State, and Social Welfare in Britain 1830–1990* (Clarendon Press, Oxford, 1994), Ch. 1.

27. See, for example, N. H. Carrier and J. R. Jeffery, *External Migration: A Study of the Available Statistics* (HMSO, London, 1953), pp. 95, 97, 99.

28. We have to keep in mind that, in contrast with continental countries such as France, the British conception of the relationship between the individual and the state under the influence of the common law developed around notions of negative liberty or freedom rather than positive rights. It has been famously said, for example, that 'England is not a country where everything is forbidden except what is expressly permitted: it is a country where everything is permitted except what is expressly forbidden'. *Malone v. Commissioner of Police of the Metropolis* (2) (1979), 2 All ER 620, 630, per Sir Robert Megarry V-C. Quoted in Garder, *White Paper*, p. 15.

29. The increasing movements of people between colonies in the nineteenth century also drew public attention to the system of granting British subjecthood especially with regard to the complicated system of naturalization within the Empire. The issue of naturalization is discussed in the next section of this chapter.

30. Kettner concludes that with the absolute clash between two contrasting views on allegiance – indelible and volitional – the Americans were left to choose either absolute dependence or total independence. Kettner, *Development of American Citizenship*, Chs 6 and 7.

31. Blackstone, *Commentaries*, pp. 357–8.

32. Ibid., p. 358. Blackstone distinguishes between natural and local allegiance. Natural allegiance is supposed to be perpetual while local allegiance is due from an alien. It is thus only temporary, lasting as long as the alien remains within the king's protection.

33. Ibid.
34. This chapter follows the Report of the Royal Commissioners of 1869 in its use of the terms 'British subject' and 'American citizen'. *Report of the Royal Commissioners for the Inquiring into the Laws of Naturalization and Allegiance*, 4109, HMSO, 1869.
35. Even in 1860, the number of American citizens who were British subjects by birth was 2,450,468, out of the total population of 27,489,561. *Report of the Royal Commissioners*, Appendix, p. 18.
36. Blackstone, *Commentaries*, p. 357.
37. Naturalization Convention 1870, concluded 13 May 1870. The treaty promised the right of expatriation and provided the means for people to resume their original nationality.
38. Treaty of Amity Commerce and Navigation, 1794, Article II.
39. Ibid. Kent later emphasizes the test of adherence for determining the subject status of the *antenati*. James Kent, *Commentaries on American Law* (Little Brown, Boston, 1866), p. 22.
40. Their views on the doctrine of perpetual allegiance were fully cited in William Forsyth, *Cases and Opinions on Constitutional Law* (Stevens & Haynes, London, 1869), pp. 257–324. For an analysis of their views see James H. Kettner, 'Subjects or Citizens? A Note on British Views Respecting the Legal Effects of American Independence', *Virginia Law Review*, 62, 873 (1976), pp. 961–5.
41. *Doe v. Acklam*, 2 B. & C., 1824.
42. Rising Lake Morrow, 'The Early American Attitude toward the Doctrine of Expatriation', *American Journal of International Law*, 26 (1932), pp. 552–64.
43. Kent, *American Law*, p. 10.
44. *Report of the Committee on Foreign Affairs concerning the Rights of American Citizens in Foreign States*, cited in *Report of the Royal Commissioners*, p. 105.
45. Morrow, 'Early American Attitude', p. 563. Kettner also emphasizes the power struggle between the states and the federal government. Kettner, *Development of American Citizenship*, Ch. 9.
46. For example, Parliamentary Debates, House of Commons, vol. 190, col. 1992, 20 March 1868 (Mr W. E. Forster, the former Under-Secretary for the Colonies).
47. *Report of the Royal Commissioners*, p. 33. This issue of impressment led in 1812 to the war between the two countries. The Treaty of Ghent, which ended the war in 1814, did not touch upon impressment at all, simply because the ending of the Napoleonic wars rendered impressment unnecessary. As a result, the two countries decided to drop the issue.
48. *Report of the Royal Commissioners*, p. 33. The conflict of opinion between the two governments regarding the status of the naturalized citizens of British origin in the States was repeated when the Civil War broke out in the United States. On the one hand, the British government tried to respond to the claims from the emigrants to protection on the grounds of their indelible allegiance. The US government, on the other, insisted that a natural-born British subject who had been naturalized in the US would not be recognized within the United States as a British subject. See, for example, 'Status in Confederate States of Persons Naturalized in the United States', *Report of the Royal Commissioners*, p. 42.
49. For details, see *Report of the Royal Commissioners*, pp. 40–52. Also see Alexander Cockburn, *Nationality: The Law Relating to Subjects and Aliens Considered with a View to Future Legislation* (William Ridgeway, London, 1869), pp. 70–106.
50. The order was modified later in the same year so that it allowed only the arrest of suspicious persons and the search of American baggage.
51. *Report of the Royal Commissioners*, p. 41.
52. The sentence of death was later commuted. The Fenian Society, formed in New

York in 1858, was an Irish revolutionary society committed to the establishment of an independent republic of Ireland. Its members were known at that time as the Fenians and later as the Irish Republican Brotherhood.

53. *Report of the Royal Commissioners*, pp. 49–50.
54. Ibid., p. 50.
55. Act of July 25, 1868, s. 1.
56. Act of July 25, 1868, s. 1.
57. PRO. FO 5/1356. American Naturalization Treaty 1868. Numerous dispatches demonstrated the strong determination of the US government on this issue.
58. Parliamentary Debates, House of Commons, vol. 190, cols 1986–1987, 20 March 1868.
59. Ibid., col. 2010.
60. *Report of the Royal Commissioners*. Protocol Showing the Principles Agreed upon the British and the United States' Governments on the Question of Naturalization – Signed in London, 9 October 1868.
61. *Report of the Royal Commissioners*, p. v.
62. Ibid.
63. Ibid., p. vii.
64. Dummett points out that the 1870 act ended the tolerance of plural nationality for the first time in British history in return for providing the means of renouncing British subjecthood by naturalization abroad. Dummett and Nicol, *Subjects, Citizens, Aliens and Others*, p. 87.
65. For the practice of naturalization and denization prior to Calvin's Case, see Parry, *Nationality and Citizenship Laws*, pp. 34–40.
66. The development of national citizenship, and the impact of the Second World War upon it, are discussed in relation to the principle of national self-determination in Ch. 4.
67. PRO. HO 45/10063/B2840. The Early Legislation. Memorandum of Laws relating to the Landing and Residence of Aliens in Great Britain, 18 March 1845.
68. For details of denization and naturalization prior to the twentieth century, see W. E. Davies, *The English Law Relating to Aliens* (Stevens & Sons, London, 1931), pp. 262–73.
69. For example, 15 Car. II., c. 15 (1663) for all aliens in certain specified trades (lines, spinning, new weaving etc.); 13 Geo. II ., c. 3 (1740) for all foreign seamen serving for two years on board English men-of-war; 13 Geo. II., c. 7 (1740) for all foreigners residing for seven years in any of the colonies in America; 22 Geo. II., c. 45 (1749) for foreign Protestants serving three years upon certain vessels and employed in the whale fishery. For British and colonial laws enacted before 1844, see *Report of the Royal Commissioners*, pp. 5–8.
70. *Report from the Select Committee on the Laws affecting Aliens Together with the Minutes of Evidence and Index*. HC. 307, 2 June 1843, p. iv.
71. It was not clear even after the enactment of the 1870 act whether the political disadvantages introduced by the Act of Settlement (12 & 13 Will. III., c. 2), such as prohibiting a naturalized alien from being a member of the Privy Council or of either House of Parliament, were removed. This is discussed in detail in a later part of this chapter. *Report of the Inter-Departmental Committee Appointed by the Secretary of State for the Home Department to Consider the Doubts and Difficulties which Have Arisen in Connexion with the Interpretation and Administration of the Acts Relating to Naturalization*, Cd. 723, HMSO, 1901, p. 10.
72. 10 Car. I., c. 4, (1634).
73. *Craw v. Ramsey* (1669), Vaugh. 274, 124, E. R. 1072.
74. See Shaw, *Letter of Denization*. For the practices of colonial naturalization in the

American colonies, see Edward A. Hoyt, 'Naturalization under the American Colonies: Signs of a New Community', *Political Science Quarterly*, 2 (1952), pp. 248–66.

75. Ibid.

76. Hoyt claims, for example, that none of the royal charters to the 13 colonies in America granted them the power of naturalization. Ibid., pp. 248–9. It was only by the enactment of the Act of 10 & 11 Vict., c. 83 (1847) that the power of colonial governments to confer naturalization within their territories was affirmed.

77. *Report from the Select Committee*, HC. 307, p. viii. The committee criticized the previous practices of the government, which had deterred foreign residents from settling in Britain because of its tough naturalization measures.

78. Kettner also seriously questions the extent to which the Act of Settlement was enforced in the north American colonies. Kettner, *Development of American Citizenship*, pp. 122–3.

79. Hoyt, 'Naturalization under the American Colonies', pp. 257–60.

80. Parry, *Nationality and Citizenship Laws*, pp. 53–7.

81. After the Second World War, all Commonwealth citizens, whether in the OCW or in the NCW countries, secured citizenship rights in Britain. As is discussed in Ch. 5, however, although it is not specifically mentioned in legislation, immigration polices in the 1960s were enacted in such a way as to limit NCW immigration and effectively prevent the NCW citizens from enjoying their citizenship right in Britain.

82. It was, after all, the local government's responsibility to decide precisely how the rights were conferred upon British subjects in its territory. Westminster did not actively intervene, for example, in the cases of maltreatment of Aboriginal peoples in Australia. Thus in spite of holding the status of British subjecthood they were denied their rights and entitlements by the Australian colonial government until very recently. For details, see John Chesterman and Brian Galligan, *Citizens without Rights: Aborigines and Australian Citizenship* (Cambridge University Press, Cambridge, 1997).

83. After the acts of 1731 and 1773, the rule for acquiring subjecthood by descent remained intact until the BN & SA act 1914. The 1914 act limited transmission of the status to the first generation born abroad, but extended the earlier laws by providing that naturalized subjects could also transmit their status.

84. There are no reliable statistics which gives us an accurate and satisfactory account of the movement of peoples in Britain in the nineteenth century. The series of Passengers Acts in the nineteenth century required the recording of outward bound movement in the form of passengers lists, but they were never fully implemented. For data on inward movement, no records of incoming passengers were required until 1855. Not until 1876 was a ship's master required to deliver separate lists for foreign and British passengers. Furthermore, because all Ireland was part of the United Kingdom until 1922, Irish migrants were not 'foreign' and no control or statistics on immigration existed. Carrier and Jeffery, *External Migration*, pp. 17–19.

85. PRO. HO 45/10063/B2840. The Early Legislation.

86. The Aliens Act 1793, which was amended in 1798, required masters of vessels to present the list of foreigners on board, and such foreigners, even after landing in Britain, needed to observe certain regulations with respect to their places of residence and their movements within Britain. The Registration of Aliens Act 1826 required the masters of all incoming vessels to produce a list of all aliens aboard and the officers of the customs to deliver a certificate to aliens on their arrival. The 1826 act soon fell into disuse. The 1848 act enabled a secretary of state to remove any

aliens in order to preserve the peace and tranquillity of the realm. This act was in force for only one year.

87. Dummett, for example, explains that for the government the main purpose of these Aliens Acts was 'not to keep out aliens in general but to identify, and restrict, subversives, who might collude with revolutionary subjects'. Dummett and Nicol, *Subjects, Citizens, Aliens and Others*, p. 83. Porter also stresses that 'from 1826 until 1848, and again from 1850 to 1905, there was nothing on the statute book to enable the executive to prevent aliens from coming and staying in Britain as they liked'. Bernard Porter, *The Refugee Question in Mid-Victorian Politics* (Cambridge University Press, Cambridge, 1979), p. 3.

88. *Report from the Select Committee on the Laws Affecting Aliens*, HC. 307, p. iv.

89. Parliamentary Debates, House of Commons, vol. 66, col. 1024, 20 February 1843, and vol. 67, cols. 427–35, 8 March 1843.

90. Ibid., col. 1024, 20 February 1843.

91. Cunningham, for example, published a book at the end of the nineteenth century emphasizing how much the British economy benefited from the past immigration. Yet even he was sceptical about the Jewish immigration inflows around the time of his publication. W. Cunningham, *Alien Immigrants to England* (Frank Cass, London, 1969 [1897]).

92. Parliamentary Debates, House of Commons, vol. 67, col. 433, 8 March 1843.

93. Support for free trade grew steadily among politicians after the report by the Select Committee, and three years later, the Corn Law was successfully repealed in 1846.

94. *Report from the Select Committee on Laws Affecting Aliens*, HC. 307, p. vii.

95. Ibid.

96. Ibid.

97. For the details of the 1844 act, see *Report of the Royal Commissioners*, pp. 8–9.

98. Fransman argues that the 1844 act 'reintroduced' a simple, administrative, form of naturalization, after the Act of 7 Ann., c. 5 (1708) was repealed in 1711 (10 Ann., c. 5). Because of the large upsurge of immigrants which took place after the 1708 act had simplified the naturalization procedure, it was feared that the national identity of the time was under threat, and so it was repealed. Fransman, *Fransman's British Nationality Law*, p. 29.

99. J. Mervyn Jones, *British Nationality Law* (Clarendon Press, Oxford, 1956), p. 68. First published in 1947.

100. A liberal naturalization policy was promoted as a corollary to a free-trade policy during this period, whereas immigration control was strongly advanced by trade restrictionists at the end of the nineteenth century. See Bernard Gainer, *The Alien Invasion: The Origins of the Aliens Act 1905* (Heinemann, London, 1972).

101. 'Responsible government' was defined as a 'Ministry consisting of Ministers who were members of the legislature and responsible to that legislature'. Manfred Nathan, *Empire Government: An Outline of the System Prevailing in the British Commonwealth of Nations* (Harvard University Press, Cambridge, MA, 1930), p. 32. Those colonies which did not have representative institutions and sometimes no local power of legislation were called Crown colonies and Trinidad was one of them. Trinidad was under the least liberal form of Crown colony government, Britain having reserved for itself entire control of its affairs. See for details John Manning Ward, *Colonial Self-Government: The British Experience 1759–1856* (Macmillan, London, 1976), pp. 82–91.

102. An Ordinance Enacted by the Governor of Trinidad with the Advice and Consent of the Legislative Council thereof, for Enabling Aliens to Obtain the Privileges of British-born Subjects in the Island of Trinidad. No. 26, 2 November 1868.

103. This is proved by the opinion of the Law officers, which was given on 10 March 1865. See *Report of the Royal Commissioners*, p. 14. Between 1870 and 1914, the British government treated locally naturalized British subjects as 'British protected persons' everywhere except in the country of which they were formerly subjects. The debate which led to the enactment of the BN & SA act 1914 is dealt with in the next chapter.

104. It was unclear whether naturalization under the 1870 act was effective outside the United Kingdom. Both Jones and Parry seem to take the view that its effect was limited to the United Kingdom. Yet in introducing the British Nationality & Status of Aliens Bill 1914, the then Secretary of State for the Colonies, Mr Harcourt, took the view that it had been valid throughout the world. Parliamentary Debates, House of Commons, vol. 62, col. 1198, 13 May 1914. E. L. De Hart, 'The Colonial Conference and Naturalization', *Journal of the Society of Comparative Legislation*, 8 (1907), pp. 135–7. Jones, *British Nationality Law*, pp. 77–8. Parry, *Nationality and Citizenship Laws*, pp. 80–1.

105. Parry, *Nationality and Citizenship Laws*, p. 77.

106. 52 Vict., 4 (NSW), 1888, s. 3.

107. Kettner demonstrated, for example, that the basis for the American concept of citizenship was forged through the practice of colonial naturalization. See Kettner, *Development of American Citizenship*.

108. It was still possible under the BN & SA act 1914 for the colonial governments to pass colonial naturalization acts. BN & SA act 1914, s. 26.

109. Parliamentary Debates, House of Commons, vol. 112, col. 444, 25 June 1850.

110. For details of the Don Pacifico Affairs, see Jasper Ridley, *Lord Palmerston* (Constable, London, 1970), pp. 374–6.

111. Linda Colley, *Britons: Forging the Nation 1707–1837* (Yale University Press, New Haven, 1992).

112. Colonial naturalization and immigration laws which were discriminatory against British subjects of Asian origin are discussed in more detail in the next chapter.

113. Even as late as 1931, an Order-in-Council stipulated four preferred classes of immigrants to Canada. They were: British subjects with sufficient means from the United Kingdom, Ireland, Newfoundland, New Zealand, Australia and South Africa; US citizens; dependants of Canadian permanent residents; and agriculturalists with sufficient means. Racial and ethnic exclusions remained in force along with it.

114. It is of course the case that feelings in the peripheries towards the imperial metropole vary from one colony to another and from one period to another. This section does not intend to claim that all the colonial peoples were content with, or proud of, being British subjects, but to point out that some colonial subjects had not thought of leaving the British Empire.

115. Nicholas Deakin *et al.*, *Colour, Citizenship and British Society* (Panther Books, London, 1970), p. 283.

116. Post-Second World War immigration is dealt with in Ch. 5. To commemorate the fiftieth anniversary of the arrival of the *Empire Windrush*, several first-hand accounts of the history of immigrants from the West Indies were published in 1998. See, for example, O. Wambu, *Empire Windrush* (Gollancz, London, 1998).

— 3 —
The Common Code System:
Britain and the Dominions in the
Pre-Second World War Period

THE IMPERIAL concepts of formal membership prior to the twentieth
century developed in parallel with the expansion of the British
empire into a global institution. Under the common law principle of
allegiance, it was by the unilateral decision of the imperial government
that the concepts of formal membership were modified whenever a new
group of people was included or excluded. It was also the imperial
government which ultimately decided whether the status of British
subjecthood could be granted through colonial legislation. In 1901,
however, an interdepartmental committee published a paper recommending that the systems of colonial naturalization should be consolidated in such a way that their effects could be recognized throughout
the empire.[1] In establishing the system of imperial naturalization, the
method of maintaining British subjecthood also changed, at least in the
Dominions and Britain, where British subjecthood was granted on the
grounds of the 'common code' (a set of statutory provisions which
defined who were British subjects and in what circumstances this status
was acquired or lost).[2] Unlike in previous periods, the common code
resulted from consultation and mutual agreement between the British
and Dominion governments in the colonial (later, imperial) conferences
– the conference system which had developed since 1887 among the self-
governing parts of the empire.[3] The common code was embodied by the
British Nationality and Status of Aliens Act 1914 (BN & SA act 1914), and
subsequently adopted by the Dominions.

In 1929, according to the then Attorney-General, Sir William Jowitt,
the legal nexus of the 'British Commonwealth' was based on 'the Crown
and the person of the Sovereign, a Common Nationality, certain aspects
of the Prerogative, and the powers of the Parliament at Westminster'.[4]
Existing works on the Commonwealth have studied its constitutional
aspects and the political and economic relations among its member
countries.[5] The issue of a 'common nationality' during the period under
discussion, however, has received less scholarly attention than previous
periods. It was the least examined of the four pillars of the 'British

Commonwealth' which Jowitt mentioned.[6] In order to fill this gap, this chapter, as the previous one, attempts to demonstrate the link between the rule of the construction of the political unit (in this chapter, the British Commonwealth) and that of the population organization (the common code system). In this way, it attempts to highlight the unique place of the common code system in the history of British nationality and immigration laws and to discuss the construction of the British Commonwealth by examining the way in which its formal membership was organized.

This chapter examines developments in two contradictory processes under the common code system. First, painstaking efforts were made by leaders of the Dominions and Britain to maintain the common status of British subjecthood. Second, colonial citizenship in the Dominions became further delineated through either immigration or citizenship laws, on the basis of what had begun to emerge in previous periods. My study follows the accommodation and clashes between the two processes by focusing on the debates at imperial conferences and also within the British government, dividing the period into two: before and after the establishment of the common code system in 1914. In so doing, this chapter will analyse the impacts of these two processes on the configuration of diverse groups of people, all of which were composed of British subjects. The common code system, on the one hand, gave an institutional expression to the psychological link between Britain and the Dominions, sharpening the division between them and the rest of the empire. On the other hand, local citizenship was established in the Dominions for the purpose of their immigration control; their identity, which was separate from that of British subjecthood, was further strengthened. By the time the common code system was destroyed in 1946, therefore, it had become clear that the identities of British subjects in the Dominions were multi-layered, while affinity between the British public and their descendants abroad was also expanded.[7] In short, it was possible to maintain the common code system, precisely because the common status of British subjecthood was not entirely common throughout the Empire in terms of the sense of affinity and the citizenship rights and obligations it engendered, because of local legislation on immigration.

THE IMPERIAL LAW OF NATIONALITY AND THE LOCAL CONTROL OF IMMIGRATION

It is important to remember that the common code system was preserved as a result of co-operation between the British and

Dominion governments. The arguments for abandoning the common code system during this period remained purely theoretical.[8] The Dominion governments were content to have the choice of leaving the system, while preferring to stay within it.[9] Their citizenship laws were strictly limited to immigration purposes, and, what is more, citizenship rights and obligations remained to be granted on the basis of holding British subjecthood.[10]

As a result, the issues of 'common status' during this period seem largely to have been overlooked by scholars, as if nothing had changed from the previous periods. This chapter, however, aims to challenge this view, stressing that the significance of the common code system lay in the consultative method used to define the common code as well as the shared recognition between the British and Dominion governments that the common code system had to be preserved as the foundation of the British Commonwealth. It was also on the basis of what had been achieved under the common code system that the composite type of citizenship and citizenship structure were finally completed by the British Nationality Act 1948 (BNA 1948) under the framework of Commonwealth citizenship. In comparison with British subjecthood, the common code system increasingly clarified the power of the Dominion governments to decide who were entitled to citizenship rights and obligation within their territories. Local identity in the Dominions also developed alongside that of British subjecthood. Nonetheless, the status of British subjecthood was shared alike by people in both the Dominions and the colonies, and this nominal uniformity was considered by politicians as crucial for the British Commonwealth and Empire.

Towards imperial naturalization

The first step to establishing the system of the common code was taken not as a result of careful planning, but simply as an attempt to overcome the inconveniences of naturalization practice in the previous centuries. Towards the end of the nineteenth century, the practice of naturalization within the Empire was re-organized by the Naturalization Act 1870. Although it eliminated the long-standing dispute with the United States over dual nationality, the act did not clarify all the doubts in relation to the laws and practices of naturalization. First, even after its enactment, naturalized subjects did not have the same rights and privileges which natural-born subjects enjoyed. Section 7 of the 1870 act confirmed that naturalized subjects were entitled in the United Kingdom to 'all political and other rights, powers, and privileges, and be subject to all obligations, to which a natural-born British subject is entitled or subject' except in the country to which they were subject before naturalization. Yet, the disqualifying clause of the Act of Settlement (1700) was never expressly repealed. The 1870 act thus left uncertainty over whether its section 7 enabled a naturalized subject to become a member of the Privy Council or of either House of Parliament.[11] Second, the system of local naturalization was re-confirmed, although its effect remained within the territory of the colony where local naturalization was granted (s. 16). The 1870 act, however, did not specify whether the certificate of naturalization granted by the British government was effective outside the United Kingdom. Even within the British government, views on the interpretation of the act were divided.[12]

Without any guidelines for naturalization in the Empire, the naturalization laws and practices of each colony diverged in accordance with their need to attract immigrants and the kind of immigrants they wanted. For example, a person could apply for naturalization immediately after arrival in New Zealand. On the other hand, five years' residence in its territory was a prerequisite in the United Kingdom. Furthermore, the certificate of colonial naturalization was not recognized throughout the Empire. The conditions for naturalization had to be fulfilled in the territory where a person applied for it, and previous residence in other parts of the Empire did not count.[13] Naturalized subjects from New Zealand were therefore not only regarded as aliens in the United Kingdom, but also had to wait for another five years to apply for naturalization in the United Kingdom. As the flows of movement of people between each part of the Empire increased, so demands for uniform naturalization laws grew.

As a response to these two problems created by the 1870 act, an interdepartmental committee published a report in 1901. The committee recommended legislation, which would enable 'a Secretary of State, or the Governor of a British possession, to confer the status of a British subject upon persons who fulfil the requisite conditions *in any part of the British Dominions'*.[14] The status so conferred, they continued, should be 'recognized by British law everywhere, *both within and without His Majesty's Dominions'*.[15] This report, which proposed imperial naturalization, was circulated to the governments of the various parts of the Empire for consideration and discussion at the colonial conference 1902. It was through this procedure – circulation of a report (or a draft scheme) prepared by the British government and its discussion at colonial conferences – that the concept of the common code would be maintained for almost 30 years.

The issue of imperial naturalization had been on the agenda for three conferences – 1902, 1907 and 1911 – until the participating countries unanimously agreed to create the common code. As the system of imperial naturalization required concerted action if it was to succeed, the colonial conference – a newly developing institution for inter-imperial communications – provided a suitable forum. The conferences provided a regular meeting place where all the heads of government of the self-governing colonies and Britain could discuss matters affecting the Empire as a whole. The first colonial conference was held in 1887 at the time of the Golden Jubilee of Queen Victoria.[16] Although it was not originally intended to convene the conferences regularly, the colonial conference in 1902 – the third of this sort – decided that conferences should be held at least every four years. The rule was established in 1907 that the conference was to be called the imperial conference, at which 'questions of common interest may be discussed and considered as between His Majesty's Government and the Governments of the self-governing Dominions beyond the seas'.[17] Providing a forum for consultation and debate, imperial conferences came to symbolize the new form of inter-imperial relations which was based more on 'the voluntary action of free partners' than on 'superiority and subordination'.[18] In reality, however, it remained true that Britain was the predominant partner in fields such as the economy and military affairs. Furthermore, the agreements made at colonial conferences (later, imperial conferences) did not have any binding powers over the participating countries, and controversial issues were often dropped from the agenda.

In response to a suggestion made in the 1901 report, the governments of the Cape Colony and Natal asked in the colonial conference of 1902 that Dominion governments should have the right of naturalization which was effective throughout the Empire.[19] Although no resolution was reached then, a bill was drafted after the conference and passed round the colonial governments. In the next colonial conference in 1907, it was generally agreed that uniformity of naturalization laws should be attained by imperial legislation. However, there was disagreement on the details of the bill. The most serious was over whether the bill should apply equally to aliens of European and non-European descent. The Australian and the Cape governments were most concerned with this provision, claiming that they would refuse to 'recognize as a British subject any coloured person coming to reside therein, who [had] been naturalized in some other portion of His Majesty's Dominions where no colour distinction is made'.[20] In the end, a resolution was passed only to give further consideration to the question of naturalization.

In order to break this deadlock, an interdepartmental committee was formed by the British government.[21] It refused to introduce a distinction between persons of European and non-European descent in an imperial act on the grounds that, first, the number of people of Asian or African origin who might become naturalized would be 'but a drop of the ocean compared with the natural-born subjects of coloured race'.[22] Second, the discriminatory provision was considered as unworkable in practice as well as invidious. Nonetheless, in order to earn the support of Dominion governments, the committee assured them that the imperial act of naturalization would not confer any greater or other rights than those possessed by natural-born subjects. In promising that the imperial act would not nullify any of the existing colonial laws affecting natural-born subjects of non-European origin, the committee indirectly acknowledged that racial discrimination in the Dominions could continue through local legislation and that the British government had no intention of interfering.[23]

At the next conference, in 1911, the government of the Commonwealth of Australia, with New Zealand and the Union of South Africa, introduced resolutions in favour of creating a system of imperial naturalization.[24] The assurances given by the British government that the full power of the Dominion governments over local naturalization would be respected had already relieved the previous anxiety of the Australian government.[25] In moving the resolution, however, E. L. Bachelor, the then Australian Minister of External Affairs, asked for confirmation again that the system of imperial naturalization would not limit the right of a Dominion to legislate for local naturalization. In reply, the chairman of the conference, the then Secretary of State for the Colonies, L. Harcourt, frankly admitted that the Dominion governments would have 'more than the power of exclusion of aliens left for [them]: [they] have the power of exclusion of British subjects, if of a particular colour or a particular race'.[26] '[O]r any other conditions you may choose to make at any time by your law',[27] Winston Churchill, the then Secretary of State for the Home Department, added. In line with these arguments, Churchill proposed at the imperial conference in 1911 five principles which would underlie the system of imperial naturalization and also the common code system. Under Churchill's principles,

1. Imperial Nationality should be world wide and uniform, each Dominion being left free to grant local nationality on such terms as its legislature should think fit.
2. The Mother Country finds it necessary to maintain five years as

the qualifying period. This is a safeguard to the Dominions as well as her, but five years anywhere in the empire should be as good as five years in the United Kingdom.

3. The grant of Imperial Nationality is in every case discretionary, and this discretion should be exercised by those responsible in the area in which the applicant has spent the last twelve months.

4. The Imperial Act would not apply to the self-governing Dominions unless adopted by them.

5. Nothing now proposed would affect the validity and effectiveness of local laws regulating immigration or the like or differentiating between classes of British subject.[28]

In other words, each Dominion was not only left free to grant local nationality on its own terms, but to regulate immigration and to differentiate between classes of British subjects through its local legislation. The general rule for imperial naturalization was that there would be two standards of naturalization: the local legislation and an imperial standard. On the basis of these principles, unanimous agreement was finally reached between the British and Dominion governments, and the BN & SA bill was tabled in Parliament in 1914.[29]

Here, it has to be stressed that the common code system was only accepted because it allowed discrimination against substantial sections of British subjects in terms of their enjoyment of citizenship rights and privileges. As one scholar puts it, the common code was 'only a half-truth, for it did not explain that in practice the [Dominions] were at liberty to discriminate against subjects of the same Crown' through immigration and naturalization laws.[30] Just as discriminatory laws in each colony had been made under the universal status of British subjecthood prior to 1914, so it remained under the common code system. Sharing a common status as they might, the right of British subjects of Asian origin to enter or settle in other parts of the British Empire was much more restricted than those of European origin. In the colonial (later, imperial) conference, which consisted only of the 'white Dominions' and Britain, the common code ended up being common only in name.[31]

The roles of immigration control and naturalization in the Dominions and Britain

In short, the negotiations over the system of imperial naturalization took nearly two decades because of two obstacles. First, the British government insisted from the beginning of the debate that persons applying for naturalization had to have five years' residence. The

British government had later made some concessions, responding to the recommendation in the 1901 report that a person could qualify for naturalization by residing in any part of the Empire rather than only the United Kingdom. The future location of residence was also not confined to the United Kingdom but anywhere in the Empire. Five years' residence was considered, however, to be requisite proof that an applicant would continue, and be fit, to reside within the Empire, and this period was not to be shortened.[32] In successive conferences in 1907 and 1911, the British government remained adamant, showing no willingness to compromise on this point.

The second hurdle was immigration policies in the Dominions. Immigration control in Britain in the nineteenth century, especially after the end of the Napoleonic wars, was sporadic and sketchy.[33] Although the Aliens Act was passed in 1905, its purpose was only to prevent 'undesirables' from coming into the country.[34] In contrast, other parts of the Empire had been restrictive and selective about the character of immigrants whom they received. By the turn of the century, as a result, all the self-governing colonies had developed some sort of law to restrict immigration.[35] Those colonies even targeted British subjects from other parts of the Empire from India and Hong Kong, for example, to prevent them from immigrating. They employed several ingenious methods in order to avoid criticism of their exclusive immigration control over British subjects from other areas, such as requiring a language test, or introducing a higher poll tax for Asian immigrants. Typically, one Canadian immigration law in 1909 (ch. 19) was enacted specifically to ban immigration from Hong Kong. Knowing that there was no direct link between Hong Kong and Canada, the Canadian government prevented Hong Kong immigrants from entering Canada, on the grounds that they had to arrive directly on a through ticket from their country of nationality or domicile. Dominion governments were afraid that their immigration laws, which were often discriminatory towards people of non-European origin, might be hampered by the introduction of imperial naturalization.[36]

People of non-European origin were not only discriminated against by immigration laws, they were also disqualified from obtaining naturalization in some of the Dominions.[37] The difference in the composition of the population of Britain and the Dominions largely explained the difference in their attitudes towards naturalization. The large indigenous population in Britain meant that policy had always been stringent, and the basic rule for subjecthood had always been to be 'born within ... the allegiance of the king'.[38] In contrast, the lack of population in the Dominions led to elaborately developed immigration and naturalization controls in order both to attract new immigrants and to control their character. Because acquisition of subjecthood by naturalization was understood as something of an anomaly, no systematic method of naturalization developed in Britain until the mid-nineteenth century. Even in the 1870 act, naturalization in Britain could be accepted or rejected 'as he [the Secretary of State] thinks most conducive to the public good'(s. 7). If an application was rejected, no appeal was allowed and the reason for rejection did not need to be explained to the applicants. As a populous and fairly urbanized country, the emphasis vis-à-vis naturalization was on exclusion.[39] Moreover, the British government had been worried since the beginning of the twentieth century that the establishment of its welfare services might attract a large inflow of immigrants.[40] It feared that welfare services, however limited they were by today's standard, might entice larger numbers of immigrants than before, who would simply end up becoming a burden on the government and swamp the already tight labour market.[41] Thus, the government was determined to keep a firm attitude towards naturalization.

The Dominion governments had always taken a totally different view on naturalization and immigration. As they started with a relatively small population, they were in constant need of more workers and settlers.[42] They were thus forced to develop immigration controls in order to select the kind of immigrants they would like to attract. With the increase in the number of immigrants, the composition and character of the population in those Dominions were increasingly influenced by their immigration and naturalization laws. Owing to the domestic tension between ethnic groups, some Dominions – especially Canada and the Union of South Africa – were adamant, insisting that they had to be more than sensitive about population inflows.[43] As the number of immigrants grew, therefore, so also did the importance of their immigration and naturalization policies. In short, for those Dominion governments, their definition of membership was increasingly dependent upon, and influenced by, their immigration and naturalization laws, rather than the all-embracing principle of allegiance.[44]

The imperial concept of membership – British subjecthood – which was supposed to provide unity among British subjects anywhere in the Empire, also augmented the importance of immigration control in the Dominions. British subjects, wherever they lived within the Empire and whichever racial or ethno-cultural group they belonged to, shared a single status – 'British subject' – tied to a common superior. Under this principle, therefore, the system of immigration control became more crucial in distinguishing those British subjects who belonged to a particular Dominion, and enjoyed a special tie with it, from all other British subjects. As the rights and privileges were attached to the status of British subject, British subjects in a Dominion other than the one to which they originally belonged could claim the rights and privileges guaranteed in that Dominion. The imperial government feared that inter-Dominion disputes might flare up if some Dominion governments discriminated against the rights and privileges that British subjects from other parts of the Empire could enjoy by enacting some sorts of local legislation. In order to reduce friction within the Empire, therefore, Britain's preferred choice was for the Dominion governments to limit, by immigration law, the actual inflows of those British subjects against whom they would have discriminated once they were inside.[45] During the 1907 conference Sir Joseph Ward, the then Prime Minister of New Zealand, for example, made a famous speech, claiming that New Zealand is 'a white man's country, and intends to remain a white man's country', and '[we] intend to keep our country for white men by every effort in our power'.[46] Herbert Gladstone, the then Secretary of State for the Home Department, suggested in response that the New Zealand government should maintain its population balance through immigration laws, so that those who met the requirements of the immigration laws and entered New Zealand could be treated equally in terms of their rights and duties with those who were already in New Zealand.[47] In this way the imperial practice of conferring the same rights and privileges on all British subjects throughout the Empire could be maintained, while New Zealand remained 'a white man's country' through immigration control.

In the middle of the debate over creating a system of imperial naturalization, the Canadian government under Sir Wilfred Laurier enacted the Immigration Act 1910 (CIA 1910). The introduction of the CIA 1910 was officially understood to facilitate the administrative control of immigration by providing some criteria for determining who were to be considered 'Canadians'.[48] However, this action, although its effect was limited, was also an indication that Canada was developing its own national consciousness.[49] For the first time in the history of the British Empire a Dominion defined its own 'citizenship' while maintaining the status of British subject.[50] The CIA 1910, in short, created two kinds of British subjects in the Empire: a British subject with Canadian citizenship and a British subject without it. It also expressly stated that, as far as immigration was concerned, British subjects, unless they possessed Canadian citizenship or Canadian domicile, were subject to the same control as aliens. While working on creating a system of imperial naturalization, the Canadian government, nevertheless, took the first concrete step among the Dominions towards distinguishing its own concepts of membership from those of Britain.

The CIA 1910, surprisingly, neither received much attention in the British Parliament or the imperial conference, nor led to the Canadian government being opposed to the idea of imperial naturalization. First, it was apparent that Sir Wilfred Laurier was in favour of making the naturalization effective everywhere in the Empire, as long as a diversity of methods for granting naturalization was preserved.[51] As was discussed in Chapter 1, the holding of British subjecthood, unlike that of national citizenship, did not necessarily mean that people felt a shared sense of belonging to the Empire. It was up to the imperial government to decide the criteria for formal membership of the Empire, so that someone could be both a Canadian citizen and a British subject. The creation of local citizenship should not in itself challenge the holding of British subjecthood. Second, the purpose of Canadian immigration policy – to exclude those of non-European origin – had always been clear. Westminster could therefore be certain that the creation of Canadian citizenship would affect neither British subjects in Britain nor those in the other Dominions. In that sense, the CIA 1910 did not in any way go against the type of common code which the Dominion and British governments had been negotiating at imperial conferences.

The common code under the British Nationality and Status of Aliens Act 1914

As the outcome of a series of imperial conferences, the proposed BN & SA 1914 bill had already been agreed to by all the governments of the Dominions by the time it was tabled in Parliament. The BN & SA act 1914, dealing with issues of both nationality and naturalization, consisted of three parts.[52] Part I defined a natural-born British subject, providing the principle of *jus soli* with a statutory form. Part II established the scheme of imperial naturalization. In response to the stipulation of the British government, a person could only apply for imperial naturalization after five years' residence within the Empire, which included 12 months' residence, just before the application, in the place where naturalization would be granted (s. 2(2)). To satisfy the Dominions, an applicant was also required to possess an adequate knowledge of the English language (s. 2(1)(b)). Finally, general provisions were stated in part III. The act maintained local naturalization. It also affirmed, in line with the five principles which had been decided at the 1911 imperial conference, that no power would be taken away from the Dominions, and that the operation of any existing law in force would not be affected. The Dominions would not be prevented, under the 1914 BN & SA act, from 'treating differently different classes of British subjects'(s. 26). The drafters intended that both parts I and III would apply to all the Dominions by virtue of the authority of the imperial parliament, with only part II not being effective unless each Dominion government adopted it. Yet all the Dominion governments re-enacted the whole act at different times, modifying it to fit into their local needs.[53] The local laws which adopted the BN & SA act 1914 therefore ended up being different from each other.[54] As a result, not only was the common code which the BN & SA act 1914 had created not common to British subjects of Asian origin, but it was also not as common as its name implied even among the Dominions and Britain.

Chapter 2 discussed how the principle of allegiance developed and became more complicated in response to the British Empire's growing into a global institution. Again, the changing nature of the political unit, in this case the constitutional relationship between the Dominions and Britain, influenced, and was influenced by, the nature of formal membership which was embodied in the common code. Although Britain remained the predominant actor in the Empire, the Dominions were no longer submissive juniors. When the BN & SA act 1914 was enacted, for example, the judicial and political powers of the Dominion governments were still restricted, and their autonomy in the matter of foreign policy was controlled by the imperial government.[55] The paramount authority of Westminster over all the colonies in terms of legislation had also been confirmed and was not yet challenged.[56] The Colonial Laws Validity Act (28 & 29 Vict., c. 63) still gave the imperial government the legal power to legislate for the whole Empire and to repeal any colonial laws which would conflict with those of Britain. Nevertheless, the governments of the self-governing colonies (later, the Dominions) had been exercising increasing control over their internal affairs since the late nineteenth century.[57] At the beginning of the twentieth century they came to acquire some autonomy even in external affairs, such as commerce and trade, and even attended international conferences on purely administrative issues, such as that on the universal postal union, which was held in 1906.[58]

Nevertheless, in examining the process of transforming the inter-imperial relationship at the time, we find that the difference in views between the British and Dominion governments was not as great as had earlier been feared. The separatist attitude of the Dominion governments was not as radical and determined as it looked, while the British government was aware that 'the cultivation of unifying symbols' was enough to mobilize the loyalty of people in the empire.[59] In other words, the Dominion governments did not yet intend to leave or bring about the dissolution of the Empire. Their goal was to achieve as much autonomy as they could manage within the Empire. The British government had by then also recognized that constitutional control was outdated, preferring softer methods such as consultation and persuasion. Overall, the self-interest of both the imperial and the Dominion governments ensured their agreement that it was beneficial to maintain the unity of the Empire.

More specifically, the British government had been worried about the decline in its economic competitiveness in comparison with the rising industries in countries such as Germany and United States since the start of the so-called 'Great Depression' in the 1870s.[60] Concerned about the new rivals, some politicians in Britain, notably Joseph Chamberlain, came to question whether free trade would still meet Britain's economic interests.[61] In order to maintain the country's predominance, they started to search for a way to strengthen the unity of the Empire, for example, in the form of imperial preferential tariffs.[62] Although the movement for imperial preference did not succeed until the 1930s, co-operation and unity in imperial trade were continuously discussed in colonial and imperial conferences.[63]

The Dominion governments, on the other hand, were also attracted to closer economic co-operation with Britain. Unlike British industries, whose main trading partners were outside the Empire, those of the Dominions relied heavily upon intra-Empire trade.[64] Therefore, for example, although the Canadian government was not enthusiastic about naval co-operation and established its own fleets in 1909, it strongly supported an imperial preferential tariff in order to expand its agricultural exports to Britain.[65] The Dominion governments did not want to erode the autonomy which they had already achieved, but at the same time the unity of the Empire was to their advantage and could even be increased in some areas, such as trade relations.

In short, the common code system was a product of the time. It was agreed that the Dominion governments were to preserve their own immigration laws and to be allowed to grant local nationality on their own terms. As a basis of unity, however, imperial nationality should remain world-wide. Nonetheless, the common code system had been created at imperial conferences which were attended only by the Dominion and British governments. It therefore allowed immigration control in the Dominions which had been discriminatory to British subjects of non-European descent to persist. In reality, the Dominions were free from imperial control in the field of immigration and naturalization; their increasing demand for equality with the British government was met by the system of consultation over the common code; and the division between the 'white Dominions' and the rest of the Empire was strengthened under the *common* code system. The BN & SA act 1914 thus demonstrates that while the Dominion governments were not yet ready to go further to establish their own nationality laws and to depart from British subjecthood, they wanted to keep the power to determine who belonged to them, and participated, as equal partners with Britain, in defining the formal membership of the Empire. Prior to the Second World War, after all, the principal aim of politicians in the Dominions was to reconstruct their relationship with Britain by reducing, as much as possible, control from Westminster.[66]

THE COMMON CODE AND LOCAL CITIZENSHIP AFTER THE FIRST WORLD WAR

The development of the British Commonwealth and the common code system

The First World War further changed the nature of the relationship between Britain and the Dominions and, in consequence, the position of British subjects and aliens in immigration and nationality laws. There were two major developments in British law during this period which affected the concepts of British subjecthood and Britishness. First, outside the system of the common code, controls on aliens and on British subjects became sharply demarcated. Until this time, especially during the nineteenth century, the main focuses of the immigration and nationality laws in Britain were various systems of naturalization and the development of the common law principle of allegiance.[67] However, with the enactment of the Aliens Act 1905 (AA 1905) and the more elaborate Aliens Restriction Acts in 1914 and 1919, efforts to define aliens and to control their immigration based on these definitions developed more systematically than before. The war sentiment intensified this dichotomous approach – one immigration law for aliens and another for British subjects as a whole – which persisted until 1971. Second, within the system of the common code, the acquisition of British subjecthood by descent was expanded, as a result of the wartime contribution made by overseas communities of British descent.[68] Although these developments were both discussed at imperial conferences and agreed in principle, they had to be applied by local legislation in each Dominion and were often modified in the process.[69]

With regard to immigration control on aliens, the day after Britain entered the war against Germany, the Aliens Restriction Bill 1914 was rushed through Parliament in one day. Anti-alien feelings, which were still rudimentary at the time of the AA 1905 (at that time they were mainly directed against Jewish immigrants), were aggravated by the outbreak of war. R. McKenna, the then Secretary of State for the Home Department, explained that the main purpose of the 1914 bill was to 'remove or restrain the movements of undesirable aliens, especially with a view to the removal or detention of spies'.[70] He also confirmed that '"alien enemies"[71] against whom there is no reason whatever to suppose that they are secretly engaged in operations against this country' would only face registration and prohibition from living in a certain area.[72] However, restrictions on them tightened as the war became prolonged.[73] Although the Aliens Restriction Act 1914 (4 & 5 Geo. 5., c. 12, ARA 1914) was originally considered as an emergency measure, it was not repealed after the war but was extended by one year by the Aliens Restriction (Amendment) Act 1919 (9 & 10 Geo. 5., c. 92). The 1919 act, along with the Aliens Orders 1920 and 1925, controlled the immigration of aliens until amended in 1953, giving the Home Secretary wide powers to control the entry and deportation of aliens.[74]

Anti-alien feelings were also directed against naturalized subjects of German origin or descent. The Home Office submitted a memorandum to the imperial war conference in 1917, suggesting that the power should be given to governments to revoke naturalization for reasons other than false representation or fraud, such as not being 'conductive to the public good'.[75] After the conference, the British Nationality and Status of Aliens Act 1918 (8 & 9 Geo. 5., c. 38, BN & SA act 1918) was introduced. Sir W. Dickinson, a Liberal MP, proposed that the provision to expand the power of the Secretary of State to revoke a certificate of naturalization should be limited to being a wartime measure.[76] His was a minority voice, however, and the BN & SA act 1918 was passed to amend the BN & SA act 1914.[77]

While immigration control on aliens was strengthened after the war, the British government and public had become more aware of their links with overseas communities of British descendants.[78] When the BN & SA act 1914 was prepared, it was strongly felt that the opportunities for holding dual citizenship should be as limited as possible.[79] After all, the 1870 act was enacted after nearly a century-long dispute with the United States over dual citizenship. Acquisition by descent was therefore confined, under the BN & SA act 1914, to only the first generation born abroad, where the father was a British subject at the time of the birth (s. 1(b)). During the war, however, the number of

British subjects who were serving the Crown abroad increased, as did the number of children born abroad in occupied territories. Under the influence of war sentiment, the British government considered that it had to respond to the allegiance of British descendants abroad and conferred upon them the status of British subjecthood. Thus, the BN & SA act 1918 acknowledged that persons born abroad would become British subjects if their father was serving the crown at the time of their birth (s. 2), amending the provision of the BN & SA act 1914. In other words, even children born in German-occupied territories while their fathers were in service could pass their status of British subject to their children born in France.[80]

The amendment introduced by the BN & SA act 1918 did not fully satisfy the demands of the overseas communities of British descendants. Both the British public and policy-makers were also willing to include generations of British descendants abroad among the holders of British subjecthood. After discussion at the imperial conference 1921, therefore, a bill was tabled the following year which later became the British Nationality and Status of Aliens Act 1922 (12 & 13 Geo. 5., c. 42, BN & SA act 1922). In introducing the bill, Sir J. L. Baird gave an example of a soldier at the front who grew up in Argentina as a British subject.[81] Although he had fought for Britain and the British Empire, his son could not be a British subject. In response to this kind of appeal, the bill allowed the transmission of British subjecthood by descent indefinitely, provided that the child's birth was registered at a consulate within 12 months and it was declared that the child would remain British at the age of majority.[82] The bill was received enthusiastically in Parliament, and some MPs even tried to ease these two conditions for transmission.

Furthermore, for the purpose of covering '[all] the children of the men who went out and fought for us, and ... all the children who were born after the Act of 1914 was passed', the government made the BN & SA act 1922 retrospective to 1 January 1915.[83] It even allowed a naturalized British subject, who had not previously been allowed to transmit the status of British subjecthood to a child born abroad, to do so if a child was born abroad on or after 1 January 1915 (s. 1(1)(b)(ii)). The conditions for acquisition by descent were simplified even further by the British Nationality & Status of Aliens Act 1943 (6 & 7 Geo. 6., c. 14, BN & SA act 1943).[84] During the inter-war period the criteria for formal membership of the British empire ultimately shifted from the long-time principle of *jus soli* to include the aspect of *jus sanguinis*.

These two changes in nationality and immigration laws – tightening immigration control for aliens and expanding the principle of *jus sanguinis* – responded to, and reflected, the changing concepts and role of formal membership in the British Empire as well as Britishness in the United Kingdom. First, the division between aliens and British subjects became firmly demarcated by immigration laws. Although the tightening of immigration control against aliens was originally considered to be temporary and was targeted at enemy aliens, the ARA 1914 and subsequent laws had changed the premise of immigration control. Until then, it was only 'undesirable' aliens who were prevented from entering the United Kingdom. However, after the enactment of the ARA 1914, all aliens were subject to immigration control, being allowed to enter only exceptionally. Immigration control was further embedded by the enactment of the ARA 1919 and the Aliens Order 1920, which extended the validity of previous restrictions into peacetime.[85] In the case of Britain, therefore, the separation between formal members and aliens was completed in the context of First World War fervour.

Second, for politicians and the public in Britain, the blood relationship as a criterion for formal membership became increasingly significant during this period. Surprisingly, this point has hardly been stressed by previous research. The wartime participation of British descendants abroad strengthened the attachments towards them. These feelings of affinity between the two communities led to the intensification of the aspect of *jus sanguinis* in Britain's immigration and nationality policy.

This development, however, unexpectedly damaged the common code system and also led to a further divergence between the sense of holding British subjecthood and belonging to Britain itself. Although there were always consultations with the Dominion governments at imperial conferences whenever those changes were made, not all the Dominions followed the full series of changes of the BN & SA acts.[86] As a result, the difference between the nationality laws of each Dominion and Britain widened. Unlike with a national type of citizenship, as previously described, the holders of British subjecthood were allowed to have multiple identities if they wished. Not everybody in the Dominions shared the same sentiment towards overseas communities of British descent as did those in Britain. Moreover, some Dominions contained a number of British subjects who had no British connections. It was, for example, unrealistic to expect a Québécois to identify with a third-generation British descendant in Argentina. In other words, the Canadian government, with a substantial number of non-British residents, was not keen on enacting nationality laws which might appear too pro-British. Within Britain, in contrast, a blood relationship became one of the key elements in defining who 'belonged' to Britain. After all, British subjecthood continued to include not only those of British origin but also those of other backgrounds, in order to give unity to racially and culturally diversified groups of people within the British Empire. Consequently, it was inevitable that the holders of British subjecthood included a group of people who had no substantial links with Britain and at the same time excluded those whom the British public thought should be included.

Managing the common code system after the First World War

So far, this section has argued that the effect of the First World War was to consolidate the boundary between British subjecthood and aliens while at the same time expanding the bounds of British subjecthood to include British descendants abroad. Within the bounds of British subjecthood, however, efforts to define colonial citizenship intensified, as did those to redefine the imperial relationship between Britain and the Dominions and to manage the common code system.

During the First World War, discussions continued between leaders in Britain and the Dominions on how relations between Britain and the Dominions, and consequently the common code system, should be developed after the war. Since the mid-nineteenth century, relations between Britain and the Dominions had always been different from those between Britain and the rest of the Empire.[87] The Dominion governments had enjoyed greater autonomy, as if they formed an inner community within the Empire, with increasing freedom from the control of the imperial government. However, as the confidence of the Dominions expanded through their experiences in the war, their demand for a redefinition of their relationship with Britain intensified. The privileged status of the Dominions was, finally, expressly stated in a resolution approved by the Imperial War Conference 1917.[88] It confirmed that readjustment of the constitutional relations among the participating countries should be based upon (i) 'a full recognition of the Dominions as autonomous nations of an Imperial Common-wealth'; and (ii) 'the right of the Dominions ... to an adequate voice in foreign policy and in foreign relations'; and should provide (iii) 'effective arrangements for continuous consultation in all important matters of common Imperial concern, and for such necessary concerted action, founded on consultation'.[89]

When the 1921 imperial conference – the first imperial conference after the war – was held, however, the Dominion governments were still too preoccupied with their domestic issues, especially economic recovery, to tackle the issues of constitutional change in the British

Commonwealth. Yet, at the time of the subsequent imperial conference in 1926, the issue of constitutional reform had been revived in some Dominions, especially South Africa.[90] After a series of heated talks, the Inter-Imperial Relations Committee under Earl Balfour in 1926 published a report which confirmed that the communities of the Commonwealth were autonomous and equal to each other.[91] It was nonetheless vague in detail, and basically repeated what had been agreed before.[92] The practical application of the Balfour report therefore had to be negotiated in 1929, with special reference to three legal issues: statutory provisions relating to the disallowance and reservation of Dominion legislation, the Colonial Laws Validity Act 1865, and extra-territorial legislation by the Dominions.[93] The last two issues had special implications for the system of the common code. First, abandonment of the Colonial Laws Validity Act 1865, enabling the Dominions to repeal the BN & SA act 1914 itself, could destroy the statutory basis of the BN & SA act 1914 on which the system of the common code was established. Second, the problem of extra-territorial legislation was directly related to the difficulty of finding a way to define persons who belonged to a particular Dominion without harming the system of the common code. The question, therefore, became 'whether some species within the genus "British subject" could not be found to which alone Dominion legislation would apply extra-territorially'.[94]

The result of the 1929 conference was published as a report, which urged that the Dominion governments ought to recognize 'a particular status of membership of those communities for legal and political purposes'.[95] The report further confirmed that the common status, which was based on common allegiance to the Crown, was not inconsistent with 'the recognition within and without the Commonwealth of the distinct nationality possessed by the nationals of the individual states of the British Commonwealth'.[96] In view of the possibility of breaking the system of the common code, however, the report only recommended reciprocal action if any changes were to be made to the existing system. Nonetheless, after the 1929 report, both the excessively centralizing and separating movements within the Commonwealth were checked in the face of the more pressing issue of a world economic crisis. The Dominion governments in the 1930 imperial conference thus acknowledged the two principles: maintenance of the common code system and the right of the Dominion governments to establish their own nationality. Granted that each member of the Commonwealth was entitled to define its own criteria of nationality, each member agreed to ensure, as far as possible, that those nationals should also possess the common status.[97] The repeal of the Colonial Laws Validity Act by the Statute of Westminster in 1931 finally gave legal recognition to the fact that the Dominion governments could abolish the BN & SA acts and leave the common code system.

In 1937, General Hertzog, the head of the Union of South Africa government, once again challenged the common code system. His submission of a memorandum raising the issues of separate nationality laws at the imperial conference 1937, suggests that he needed to find out how far each Dominion could push its demands to define its own nationality criteria. His memorandum contained two proposals: first, each Dominion should establish nationality laws of its own, and second, the common status should be granted only on the basis of the nationality of each Dominion.[98] The British government feared that these proposals might risk the then structure of the Commonwealth by strengthening separatism among the member countries.[99] For example, the proposals could end up forcing Australia and New Zealand, which had not enacted their own nationality laws, to do so. It was also uncertain whether the Irish Free State would join this scheme. Under the Union proposals, furthermore, the common status of British subject would depend exclusively upon the nationality laws of each member country, including Britain. Until then, the British government, as the head of the British Empire, had never intended, or even imagined the need, to establish UK nationality. In the face of these problems which the proposals raised, the then Secretary of State for Dominion Affairs, Malcolm MacDonald, claimed that the British government should aim at regaining the balance between 'freedom' and 'co-operation', on which the Commonwealth was based.[100] He warned that the Dominion governments had been emphasising only 'freedom' and neglecting 'co-operation', which would harm the principle of the Commonwealth.

The British government, after all, did not need to worry about the Union proposals. The Dominion governments were not keen on them, as neither Australia nor New Zealand had ever shown any interest in establishing citizenship laws of their own, and Canada, with its nationality law already established, would not wish to take a further step. Furthermore, the Union government itself was not as eager to put its proposals into practice as might be supposed.[101] General Hertzog had no intention of upsetting pro-British voters by forcing his way in the face of opposition from other Dominions. In the end, all the Dominions governments wanted was to establish their ability to define citizenship in their own way. Far from wanting to abolish the common code system, all the other Dominions, the Irish Free State aside, were satisfied with securing the option to leave the system of the common code if they wished, without planning to take it up.[102] For the Dominion leaders, a further separation would lead to the loss of conservative support, and moreover, they needed the Commonwealth in order to survive the economic crisis and political instability of the world in the 1930s.[103] A report published by a committee on the constitutional question at the 1937 conference reflected the ambivalent mood of the Dominion governments.[104] It admitted that each member of the Commonwealth had the right to decide who would possess definite connections with it, and even encouraged those countries which did not wish to enact nationality laws to define who belonged to them administratively. Nonetheless, all the participants there agreed that uniformity in the definition of nationality was desirable in principle. In the end, the Dominions still needed the common code system as much as Britain, although they preferred to keep it in name only and without constraints.

Defining separate Dominion citizenship within the common code

In parallel with the process of managing the common code system at imperial conferences, each Dominion also defined its local 'citizenship',[105] either through laws or administrative measures. Increasingly, citizenship rights and privileges were determined by the Dominion governments rather than by the imperial government, as they established citizens of their own and tied their status to immigration control. In consequence, the bonds between the Dominion governments and their citizens became stronger, which led to a weakening of their link with the British Empire. By the time the Canadian Citizenship Act 1946 (CCA 1914) broke the common code system, all the Dominions had developed local citizenship of their own in one way or another, albeit to an extent which did not deny the common code.

The common code system, after all, never succeeded in weakening the separatist tendency in the Dominions. As was pointed out earlier, although the BN & SA act 1914 had been introduced to the British Parliament as an 'agreed plan' and 'so greatly desired by the Dominions beyond the seas',[106] it was not implemented simultaneously throughout the Empire. Furthermore, except for Newfoundland, which was too small in population and in economic capability to be independent of the Empire, all the other Dominions intended under the common code system to differentiate between those people who specifically belonged to them and British subjects as a whole. However, their pursuit of a separate status for their 'citizens' was not uniformly paced or enthusiastic. After the Irish Free State received Dominion status in 1921, its eagerness and determination to create its own citizens was always greater than that of the other four Dominions, among which Canada and the Union of South Africa were more supportive of the idea of a separate citizenship status for each Dominion.[107]

The first decisive move for separation from the common code came from the Canadian government. It enacted the Canadian Nationals Act in 1921 (CNA 1921). The direct purpose of this act was to enable the Canadian government to put forward a candidate of its own to the newly established Permanent Court of International Justice (PCIJ). The PCIJ was founded under the League of Nations in 1920, no country being allowed, according to the Statute of the Court, to send more than one of its own citizens as judges. Canada, as an independent member of the League of Nations, was also an independent member of the PCIJ.[108] Unless 'Canadian citizens' were distinguished from other British subjects outside Canada, however, a Canadian candidate might be turned down if a British subject, for example, from Australia, had already been elected. The Canadian government, therefore, defined by the CNA 1921 'a Canadian national' as 'any British subject who is a Canadian citizen within the meaning of the Immigration Act 1910' (s. 1).[109] The CNA 1921 maintained the status of British subject as a condition of becoming a Canadian national, and thus had not in theory departed from the system of the common code. Yet after its enactment, if the Canadian government signed a bilateral international treaty such as a fishery treaty, it could confer the privilege derived from that treaty only on its citizens.[110] Thus the Canadian government earned another way of claiming its individuality in the international arena.

Following in Canada's footsteps, the Union government defined its own citizens by passing the Union Nationality and Flags Act of 1927 (no. 40 of 1927, UNFA 1927). It did this as soon as it had finally adopted the BN & SA act 1914 by enacting the British Nationality in the Union and Naturalization and Status of Aliens Act of 1926 (no. 18 of 1926).[111] These two acts constituted the basis of nationality and naturalization in South Africa up to the end of the Second World War. Compared to the BN & SA act 1914 and the CNA 1921, the UNFA 1927 was more restrictive on the principle of *jus soli*; the status of Union national could not be conferred on prohibited immigrants and their children, or on foreign diplomats.[112] As regards the effect on British subjects of the acquisition of the status of Union national, the representatives of the Union government guaranteed that the UNFA 1927 did not deprive Union nationals of any of the rights or status of a British subject. Instead, they explained, the UNFA 1927 created 'within the class of persons who are British subjects a class of persons who are Union nationals', only the latter class being granted new rights to take part in the public life of the territory of the Union.[113] The Union's separatist tendency in the field of nationality law led to General Hertzog's proposals at the 1937 conference. Not only did he claim that every Dominion should have its own nationality act, he also asked for a change in the title of common status from 'British subject' to 'His or Her Majesty's subject'.[114] Emphasizing that the Empire was a collection of several monarchies, he pointed out that the maintenance of the term 'British subject' would mean ignoring the Dominions' claim to recognition.[115] Given the large non-British population within its territories, the Union government had to be careful not to appear too pro-British. Therefore for Hertzog to demonstrate his separatist stance once in a while was politically more important than to actually achieve separation from the Empire.

The toughest challenge to the common code system came, to nobody's surprise, from the Irish government in 1935, when the Irish Nationality and Citizenship Act 1935 (IN & CA 1935) was enacted. The IN & CA 1935 repealed the previous BN & SA acts and the common laws, resulting in Irish citizens losing the status of British subjecthood. The status of Irish citizenship was reconfirmed by a new constitution which was established in 1937. The Irish government, however, continued to confer citizenship rights on the holders of British subjecthood within Éire in exchange for the rights and privileges given to Irish citizens in the Commonwealth outside Éire. In practice, therefore, the common code system survived. In the face of the IN & CA 1935, the British government had two choices.[116] It could have either accepted Irish citizenship as an anomaly within the common code system or acknowledged the departure of the Irish government from the common code system and recognized Irish citizens as aliens. Neither of the choices was ideal for the British government. Accepting the Irish decision to renounce the status of British subjecthood could have risked weakening the common code system and the unity of the Commonwealth. If Irish migrants were reduced to the status of aliens, the administrative costs and burden of controlling the borders and issuing work-permits were expected to be enormous. It was also feared that the British labour market would lose a valuable labour supply. In the end, MacDonald stated at the 1937 imperial conference that the British government 'would be prepared to treat it as not making such a fundamental alteration'.[117] Other participants at the conference agreed, as they were unanimously in favour of keeping Ireland in the Commonwealth and maintaining its unity.

The two other Dominions, Australia and New Zealand, were considered to be less inclined towards separatism. In response to Hertzog's proposal at the 1937 conference, for example, the Australian delegate was even opposed to the introduction of administrative action which would distinguish certain people with a strong tie with Australia from other British subjects. The Australian legal adviser emphasized that the use of the concept of 'Australians' was limited to immigration and deportation purposes, and that the government would not want to take any measures which might enhance its implications. The delegates from both Australia and New Zealand were united in their disapproval of any statement 'which would tend to emphasize divisions between the members of the Commonwealth' such as that of separate nationalities.[118] Indeed, they did not enact their nationality laws until the system of the common code finally collapsed.

However, it is wrong to think that the Australian and New Zealand governments were not interested in expressing their own identities. They were more assertive than the other Dominions in supporting their own concept of membership on issues which were important to them, such as the status of married women.[119] The New Zealand government, by enacting the BN & SA (in New Zealand) Amendment Act (25 Geo. V., no. 38) in 1934, conferred on a woman marrying an alien husband the right to opt to retain her status of British subject, even though she acquired her husband's nationality upon marriage. In the following year, the Australian government passed similar legislation (no. 62). Although there was no agreement among the Dominion governments on this issue, it had already been confirmed in the 1930 conference that all the Dominion governments possessed the power to confer local rights within their territories. Therefore as long as those two laws in Australia and New Zealand only conferred local rights, and not the status of British subject, to women marrying aliens, they did not require prior consultation at imperial conferences.[120]

The final blow to the common code system came, again, from Canada after the Second World War, when the Canadian government passed its own citizenship act in 1946.[121] Under the Canadian system, the status of British subject was conferred on the basis of holding Canadian citizenship, exactly in the way General Hertzog had suggested in 1937. Although the Canadian government informed its British counterpart of the existence of the Canadian Citizenship bill just before it was introduced in the Canadian parliament, the bill was prepared without consultation with the other members of the Commonwealth.[122] The Canadian government wished neither to be deterred from introducing the bill nor to have to amend it. The common code system, as a result, came to an end through the unilateral action of the Canadian government in spite of all the previous consultative efforts.

THE COMMON CODE SYSTEM: BRITISH SUBJECT, COLONIAL CITIZEN AND ALIEN

We have seen how the Dominions attempted to acquire constitutional equality with Britain. It was not a straightforward process of decentralization. After the enactment of the Statute of Westminster in 1931, they could legally leave the Commonwealth. The Dominion governments were, however, content with their theoretical freedom and chose to remain inside the Commonwealth due to shared sentiments and also to their self-interest in economic and security areas.[123] For the Dominions, for example, Britain continued to provide an export market and capital as well as protection in an increasingly unstable world. It was also true that Dominion leaders were in close contact with their British counterparts during the period under discussion, dealing jointly with issues of mutual interest at imperial conferences such as the common code system. More importantly, among the ordinary people in the Dominions, especially in Australia and New Zealand, there is no denying that a strong sense of pride to be British subjects persisted all through the period.[124] Feeling bound up with Britain, all the Dominions except Éire voluntarily joined the war against Germany in 1939. On the surface, just as in previous periods, the common status of British subjecthood was maintained throughout the Empire.

Nonetheless, the common code system was repeatedly reinterpreted in response to the strengthening of colonial identity. Nominally, the common code system had already accepted the existence of multiple citizenships – British subjecthood and colonial citizenship – since 1910. More importantly, the system of the common code came to form, to a greater extent than in the previous period, a multi-layered structure as regards both the substantive and functional aspects of citizenship. Although citizenship rights and obligations were still granted through the holding of British subjecthood, the Dominion governments could in practice decide through immigration control upon whom they conferred these rights and obligations within their territories. In addition, in terms of domestic legislation and even international laws, the Dominion governments were able to identify from all the holders of British subjecthood those who belonged to them, especially with their entitlement after 1931 legally to define their 'citizens'. By doing so, their international standing was further strengthened, for example, as individual members of international organizations such as the League of Nations and as signatories to commercial treaties in their own right.

From the perspective of nationality laws in the British Empire, when the system of the common code broke down in 1946, the world population was not divided into two clear groupings – citizens and aliens – which the national type of citizenship presupposed. The division between British subjects and aliens existed, but contrary to what we normally assume, it had been vague until the beginning of the twentieth century, and was only properly established after 1914. Under the concepts of allegiance, for example, even foreigners were expected to have 'local allegiance' while in the territory.[125] Furthermore, naturalized citizens were deprived of the rights which the natural-born enjoyed until as late as 1914. Neither did the holding of British subjecthood necessarily guarantee a free entry in some Dominions. Only as a result of the First World War was the definition of aliens clarified, with legislation on aliens being tightened. Yet, as was pointed out earlier, while the division between British subjects and aliens became hardened, British descendants abroad who had been previously been denied the right to inherit the status of British subjecthood were increasingly included. Although this expansion of the rule of *jus sanguinis* during this period has received little scholarly attention, this work stresses that this trend shows the persistent influence of the principle of indelible allegiance legally abolished in 1870.

Under the common status of British subjecthood, there developed two groupings: British subjects under the common code system, which the Dominions and Britain jointly maintained, and those in the colonies. The former grouping under the common code system, in combination with the expanded rule of *jus sanguinis*, naturally received more favourable treatment as OCW citizens under post-Second World War immigration policy in Britain.[126] Britain's special relationship with the OCW countries receives much attention in recent studies of British immigration policy after the Second World War.[127] They point out that emotional links existed between peoples and leaders in Britain and the OCW as a result of the history of population movements from Britain. Yet, their analysis does not mention the influence of the common code system on post-Second World War immigration and nationality policy. In addition to the emotional bonds, this chapter has shown that the Dominion governments, along with Britain, engaged in establishing the definition of British subjecthood under the common code system, and jointly preserved it. After these experiences at imperial conferences, it is not surprising that some of the OCW governments in the mid-1960s still felt that, unlike those in the NCW countries, their citizens should always be treated equally to those in Britain, as had been the case under the common code system.[128]

Lastly, local citizenship in the Dominions, which had originally been established for immigration purposes, began to nurture a local identity, accommodating itself with that of British subjecthood. Here, we see that, alongside the alternative type of citizenship – British subjecthood – the national type of citizenship was developing into a clearer form than before. The main difference between the national and the alternative types of citizenship is that, in theory, the former is based on, and refers to, both political and national membership.[129] National citizenship can, therefore, count on an inner sense of shared identity which is supposed to emerge among its holders and be nurtured from below.

In contrast, British subjecthood in the colonies, and in the Dominions under the common code system, was simply the status of formal membership of the political unit, which had been granted from above (through unilateral colonization in the case of colonies, and bilateral agreement in the Dominions), not necessarily on the grounds of shared identity or belonging to a political unit. There was no systematic effort made by the imperial government to develop a sense of belonging among the holders of British subjecthood, either.[130] The common monarchy and the common status remained as symbols that unified the holders of British subjecthood, with their diversified cultural and linguistic backgrounds. Yet the common status was based on legislation (the BN & SA act 1914) which could be abolished by unilateral decision of a Dominion government after 1931. Furthermore, as was pointed out earlier, the common status under the common code system was not in practice common to all the holders of British subjecthood, British subjects of non-European descent being deprived of certain citizenship rights in some Dominions. After two world wars, it was inevitable that the Canadian government in 1946 chose to confer Canadian citizenship upon those people whom it had acknowledged as belonging to it. The status of British subjecthood became secondary, granted on the grounds of holding Canadian citizenship.

There is no denying that the local identity in each Dominion often merged with that of British subjecthood. Even during the parliamentary debates in 1946 over the Canadian Citizenship bill, for example, several MPs were opposed to its introduction, claiming that they were proud of being British subjects. For them, a Canadian citizen and British subject were 'both the same'.[131] Yet, after all, emergencies such as wars aside, it was the Dominion governments that were accountable to peoples in the Dominions in their everyday lives, and it was these governments that represented the people. The process of separating local citizenship from British subjecthood certainly progressed during this period. Eventually, after the Second World War, British subjecthood was re-invented to take the form of the composite type of citizenship called Commonwealth citizenship.[132]

NOTES

1. *Report of the Interdepartmental Committee Appointed by the Secretary of State for the Home Department to Consider the Doubts and Difficulties which Have Arisen in Connexion with the Interpretation and Administration of the Acts Relating to Naturalization*, Cd. 723, HMSO, 1901.
2. PRO, CAB 133/87. Meeting of Prime Ministers. Committee of Officials on Nationality Question. Minutes of Meeting of the Committee. 30 May 1946.
3. For details of the early development of the colonial (later, imperial) conferences, see Kendle, *Colonial and Imperial Conferences*. From 1907, the name changed from imperial to colonial conference.
4. PRO, CAB 32/69. Conference on the Operation of Dominion Legislation 1929. Minutes of Meetings and Reports of Committees. 8 October 1929. The Commonwealth during the period under discussion was officially called the British Commonwealth of Nations. After the Second World War the Commonwealth included Asian and African countries as they became independent, while the British Commonwealth consisted only of the Dominions. When the Commonwealth prior to the Second World War is being specifically referred to, the term 'the British Commonwealth' will be used. Otherwise, 'the Commonwealth' will be used.
5. Among many valuable works on legal aspects of the British Commonwealth, this chapter owes a special debt to the following: R. T. E. Latham, 'The Law and the Commonwealth', in W. K. Hancock, *Survey of British Commonwealth Affairs: Problems of Nationality 1918–1936* (Oxford University Press, London, 1937), pp. 510–615; Keith, *Constitution Law of the British Dominions*; Nicholas Mansergh, *The Commonwealth Experience* (Weidenfeld & Nicolson, London, 1969); K. C. Wheare, *Constitutional Structure of the Commonwealth* (Clarendon Press, Oxford, 1960).
6. Wheare at least spares one chapter for the issues of nationality: *Constitutional Structure of the Commonwealth*, Ch. 6. The way in which Latham deals with the issues of nationality during the period under discussion is typical of the studies on a 'common nationality'. He laments the 'welter of nationalities, citizenships, and unnamed personal statuses which exist for a multitude of purposes', but does not discuss what 'a multitude of purposes' is. Latham, 'Law and Commonwealth', pp. 591–5.
7. Canadian Citizenship Act 1946 (10 Geo. 6., c. 15, CCA 1946). Reflecting the mutual affinity between Britain and the Dominions, immigration policy in Britain after the Second World War was always more lenient towards OCW citizens than to NCW citizens. Details of immigration policy in Britain will be discussed in Ch. 5.
8. One of the biggest challenges came in 1937 from General Hertzog, the head of the Union of South Africa government, when he suggested that the status of British

subjecthood under the common code system should be conferred only on the basis of local citizenship. Details of his suggestion are discussed later in this chapter. PRO, CAB 32/131. Imperial Conference 1937.

9. Especially after the Statute of Westminster (22 Geo. 5., c. 4), the Dominion governments could choose to repeal the BN & SA act 1914 within their territory and abolish the common code whenever they wished.

10. Canadian nationals, for example, could only be defined by the Canadian act of 1921 (11 & 12 Geo. 5., Ch. 4) as 'any British subject who is a Canadian citizen within the meaning of the Immigration Act 1910' (9 & 10 Edw. 7., ch. 27).

11. For the practices of the naturalization acts prior to the twentieth century, see Ch. 2.

12. The Colonial Office, on the one hand, regarded naturalization in Britain as effective throughout the Empire. On the other hand, the law officers in 1874 expressed the opposite view. For details, see De Hart, 'Colonial Conference and Naturalization', pp. 135–7; Parry, *Nationality and Citizenship Laws*, pp. 80–1.

13. Naturalization would be granted, however, if a person had been in the service of the crown for five years and had an intention to reside in the United Kingdom or to continue in the service of the crown. 33 & 34 Vict., c. 14, s. 7. Also some colonies accepted the previous naturalization in other parts of the Empire as effective. See, for example, the Canadian Naturalization Amendment Act 1907, Cape of Good Hope, Act No. 2 of 1883, South Australian Act No. 5 of 1864, and New Zealand Act No. 19 of 1880. E. L. De Hart, 'The English Law of Nationality and Naturalization', *Journal of the Society of Comparative Legislation*, 2 (1900), pp 24–5.

14. *Reports of the Interdepartmental Committee*, Cd. 723, p. 18 (emphasis added). Other major recommendations were that (i) the acquisition of subjecthood by descent should be limited to the first generation born abroad; (ii) the system of local naturalization should be kept; and (iii) naturalization in a foreign country by a voluntary act would lead to a loss of the status of British subject.

15. Ibid. (emphasis added).

16. For details of the development of the system of colonial conferences see Kendle, *Colonial and Imperial Conferences*; Maurice Ollivier (ed.), *The Colonial and Imperial Conferences from 1887 to 1937*, 3 vols (E. Cloutier, Ottawa, 1954). Delegates from the Crown colonies were also allowed to attend the first colonial conference.

17. *Colonial Conference 1907: Minutes of Proceedings*. Cd. 3523, HMSO, May 1907. The Secretary of the State for the Colonies was responsible for organizing imperial conferences. He was also appointed as an *ex-officio* member of the conference, taking the chair in the absence of the prime minister of the United Kingdom.

18. Hancock, *Survey of British Commonwealth Affairs*, p. 28.

19. *Colonial Conference 1902: Papers Relating to a Conference between the Secretary of State for the Colonies and the Prime Ministers of Self-Governing Colonies*. Cd. 1299, HMSO, 1902.

20. *Colonial Conference 1907: Minutes of Proceedings*. Cd. 3523. 14th Day, 9 May 1907 (a comment made by General Botha). General Botha also suggested, in his memorandum submitted to the 1907 conference, that the certificate of imperial naturalization whose effect was valid throughout the Empire should be conferred only on a person of European birth or descent.

21. *Dominions No. 4. Further Correspondence Relating to the Imperial Conference*. Cd. 5273, HMSO, July 1910. No. 161, Colonial Office to Home Office. 28 January 1908.

22. *Dominions No. 4*. Cd. 5273. No. 164, Secretary of State to the Governor-General and Governors. 9 November 1908.

23. The committee also proposed to include evidence of an adequate knowledge of the English language as a condition for naturalization. A language test was new in British naturalization laws, but had been used in the Dominions as an indirect way of discriminating against British subjects of non-European origin. Ibid.

24. *Imperial Conference 1911. Precis of the Proceedings.* Cd. 5741, HMSO, June 1911.
25. The governments of both New Zealand and the Union of South Africa also supported the introduction of imperial naturalization at the 1907 conference. The New Zealand government, however, was not in agreement with all the details of the system, such as the period of residence required prior to naturalization.
26. *Imperial Conference 1911. Dominions No. 7. Minutes of Proceedings of the Imperial Conference 1911.* Cd. 5745, HMSO, July 1911. 8th Day, 13 June 1911.
27. Ibid.
28. Ibid.
29. In the House of Commons Harcourt explained that the British Nationality and Status of Aliens Bill 1914 was based on the five conclusions agreed at the 1911 conference. Parliamentary Debates, House of Commons, vol. 62, col. 1199, 13 May 1914.
30. Satvinder S. Juss, *Immigration, Nationality and Citizenship* (Mansell, London, 1993), p. 51. This study, however, will not go as far as Satvinder in claiming that the common code system encouraged discrimination against British subjects of Asian descent by accepting discriminatory immigration control by the Dominion governments. Discriminatory legislation had existed before the common code system and it is not clear whether discrimination intensified under the common code system.
31. Indian representatives were, for the first time, invited to the imperial conference in 1917. Although their claim for equality of Indians in the Dominions was 'recognized' by other participants at the imperial conference 1921, immigration policies in Kenya and South Africa remained unchanged. Hugh Tinker, *Separate and Unequal: India and the Indians in the British Commonwealth 1920–1950* (C. Hurst, London, 1976), pp. 44–53. Within India, furthermore, political rights were very much restricted until the enactment of the India Act 1919.
32. *Colonial Conference 1902: Papers Relating to a Conference between the Secretary of State for the Colonies and the Prime Ministers of Self-governing Colonies.* Cd. 1299. Appendix XIII, Naturalization, p. 151.
33. Except for a few Aliens Acts (1824, 1836, and 1848) whose object was mainly to keep out revolutionary persons, the British government had no power to deal with aliens until the twentieth century. For details of early immigration laws in Britain, see PRO, HO 45/10063/B2840. The Early Legislation. Memorandum of Laws Relating to the Landing and Residence of Aliens in Great Britain. 18 March 1845.
34. The AA 1905 defined 'undesirable immigrants' as those who (i) could not decently support themselves and their dependants (if any); or (ii) appeared likely to become a charge on public funds or were otherwise a detriment to the public; or (iii) had been sentenced in a foreign country for an extraditable crime; or (iv) were the subject of an expulsion order made under the Act: Aliens Act 1905, s. 1(2). These tests were not applicable to everyone, but only to steerage passengers (the cheapest class) who came on 'immigrant ships', defined as ships carrying more than 20 aliens (other than the crew). There are a number of pieces of research on the Aliens Act 1905: for example, Gainer, *The Alien Invasion*; John A. Garrard, *The English and Immigration 1880–1910* (Oxford University Press, London, 1971); M. H. Landa, *The Alien Problem and its Remedy* (P. S. King & Sons, London, 1911).
35. For laws and regulations enacted in the colonies before 1904, see *Papers Relative to Laws and Regulations in Force in the Colonies under Responsible Government Respecting the Admission of Immigrants.* Cd. 2105, HMSO, 1904.
36. For racism in the Dominions and the British Empire as a whole, see, for example, R. A. Huttenback, *Racism and Empire* (Cornell University Press, London, 1976).
37. For details see Parry, *Nationality and Citizenship Laws*, Chs 9–12. In addition to New Zealand (1896) and Australia (1903), Natal also had a naturalization law which

limited naturalization only to aliens 'of European birth and descent'. Act No. 18, 1905. Canada also imposed restrictions on the naturalization of Asians.

38. Blackstone, *Commentaries*, p. 354. The development of the concept of membership in Britain prior to the twentieth century is discussed in Ch. 2.

39. During a short period of the nineteenth century when the 1844 act was passed, it was considered advantageous to encourage naturalization of foreign immigrants. See the previous chapter for details.

40. Old age pensions, for example, were first introduced in 1909.

41. Harcourt, the then Secretary of State for the Colonies, attributed the government's objection to shortening the qualifying period for naturalization to proximity to the Continent as well as social welfare services. Parliamentary Debates, House of Commons, vol. 62, col. 1197, 13 May 1914.

42. When the Dominion and British governments were seeking a means of establishing imperial naturalization at the beginning of the twentieth century, Ireland had not yet been given Dominion status. Therefore, with the exception of the Union of South Africa, all the other Dominions had started, more or less, as settled colonies.

43. For example, Malan, the then Minister of Education of the Union of South Africa, justified in 1911 its discriminatory immigration measure against British Indians on the grounds that South Africa had a large African population and could not bear another coloured problem connected with Asians. *Imperial Conference 1911*. Cd. 5745. 8th Day, 13 June 1911.

44. As a country of immigration, for example, the development of the concept of citizenship in the United States depended greatly upon its immigration policy. Kettner, *Development of American Citizenship*, 1978.

45. The most famous case of intra-imperial conflict on discrimination was between the Union of South Africa and India. See Robert G. Gregory, *India and East Africa: A History of Race Relations within the British Empire 1890–1939* (Clarendon Press, Oxford, 1971).

46. *Colonial Conference 1907*. Cd. 3523. 14th Day, 9 May 1907.

47. Ibid.

48. C. F. Fraser, *Control of Aliens in the British Commonwealth of Nations* (Hogarth Press, London, 1940), pp. 91–3.

49. To illustrate Laurier's stand on the inter-imperial relationship, Wigley introduced in his work an anecdote about Laurier's insistence on using the term 'country' for Canada in the 1902 imperial discussion, while Richard Seddon of New Zealand talked of his 'colony'. Philip G. Wigley, *Canada and the Transition to Commonwealth, British–Canadian Relations 1917–1926* (Cambridge University Press, Cambridge, 1977), pp. 9–10.

50. According to the CIA 1910, an 'alien' meant a person who was not a British subject. A 'Canadian citizen' was defined as '(1) a person born in Canada who has not become an alien; (2) a British subject who has Canadian domicile; and (3) a person naturalized under the laws of Canada who has not subsequently become an alien or lost Canadian Domicile' (s. 2). For more details of the act, see Fraser, *Control of Aliens*, pp. 91–3.

51. *Imperial Conference 1911*. Cd. 5745. 8th Day, 13 June 1911.

52. For details see Fransman, *Fransman's British Nationality Law*, pp. 41–54. Parry, *Nationality and Citizenship Laws*, pp. 148–93.

53. While Canada adopted the BN & SA act 1914 in 1914, Australia did so in 1920, the Union of South Africa in 1926 and New Zealand as late as 1928.

54. For example, if a woman with British subjecthood from New Zealand married a foreigner, she would lose her status of British subjecthood in the other parts of the Empire, but was allowed to keep it in New Zealand. Parry, *Nationality and*

Citizenship Laws, p. 84.

55. Exclusive control by the imperial government over foreign affairs in the Dominions was clearly proven when the imperial government declared war in 1914 on behalf of the entire Empire without first gaining consent from the Dominion governments.

56. The jurisdiction of colonial legislatures was also confined on the territories of their colonies. *McLeod* v. *Attorney General for New South Wales* (1891), A. C. 455.

57. Keith, *Constitution Law of the British Dominions*, Ch. 1.

58. For example, in 1895, responding to requests from the Canadian government, the imperial government decided to grant self-governing colonies the autonomy to impose tariffs. In 1907 the Canadian government agreed a commercial treaty with its French counterpart, although the British ambassador in Paris jointly signed the treaty.

59. Holland argues that loyalty towards the crown among the Dominion people might not be apparent in their everyday life, but was certain to burst out at the time of emergency such as war. R. F. Holland, *European Decolonization 1918–1981: An Introductory Survey* (Macmillan, London, 1985), p. 24.

60. Britain's decline in the field of economy and politics is thoroughly analyzed in Andrew Gamble, *Britain in Decline: Economic Policy, Political Strategy and the British State* (Macmillan, London, 1994 [1981]). See also E. J. Hobsbawm, *Industry and Empire* (Penguin, Harmondsworth, 1990 [1968]), Chs 6, 7, 9).

61. Protectionist sentiment began to emerge in the 1880s; for example, the National Fair Trade League was founded in 1881. Sydney H. Zebel, 'Fair Trade: An English Reaction to the Breakdown of the Cobden Treaty System', *Journal of Modern History*, 12, 2 (June 1940), pp. 161–85.

62. T. Boyle, 'The Liberal Imperialist, 1892–1906', *Bulletin of the Institute of Historical Research*, 52, 125 (May 1979), pp. 48–82; Sydney H. Zebel, 'Joseph Chamberlain and the Genesis of Tariff Reform', *Journal of British Studies*, 7, 1 (November 1967), pp. 131–57. Under imperial preference, each self-governing colony would impose its own external tariff but admit goods from others at preferential rates.

63. Holland summarized that 'the organization of [the] Commonwealth was one way that the British state attempted to stem political and economic decline after 1918': R. F. Holland, *Britain and the Commonwealth Alliance 1918–1939* (Macmillan, London, 1981), p. 24.

64. See, for example, PRO, CAB 37/62/113. Statistics of Trade of the United Kingdom with the Various Colonies and Possessions. 18 July 1902.

65. For the position of Canada within the empire during the period under discussion, see, for example, Wigley, *Canada*, Ch. 1.

66. Hancock, *Survey of British Commonwealth Affairs*, p. 2. According to him, the Dominions changed their target for reconstructing the empire from 'liberty' to 'equality of status' after the First World War.

67. For details see Ch. 2.

68. The idea to include British people throughout the world in a 'common citizenship' was not itself new, as was seen, for example, in the proposal made by Dicey in 1897, when he insisted that a common citizenship should be formed between the United States and the United Kingdom. A. V. Dicey, 'A Common Citizenship for the English Race', *Contemporary Review*, 71 (1897), pp. 457–76.

69. As was pointed out earlier, an imperial conference was not a legislative body of the empire, nor was it intended to become so.

70. Parliamentary Debates, House of Commons, vol. 65, col. 1986, 5 August 1914.

71. 'Alien enemy' was a person voluntarily resident in or carrying on business in an enemy's country. The test of enemy character was not supposed to be nationality

but the place were a person lived and carried on their business. *Porter* v. *Freudenberg* (1915), 1 K.B. 857.

72. Parliamentary Debates, House of Commons, vol. 65, col. 1989, 5 August 1914.

73. For the details of the ARA 1914 and its enforcement, see J. C. Bird, *Control of Enemy Alien Civilians in Great Britain 1914–1918* (Garland, New York, 1986).

74. The ARA 1919 was extended on an annual basis and is still in force. The Aliens Order 1920 also transformed the passport system, which had been used as a temporary measure, into a permanent feature of immigration control in Britain. The Aliens Order 1953 controlled the immigration of aliens until 1971, when it was repealed by the Immigration Act 1971. For details about the Aliens Acts see, for example, Juss, *Immigration, Nationality and Citizenship*, pp. 37–9. For the historical development of the passport system, see Torpey, *Invention of the Passport*.

75. *Imperial War Conference 1917. Extracts from Minutes of Proceedings and Papers Laid before the Conference.* Cd. 8566, HMSO, May 1917. 'Memorandum Prepared in the Home Office', March 1917. The issue of tightening the regulation of naturalization for alien enemies was often discussed during the 1917 session of Parliament as well. See, for example, Parliamentary Debates, House of Commons, vol. 158, cols 1574–86, 31 October; vol. 159, cols 856–7, 19 November; col. 1841, 27 November.

76. Parliamentary Debates, House of Commons, vol. 108, cols 634 and 638, 12 July 1918.

77. By then, only the Canadian government had passed its own legislation on the BN & SA act 1914. As a result, the system of the common code under the BN & SA act 1914 was changed even before all the Dominion governments had adopted it.

78. The British government maintained stringent immigration controls on inflows of aliens even after the First World War. Parliamentary interest in alien immigration intensified as immigration of Jewish refugees from German occupied territories increased in the late 1930s and during the Second World War. See Bernard Wasserstein, *Britain and the Jews of Europe: 1939–1945* (Clarendon Press, Oxford, 1979).

79. *Report of the Interdepartmental Committee*, Cd. 723, p. 6.

80. The law was also amended to include as British subjects any person born abroad whose father was a British subject by annexation.

81. Parliamentary Debates, House of Commons, vol. 156, col. 521, 5 July 1922 (Sir J. Baird).

82. BN & SA act 1922, s. 1(1).

83. Parliamentary Debates, House of Commons, vol. 156, col. 522, 5 July 1922 (Sir J. Baird).

84. For details see Fransman, *Fransman's British Nationality Law*, pp. 43–7. The BN & SA act 1943 gave the Secretary of State the discretion to register a birth more than 12 months late and was also effective retrospectively. In addition, the declaration was only necessary if a child was registered when still a minor.

85. Bird, along with other scholars, regards the enactment of the ARA 1914 as the end of the traditional laissez-faire approach to immigration. Bird, *Control of Enemy Alien Civilians*, p. 14.

86. When the government of New Zealand finally adopted the BN & SA act 1914 in 1928 (it was the last of the five Dominions to do so), for example, the BN & SA act 1914 had already been amended twice, in 1918 and 1922. For details of the history of immigration and nationality laws in New Zealand, see Parry, *Nationality and Citizenship Law*, Ch. 11. In the Union of South Africa, neither the BN & SA act 1933 nor 1943 was adopted.

87. See Hancock, *Survey of British Commonwealth Affairs*, pp. 13–28, and R. M. Dawson, *The Development of Dominion Status, 1900–1936* (Oxford University Press, London, 1937).

88. Imperial War Conferences provided the place to discuss non-war problems, while issues of war and those of a political nature were discussed in the Imperial War Cabinet, which was formed in 1917. The Imperial War Cabinet, under the Prime Minister, consisted of the British War Cabinet and the Dominion representatives.
89. *Imperial War Conference 1917*. Cd. 8566, May 1917.
90. Holland argues that Hertzog needed to solve the constitutional question in order to maintain a coalition between the Afrikaner-dominated National Party and the pro-British Labour Party. Holland, *Commonwealth Alliance*, pp. 54–5. For Hertzog's policy regarding the Commonwealth relationship during the period under discussion, see C. M. van den Heever, *General J. B. M. Hertzog* (A. P. B. Bookstore, Johannesburg, 1946), pp. 203–18.
91. *Imperial Conference 1926: Summary of Proceedings*. Cmd. 2768, HMSO, November 1926. Report of Inter-Imperial Relations Committee.
92. For the details of the 1926 conference see A. Berriedale Keith, *The Sovereignty of the British Commonwealth* (Macmillan, London, 1929), Ch. 1.
93. PRO, CAB 32/69. Conference on the Operation of Dominion Legislation 1929. Minutes of Meetings and Reports of Committees. 1st Meeting, 8 October 1929.
94. Ibid.
95. *Report of the Conference on the Operation of Dominion Legislation and Merchant Shipping Legislation*. Cmd. 3479, HMSO, 1929/30, p. 25.
96. Ibid.
97. *Imperial Conference 1930. Summary of Proceedings*. Cmd. 3717, HMSO, November 1930, 'Inter-Imperial Relations'.
98. PRO, CAB 32/131. Imperial Conference 1937. Preparatory Meetings on Constitutional Questions: Proceedings and Memoranda and the Committee on Constitutional Questions – Reports, Proceedings, and Memoranda.
99. PRO, DO 34/807/7. That was the view expressed by the Secretary of State for Dominion Affairs. For details see CAB 32/127. Cabinet. Memorandum by the Interdepartmental Committee on Intra-Imperial Relations. April 1937.
100. PRO, CAB 32/127. Cabinet. Memorandum by the Interdepartmental Committee on Intra-Imperial Relations.
101. From the point of view of domestic politics, Hertzog needed to stress his separatist attitude in order to attract Afrikaner supporters. See van den Heever, *Hertzog*, pp. 261–5. In the face of unfavourable reaction from the other Dominions, however, the Union expert at the 1937 conference made it clear that the purpose of the proposal was to obtain the benefit of the opinions of the other Members of the Commonwealth. The Union proposal was eventually dropped. CAB 32/127. Cabinet. Memorandum by the Interdepartmental Committee on Intra-Imperial Relations.
102. Of the six Dominions, only the Irish Free State enacted its own nationality and citizenship law to take advantage of this newly acquired freedom to leave the common code system. The Irish Nationality and Citizenship Act 1935 (no. 13 of 1935, IN & CA 35, s. 33) explicitly abrogated both the BN & SA acts 1914 and 1918 and the common law relating to British nationality within its territory. This Irish legislation, unlike the other immigration-related laws prior to it, was a complete departure from the common code, but no other Dominion governments were ready to follow in the Irish footsteps before the Second World War.
103. By the beginning of the 1930s it became clear that the League of Nations was not as powerful as people had hoped in bringing stability and peace to the world. The first concrete sign of the breaking up of the League was the Japanese invasion of Manchuria in 1931. F. P. Walters, *A History of the League of Nations* (Oxford University Press, London, 1952).

104. PRO, CAB 32/131. Imperial Conference 1937. Committee on Constitutional Questions: Report on (1) Nationality, and (2) Treaty Procedure.
105. Under the system of the common code, two Dominions – Canada and the Union of South Africa – passed *nationality* laws of their own. In order to avoid confusion, this chapter uses the term 'citizenship' to denote the status in general which the Dominions established by local legislation during the period between 1914 and 1946. In talking of specific legislation, it follows the term used in the legislation. Unlike citizenship status after 1946, this 'citizenship' status in the Dominions prior to 1946 did not by itself grant citizenship rights and obligations to its holders.
106. Parliamentary Debates, House of Commons, vol. 62, col. 1201, 13 May 1914.
107. Demanding less control from Westminster as was seen in the issue of separate Dominion citizenship; however, each Dominion government at the same time used imperial control to manage the separatist movements among non-British population. For example, s. 7 of the Statute of Westminster specifically excluded the British North America Acts 1867–1930, so that the Canadian government could not amend them on its own by local legislation.
108. For the issue of the representation of the Dominions at the Paris Peace Conference and their international status thereafter, see Hancock, *Survey of British Commonwealth Affairs*, Ch. 2.
109. Keith, *Sovereignty*, 1929, pp. 64–5.
110. In 1923 the Canadian government, on its own, signed the Convention for the Preservation of the Halibut Fishery of the Northern Pacific Ocean.
111. As a result of the formation of the Union of South Africa in 1910, the inconvenience of local nationalization was mainly solved before the BN & SA act 1914 was established. It therefore took South Africa 14 years finally to adopt that act. For details of the development of immigration and nationality laws in the Union up to the Second World War, see Parry, *Nationality and Citizenship Law*, Ch. 12.
112. PRO, CAB 32/131. Summary of Legislation Dealing with Nationality and Naturalization in the Union of South Africa. 'Nationality in the Union of South Africa', *British Year Book of International Law*, 17 (1935), pp. 187–9. 'South Africa: Nationality Question', *British Year Book of International Law*, 18 (1936), pp. 181–3.
113. PRO, DO 35/111/3. A note from C. W. Dixon to Robertson-Fullarton. 10 March 1932.
114. PRO, CAB 32/131. Preparatory Meeting on Constitutional Question. Distinct Nationality and Common Status. Memorandum by the Delegation of the Union of South Africa.
115. PRO, CAB 32/131. Preparatory Meeting on Constitutional Question. Distinct Nationality and Common Status. Memorandum by the Delegation of the Union of South Africa.
116. Paul, *Whitewashing Britain*, pp. 95–7.
117. PRO, CAB 32/130. Imperial Conference 1937. Meeting of Principal Delegates. Notes of Meetings. 14 June 1937.
118. Ibid.
119. The issue of the nationality of married women was constantly on the agenda of both imperial conferences and the British Parliament after the First World War. The main problem was that the BN & SA act 1914 continued the rule of the 1870 act, under which the status of a wife had to follow that of her husband. Thus a British subject would lose her status upon marriage to an alien, while an alien woman would become a British subject on her marriage to a British subject. A summary of the debates on this issue both in the United Kingdom and at international conferences up to 1930 can be found in PRO, DO 35/106/4.

Nationality of Married Women.

120. The governments of both countries further amended their laws in 1946, confirming that a woman would retain her status as British subject 'unless she makes a declaration that she desired to retain or acquire the nationality of her husband' (s. 3, No. 9 of 1946, Australia). Also, British Nationality and Status of Aliens (in New Zealand) Amendment Act 1946 (10 Geo. VI., no. 20), s. 2.

121. Details of the CCA 1946 are discussed in Ch. 4.

122. PRO, PREM 8/851. Cabinet. Canadian Citizenship Bill. Memorandum by the Home Secretary. 16 November 1945.

123. For Anglo-Dominion relations before the Second World War, see John Darwin, 'Imperialism in Decline?', *Historical Journal*, 23, 3 (1980), pp. 657–79.

124. For example, R. G. Casey, the then Treasurer in Australia, strongly insisted at the imperial conference in 1937 on maintaining the term British subject, as 'the vast bulk of the Australian population treasured the term British subject'. PRO, CAB 32/137. Committee on Constitutional Question. Notes of the 1st Meeting of the Committee. 25 May 1937.

125. Blackstone, *Commentaries*, pp. 358–60.

126. Dilke once described overseas communities of British descendants as 'Greater Britain'. C. W. Dilke, *Greater Britain* (Macmillan, London, 1869).

127. For example, see I. R. G. Spencer, *British Immigration Policy since 1939: The Making of Multi-Racial Britain* (Routledge, London, 1997), pp. 65–8.

128. Both the Australian and Canadian governments officially complained when immigration control on their citizens was tightened in the mid-1960s. Governmental officials in Britain then concluded that they were complaining not because their citizens were being unfairly treated in comparison with their NCW counterparts, but because their citizens were subject to immigration control. For more details, see Ch. 5.

129. The characteristics of the national type of citizenship are discussed in Ch. 1.

130. Some scholars argued that, during the period under discussion, the image of the monarchy was greatly enhanced by stage-managing the great royal rituals, such as the Christmas broadcasts and the coronation ceremony, as the unifying symbol of the whole Empire. See, for example, Cannadine, 'Context, Performance and Meaning of Ritual', pp. 139–50. Yet efforts to establish a shared identity among all the holders of British subjecthood were hardly systematic. The common monarchy did not result in mutual affinity between those in different parts of the Empire, although it might have helped prolong the link between the crown and British subjects. In contrast, efforts are now being strenuously made to give EU citizenship more than a legal status.

131. Parliamentary Debates, House of Commons, Dominion of Canada, 1st Session 1946, vol. I, col. 598, 5 April 1946.

132. For details of the composite type of citizenship see Ch. 1. It was defined as one of the three types of alternative citizenship, and formed by mutual contract or agreement between political units.

— 4 —
Commonwealth Citizenship: From the British Nationality Act 1948 to the Commonwealth Immigrants Act 1962

THE SECOND World War began in Europe in 1939 and in Asia in 1941. By then, the Dominions had fully secured constitutional equality with Britain.[1] They joined the Second World War on the same side as Britain, but, unlike in the First World War, they did so of their own volition. Éire remained symbolically neutral. Although the British Empire emerged territorially intact in 1945, Britain's position was considerably weakened both financially and militarily.[2] In the post-war world, furthermore, the UN appealed to member countries for 'friendly relations among nations based on respect for the principle of equal rights and self-determination of peoples'.[3] It was clear to Westminster that the colonial empires, including Britain's, had to adjust themselves to this new international environment. Consequently, it was inevitable that the method of maintaining the common status within the British Empire should be changed.

Previous works on post-war immigration policy in Britain have mainly focused on the way in which it became racially discriminatory.[4] They have not asked why British governments delayed until 1981 before creating the status of British citizenship, and have remained silent about the fact that the status of British citizenship, unlike the citizenship of other Western democratic countries, is still not defined by nationhood. This chapter in combination with the next argues that, during the period after the Second World War, successive British governments struggled, as had the governments in the Dominions prior to the Second World War, to reconcile two conflicting goals: the maintenance of the common status and the development of a national citizenship. Nationality and immigration policy in Britain after the Second World War – the contrasting features of the nationality and the immigration laws, the former being inclusive to all holders of Commonwealth citizenship with the latter becoming strictly exclusive towards NCW immigrants – was a response to this struggle.

This chapter focuses on the process of creating the formula for the new common status, Commonwealth citizenship. The other side of the process, the development of national citizenship in Britain alongside Commonwealth citizenship, is dealt with in the next chapter. This chapter begins by looking at a key concept of international relations after the Second World War, the principle of national self-determination, and its impact on the British Empire. Under the influence of this new principle, the British Empire and the British Commonwealth (now called the Commonwealth) had to undergo a constitutional transformation by discarding its empire-like features based on imperial supervision and control and by stressing instead its multiracial and multicultural aspects. The focus of my analysis then moves to the features and structures of Commonwealth citizenship. The debates on a republican India's membership of the Common-wealth reconfirmed that Commonwealth citizenship was based on agreement between member countries, and that it had only the nominal aspect of citizenship. The substantive and functional aspects of Commonwealth citizenship were never acknowledged in any member countries other than Britain. Furthermore, Commonwealth citizenship had to give up a shared sense of belonging among its holders which British subjecthood, to a certain extent, could claim on the grounds of allegiance to the Crown. In short, Commonwealth citizenship was established by extending the contractual aspects of the common code system to cover the whole Commonwealth, the status being granted by virtue of the holding of citizenship of a member country of the Commonwealth. Finally, this chapter ends by examining the immigration control introduced by the Commonwealth Immigrants Act 1962 (CIA 1962). Through its enactment, Commonwealth citizenship became merely a nominal status even in Britain.

THE POST-WAR WORLD AND THE COMMONWEALTH

The decline of Britain as a world power

Britain came out of the war in 1945, still considering itself as one of the 'three Great Powers' along with the United States and the USSR. Yet, for policy-makers in Britain, the world after the war was significantly different. This was mainly due to the decline in Britain's position in world politics in comparison with that of the United States and the USSR, and the increasingly vocal demands among political leaders of non-imperial powers for acceptance of the principle of national self-determination as the key concept of international relations.[5]

First, Britain's financial and industrial positions were greatly weakened during the war, by the accumulation of a large sum of overseas financial debt (about £3,500 million) and the liquidation of almost one quarter of its overseas assets.[6] Without substantial aid from the United States, an increase in exports, and domestic austerity, Britain was facing a sudden descent to the status of 'a second-class Power, rather like the present position of France'.[7] Yet, tensions between political leaders in Britain and the United States, which had been put aside during the war, were already surfacing towards the end of the war. Although Churchill famously described the core of Britain's external policy as 'the natural Anglo-American special relationship', it had not always been as intimate as it sounded.[8] It was true that economic support through the Lend–Lease programme was invaluable to Britain during the war.[9] Nonetheless, its abrupt end within a month of Japan's defeat left a sense of betrayal among policy-makers. The joint projects which had started during the war, such as the atomic alliance, were also phased out as soon as the war was over.[10]

In spite of the country's difficult economic circumstances and its dependence on American assistance, the Attlee government was determined that Britain could, and also should, remain as a third alternative in the face of the increasing rivalry between the United States and the USSR. The Foreign Office under Ernest Bevin was especially adamant on this issue. Concerned with the development of 'a feeling [in the United States] that Great Britain is now a secondary Power and can be treated as such', its memorandum argued that 'It is this misconception which it must be our policy to combat'.[11] It then warned that the British should not 'regard [themselves] as a European Power and ... overlook the fact that [they] are still the centre of an Empire. If [they] cease to regard [themselves] as a World Power [they] shall gradually cease to be one.'[12] For Ernest Bevin, Britain was 'the last bastion of social democracy ... as against the red tooth and claw of American capitalism and the Communist dictatorship of Soviet Russia'.[13] Asked about his opinion on Britain's defence policy in the Mediterranean and Middle East, he insisted that Britain's position there should not be weakened, otherwise it would mean the end of social democracy there.

Yet Bevin was fully aware at the same time that, as long as Britain was dependent on economic assistance from the United States, it could not fully pursue its own foreign policy. He found the answer in 'the importance not only of closer trade relations with the Commonwealth and Empire but also of an intensified effort for development within them'.[14] Unlike in the period prior to the Second

World War, therefore, the Empire became no longer 'useless encumbrances, nor ... a shameful legacy best disposed of, but ... an opportunity for planned redevelopment'.[15] Nonetheless, when the British government most needed support from the Dominions and the colonies the influence of the Mother Country over them seemed to be at its weakest. The trend of decentralization in the Dominions was accelerating, and Asian colonies such as Burma, Ceylon (now Sri Lanka) and India were pressing for independence.

The principle of national self-determination and the Commonwealth

Here, the second change in the world after the Second World War – increasing demands for the principle of national self-determination as the key concept of international relations – comes into play. The principle of national self-determination had already been acclaimed at the Paris Peace Conference in 1919. However, its effects during the inter-war period were limited, partly because of the ambiguity of the concept and also because of the way in which it was then introduced. Its real impact therefore only started to spread outside Europe after the Second World War and even later. Yet there were a number of problems with the principle of national self-determination, when it came to defining it or testing its viability, let alone putting it into practice.[16] Cobban, for example, describes it, in general terms, as 'the belief that each nation has a right to constitute an independent state and determine its own government'.[17] He quickly points out, however, that there is heated argument about how to define and also identify a 'nation'. Instead of attempting its definition, therefore, he proposes that we should understand the meaning of national self-determination in its historical context. When President Woodrow Wilson addressed the principle of national self-determination in his Fourteen Points at the Paris conference, he was not fully aware of the difficulty of its application and definition.[18] Furthermore, Wilson compromised and agreed that the application of the principle should be limited only to 'the territories of the defeated empires' in order to reach a consensus among the participants of the peace conference.[19] As was typically seen in the mandate system which was introduced by the League of Nations, the principle of national self-determination during the inter-war period was selectively implemented by political leaders in the imperial powers.

The mandate system posed a theoretical challenge to the legitimacy of the imperial system. It is true that anti-imperialist movements existed before the peace conference, the history of the Irish movement for independence, for example, long pre-dating 1919. Under the mandate system, however, the imperial powers, at least superficially in certain areas, had to downplay the coercive aspects of imperialism.[20] For instance, the administering countries were accountable to the League of Nations and had to submit annual reports to the League Council. However, the system was only applied to the former colonies of Germany and the Ottoman Empire, leaving most of the colonial territories outside it. Furthermore, its goal remained unclear, except that the League of Nations claimed that 'the well-being and the development of such peoples [in the former colonies of Germany and the Ottoman Empire] form a sacred trust of civilization'.[21] Although it is too extreme to say that the mandate system was imperial expansion under another name, there is no denying that the impact of the principle of national self-determination on the imperial powers was limited. In the British Empire, for example, a series of constitutional developments took place with regard to the Dominions' equality vis-à-vis Britain, but the pace of change in the colonies was painfully slow.

In spite of the ambiguity of its definition and the limitation of its application, however, the principle of national self-determination had important consequences for citizenship during the inter-war period. The concept of citizenship became firmly linked to nationhood under the principle of national self-determination, however it was defined and regardless of whether a 'nation' existed or not. The formula of national citizenship was strengthened, indicating that people had to be members of the 'nation' of the political unit in order to be granted the status of its citizenship, and only citizens were entitled to choose the government as their representatives. It also became imperative that equality in terms of citizenship rights and obligations should be achieved in order to validate the formula, the movement for the equal franchise between men and women in Europe, for example, being boosted after the First World War.

The principle of national self-determination was far more widely proclaimed by the time of the Second World War. After all, this was supposed to be the war between the Allies, who claimed the principle of national self-determination, and the Axis powers, with their imperial ambitions. The future status of the colonies was therefore one of the main issues for the Allies. Naturally, there were heated debates on the trusteeship system, which replaced the mandate system of the League of Nations.

In discussing the trusteeship system after the Second World War, the British government was one of the most cautious members about the application of the principle of national self-determination, as it had been during the war. The principle of national self-determination was, for example, clearly stated in the Atlantic Charter which the governments of Britain and the United States signed in 1941.[22] Yet Churchill emphatically argued later in Parliament that the provisions of the Atlantic Charter did not qualify 'the various statements of policy which have been made from time to time about the development of constitutional government in India, Burma, or other parts of the British Empire'.[23] He insisted that it was the liberation of European countries from Nazi invasion which he and Roosevelt had in mind. According to Churchill, therefore, the constitutional development of the colonies in the British Empire into self-governing institutions was an issue separate from the Charter. Although he was correct in stating that he and Roosevelt meant Europe when signing the Charter, 'a geographical limitation for the application' of a principle of national self-determination was hardly welcomed in the colonies outside Europe and the Dominions.[24] The Dominions, as members of the 'free association of the British Commonwealth of Nations', had made significant contributions to the victory of the Allies.[25]

At the San Francisco Conference and its preparatory sessions, it became increasingly difficult for the British delegates to maintain the claim of 'geographical limitation for application of the principle of national self-determination', at least in the form in which it then was.[26] Furthermore, unlike the Paris conference, where the issue of colonies was decided by the imperial powers, in San Francisco non-imperial participants such as Australia, the Philippines and Egypt took an explicitly anti-colonial stand. As a result the trusteeship system, to a certain extent, elaborated on the mandate system. For example, the working principles of the trusteeship system with regard to its general administration were clarified, the goal of the trusteeship territories being specified as 'self-government or independence'.[27] Measures of international supervision over the trusteeship territories also became more sophisticated. In addition to an annual report by administering countries, a provision for periodic visits to the territories at times agreed on by the administering countries was introduced. However, the colonial powers succeeded in avoiding the word 'self-determination', using instead, the phrase, '*the freely expressed wishes of the people concerned*'(article 76(b), emphasis added). Furthermore, a distinction was drawn in the UN Charter between the territories under the trusteeship system and those outside. The only international supervision applied to the latter category was that information on economic, social educational advancement was to be transmitted regularly to the Secretary-General (article 73(e)).

In sum, the trusteeship system did not fully represent the principle of national self-determination, and most of the colonies in Africa, whether inside or outside the trusteeship system, had to wait until the 1960s to become independent. It was, however, no longer possible to argue after the Second World War that one group of people was better equipped to govern a country than another on the basis of imperial supremacy and racial superiority. Compared with the end of the First World War, international supervision of colonial administration was also strengthened under the trusteeship system, and the principle of national self-determination further penetrated among the colonized peoples outside Europe. As was seen in the debate on the trusteeship system, a group of countries made their anti-colonial stance clear, and tried, although unsuccessfully at the time, to promote the independence of colonies.

In this new international environment after the war, the idea of the Commonwealth and its extension was increasingly attractive to politicians both inside and outside Britain.[28] The Commonwealth prior to the Second World War consisted of the so-called white Dominions (later, the OCW), with their substantial numbers of British descendants. In contrast, the Commonwealth after the war would include newly independent countries in Asia, and potentially in Africa and the Caribbean region, as, in theory, equal members of the Commonwealth. The then Secretary of State for the Colonies, Creech Jones, for example, encouraged the early participation of Ceylon in the Commonwealth. He argued that its membership would '[demonstrate] to the world that our proclaimed policy for the Colonial peoples is not an empty boast, and that an independent status in the Commonwealth is not, in practice, reserved for peoples of European descent'.[29] By accepting non-European members into the Commonwealth, the British government could prove to its critics that the Commonwealth was different from the Empire. In order to provide a third ideology different from the capitalism of the United States and the communism of the USSR, furthermore, it was important to stress the multi-racial and multi-national nature of the Commonwealth. This nature was also beneficial for economic reasons. As was discussed earlier, Britain needed all possible support from the Commonwealth and as many colonies as possible to remain inside the Commonwealth, if it wished to remain a world power.

Yet extending membership to newly independent countries which shared neither historical nor emotional links with Britain had its drawbacks. As the number of members was increased by the inclusion of Asian countries, the political and economic interests of the members diversified. The Dominions also made clear their separate identity from Britain, so that they were recognized as individual members of international organizations such as the UN. In consequence, the Commonwealth as an association was likely to become less coherent than before and more like other international organizations which were formed by groups of individual countries based on common interests. It was therefore imperative for the Commonwealth that some kind of common status had to be preserved to symbolize its unity.

The rest of this chapter examines the creation of Commonwealth citizenship and the process by which it became more derivative in status, as a result of the different citizenship laws of each member country. My analysis demonstrates that, as had been the case under British subjecthood, the exact features of Commonwealth citizenship – what it entailed and how its entitlements were granted – were only determined when problems occurred.

DISSOLUTION OF THE COMMON CODE SYSTEM AND THE BRITISH NATIONALITY ACT 1948

The process of dissolution of the common code system

It was symbolic that each Dominion government signed the UN Charter separately, rather than grouping together under the general heading of British Empire, as had happened with the League of Nations Covenant. The solidarity between Britain and the Dominions, which seemed to have existed during the war, rapidly crumbled after the war.

No more than a month after the end of the war the Canadian government took another decisive step to weaken control from Westminster by notifying its British counterpart of its intention to enact its own citizenship law.[30] The Canadian government, until then, had been content to specify who 'belonged' to Canada by naturalization and immigration acts. However, it finally decided that

> for the national unity of Canada and for the future and greatness of this country it is felt to be of the utmost importance that all of us, new Canadians and old, have a consciousness of a common purpose and common interests as Canadians; that all of us be able to say with pride and say with meaning: 'I am a Canadian citizen.'[31]

With the confidence acquired during the war, the Canadian government felt that it was time to create Canadian citizenship based on its own definition of nationhood. The percentage of non-British people was expected to grow after the war because of flows of immigration from war-torn continental Europe. For the Canadian government, therefore, the creation of citizenship of its own would not only allow the government to create a Canadian citizenship separate from British subjecthood but also appeal to a large number of its non-British population.

This Canadian action was evidence that each Dominion would wish to be an internationally acknowledged individual political unit first, and a member of the Commonwealth second. Inevitably, if the common status was to be maintained, it had to be reconstructed to enable each member to fully establish a citizenship of its own. The Canadian bill, therefore, first defined *Canadian* citizenship, and then acknowledged the status of British subjecthood purely on the basis of holding Canadian citizenship.[32] The bill then confirmed that the status of British subjecthood under the laws of the other members of the Commonwealth would also be recognized in Canada. As a result, member countries could enact and amend their own citizenship laws at any time, consultation with other members becoming unnecessary. Furthermore, by creating the status of citizenship separate from Commonwealth citizenship, each government could issue its own passport, the importance of which as an administrative tool dramatically increased through two world wars.[33] The purpose of the Canadian bill was, in the end, not to destroy, but to transform the common status into 'the common denominator' of the Commonwealth by changing the method of granting it.[34] Under this new system, therefore, the fundamental status through which citizenship rights and obligations were granted became the citizenship of each member state, not British subjecthood as had been the case hitherto.

Surprisingly, the overall reaction of the British government to the Canadian bill was favourable from the beginning.[35] Ever since the passage of the BN & SA act 1914, there had been anomalous cases under the common code system. For example, the Éire government had already repudiated the system of the common code in 1935 within the area of its domestic jurisdiction, although it continued to accept that Irish citizens should be treated as British subjects outside its territory.[36] In the face of the accumulation of exceptional cases in the common code system, the British government thought that the Canadian bill provided it with a convenient opportunity to reconsider the existing system of the common status.

Furthermore, the idea of securing the common status on the basis of the citizenship laws of each Dominion was not itself new to the

British government. An interdepartmental committee had already discussed in 1930 the possibility of producing the common status by combining the separate citizenship laws.[37] At that time, the idea was dropped for fear that the status of British subjecthood which would be conferred in that way might not be recognized by international law. By 1946, however, the British government was aware that, whether the common status under the Canadian method was internationally recognized or not, the other Dominions would follow the Canadian example. Given that the principle of national self-determination should be fully applied to the Dominions, Westminster feared that they would enact their own citizenship laws in the Canadian style anyway, otherwise they might leave the Commonwealth altogether.

Taking all these things into consideration, the British government decided that it would be best to accept the Canadian bill in principle. This could preserve the common status, and moreover, it would relieve everyone of the time-consuming and cumbersome system of the common code based on consultation and unanimity. The draft scheme, which all the existing and future members of the Commonwealth could join, was eventually prepared for the prime ministers' conference held in May 1946.[38] All the participants there agreed in principle to maintain some sort of common status among them.[39] Only one sceptical voice was heard, that of Sir Alexander Maxwell, the Permanent Under-Secretary of State at the Home Office.[40] He pointed out that the Canadian method might result in very wide variations between the citizenship laws of member countries, and that the common status under the new system could therefore end up totally different in each country, being common only in name. However, his was a minority voice, even among the British delegates. Given that all the governments had the right of self-determination and could create the national type of citizenship, the others accepted that, except for the core points, divergences in detail would be unavoidable and, even more, acceptable.[41]

In February 1947 a conference of legal experts was held to discuss the details of the new scheme for the common status, with participants from the United Kingdom, Australia, New Zealand, the Union of South Africa, Éire, Newfoundland, South Rhodesia, Burma and Ceylon, with the High Commissioner for India as an observer.[42] As Sir Alexander had feared, it soon became apparent that divergence in the citizenship laws of each country would be wider than the British government had expected. For example, the representatives of Ceylon made it clear that future citizenship legislation in Ceylon would be based on domicile rather than *jus soli*, although they accepted the desirability of preserving the common status.[43] As a result, even a fundamental rule such as *jus soli* could not be preserved, once the system of the common code was destroyed. Having lost the power to influence the citizenship of other members, however, the British government had no choice other than to stand by and hope that the common status would be maintained.

The British Nationality Act 1948

The British Nationality Act 1948 was Britain's response to the conferences of 1946 and 1947.[44] Britain, unlike other Commonwealth countries, did not create a citizenship of its own.[45] Instead, Commonwealth citizenship was categorized into four different sub-groups: Citizens of the United Kingdom and Colonies (CUKC), Citizens of independent Commonwealth countries,[46] British subjects without citizenship (BSWC), and British protected persons (BPP). During the parliamentary debate it was pointed out that these sub-divisions would lead to confusion about who 'belonged' to Britain itself and who would be granted the rights and obligations of citizens.[47] From the government's point of view, the creation of these sub-groups was necessary. First, the status of Commonwealth citizenship was indispensable as 'the outward and visible sign of that sense of family relationship which is, and ... will long remain'.[48] The government also claimed that the colonial peoples should share the status of CUKC with people in the United Kingdom, because of its responsibility for the remaining colonies.[49] Unlike these two statuses, the other two – BSWC and BPPs – did not receive much attention in Parliament. The former was expected to be only a transitory position until citizenship laws were enacted by all the participants at the 1947 conference, and the latter was not even given the status of Commonwealth citizenship.[50]

Opposition to the provisions of the BNA 1948 was concentrated on the creation of the CUKC. Some MPs considered it to be artificial or meaningless.[51] Others were concerned that it might put people in the colonies in a better position than those in the Dominions.[52] Overall, they did not, however, seem to mind the fact that only the British government conferred citizenship rights and privileges on all the holders of Commonwealth citizenship, while other member countries accepted this status only nominally. Conservative and Labour MPs simply accepted that it was necessary for the 'Mother Country' to do so.[53] The consequences of granting citizenship rights and obligations through the holding of Commonwealth citizenship were never discussed, let alone the possibility of large-scale immigration from the NCW countries, which later triggered heated debate inside and outside Parliament in the 1950s and 1960s.[54]

In addition to attributing the substantive aspects of citizenship to Commonwealth citizenship, the British government made two more compromises in order to keep Commonwealth citizenship as accessible as possible to the new members of the Commonwealth. First, the term 'Commonwealth citizenship' was introduced as an alternative name to 'British subjecthood', the CCA 1946 having set a precedent for it. Uneasiness over the term 'British subject' had already been expressed.[55] After the 1947 conference of legal experts, however, the British government was fully aware that some countries such as India and Pakistan might not join the new scheme of Commonwealth citizenship, if they were required to keep the term 'British subject'. For them, the term was strongly connected with their colonial past, which they wanted to jettison. Since their presence in the new system was vital to prove that the new post-Second World War Commonwealth was different from the former British Commonwealth, the British government could not afford to lose two key countries in Asia.

The second major change which the BNA 1948 introduced was a special status for the citizens of Éire, who became neither British subjects nor aliens (s. 32(1)).[56] Because of the complex nature of the Anglo-Irish relationship, the issue of Irish citizenship had always been a source of difficulty for immigration and nationality laws in Britain.[57] From the early stages of the debate, it had been decided that the status of British subject could no longer be forced on Irish citizens against their wishes.[58] After all, the British government had admitted that the Commonwealth was, in theory, 'a free association of people, not a collection of subject nations'.[59] On the other hand, it was aware that it could not simply remove the status of British subject from some sections of the Irish population. Special treatment was required for those Éire citizens in other parts of the Commonwealth, especially those in the service of the Crown, and also for the large numbers of persons resident within Éire who were loyal to the Crown. Furthermore, the British government feared that Éire's separatist tendencies might be accelerated by officially abolishing the tie of common status with Irish citizens. Officials from the relevant ministries in the end decided that, while the Irish government would not agree to the status of British subject being forced on its citizens, it would not object to the rights of British subjecthood being granted to its citizens.[60]

In short, in order to keep Irish citizens within a scheme of Commonwealth citizenship in one way or another, the BNA 1948 separated the nominal (citizenship-as-status) from the substantive aspects of citizenship (citizenship-as-rights and citizenship-as-desirable-activity); Irish citizens were then granted only the latter. This special treatment of Irish citizens was, according to the statement by the British government, based on the 'reciprocal exchange of citizenship rights' between the member countries of the Commonwealth.[61] After all, the Irish case should not, in theory, damage a scheme of Commonwealth citizenship itself. The BNA 1948 simply showed that the common status had to be maintained by statutory agreement between equal and free member countries, and could no longer be conferred by the imperial government. Commonwealth citizenship, unlike the national type of citizenship, was formed and the details were agreed multilaterally by contract, as if it were the composite type of citizenship.[62] Just as all the member countries agreed to keep the common status as if it were a 'common denominator' without citizenship rights attached to it, so the Irish and British governments agreed to give each other's citizens citizenship rights and privileges without sharing a 'common denominator'. Under two separate agreements with different contents a scheme of Commonwealth citizenship was ultimately established. Thus the British government, just by passing another act to confirm that the reciprocal arrangement with Ireland would continue, avoided the destruction of the whole Commonwealth citizenship scheme under the BNA 1948 by Ireland's withdrawal from the Commonwealth in April 1949, four months after the BNA 1948 became effective.[63] As a composite type of citizenship, it could simply be established as long as the participating political units all agreed to do so. The mode of granting it and its entitlement were also determined by a contract, not by the will of the metropole.

Here, we have to keep in mind that most of the politicians, including government members in Britain, did not look at the enactment of CCA 1946 and that of the BNA 1948, let alone the citizenships which the BNA 1948 created, in the way in which we do today. As one scholar points out, they simply regarded it as 'a matter of technical adjustment rather than of constitutional significance'.[64] They thought that they would succeed in preserving the common status by changing the method of granting it and allowing the citizenship of member countries to become the primary status. The British government as a result felt it neither necessary to create its citizenship on the basis of nationhood, nor to stop citizens of the NCW countries or colonies from receiving the status of Commonwealth citizenship. After all, the status of formal membership of Britain, that of British subjecthood before the BNA 1948, had always been granted to all peoples in the British Empire, regardless of their cultural or racial background. Citizenship for them was different from what we think of as citizenship, which is as a unique and single status that represents both political and national membership of the political unit and on which citizenship rights and obligations are based.[65] Policy-makers of the time in Britain were therefore not concerned about the consequences of granting the status of Commonwealth citizenship to all the citizens of member countries, much less citizenship rights and privileges.[66] Commonwealth citizenship simply appeared to them to be British subjecthood under a different name.[67]

No other Commonwealth government, however, shared Britain's view on citizenship. They were acutely aware that they each had to have their own national citizenship in order to be a recognized member of the world community after the Second World War. Their determination can be found in Paul Martin's statement in introducing the Canadian Citizenship bill. He declared that

> The main purposes of the bill ... is seen in the important part Canada has taken as a nation among the nations of the world ... We have, in two wars, borne our full and serious responsibilities for the preservation of peace and civilization ... For a young nation, Canada has done great things and Canadians have derived a growing national pride from what Canada has accomplished. We feel that we have great things in common; that we can afford to hold our heads high and be proud of the fact that we are Canadians. And it is time we know what a Canadian is ... There has been too little, not too much, national pride in this country.[68]

The Canadian government did not object to the British government conferring on Canadian citizens citizenship rights and privileges in Britain. But the Canadian government itself did not wish to grant citizenship rights and privileges in Canada to, for example, people from India, because they had nothing to do with Canada and thus had no place in Canadian citizenship either. On the basis of carrying a Canadian passport – by then prima facie proof of citizenship – Canadian citizens were protected by the Canadian government, not by the imperial government in London.[69] The British government did not fully realize that other member countries were determined to establish the national type of citizenship, as was seen in the statement by Martin.

It was theoretically true that, at the time of the BNA 1948, the Crown still existed as a common link between Commonwealth citizens, and consequently that a shared sense of identity among

Commonwealth citizenship holders could be assumed. This view was soon officially challenged by India's attempt to remain in the Commonwealth on the grounds of 'common citizenship'.

THE COMMON STATUS AND CRITERIA FOR MEMBERSHIP OF THE COMMONWEALTH

While the Attlee government was preparing for the BNA 1948, its counterparts in other member countries were pursuing the same activity. The 1946 prime ministers' meeting and the subsequent 1947 conference of experts had decided only that the citizenship of each member country would become the gateway for the common status. The precise picture of this new citizenship and its citizenship structure, therefore, remained unclear until 1951, when all the participants of the 1947 conference had finished enacting citizenship laws of their own.

Around the same time, colonies in Asia such as Burma, Ceylon, India and Pakistan became independent.[70] Of these, India, Pakistan and Ceylon did so within the Commonwealth, whereas Burma left it. Before the Statute of Westminster, the members of the British Commonwealth were connected with each other by four legal links: 'the Crown, a common nationality, certain aspects of the Prerogative, and the powers of the Parliament at Westminster'.[71] However, by the end of the Second World War, only the first two links survived. In the late 1940s policy-makers in Britain debated whether or not membership of the Commonwealth and republicanism could be reconciled. When Burma and Éire left the Commonwealth, declaring that they would become republics, the answer seemed to be settled in the negative. In determining whether India could remain inside the Commonwealth as a republic and on what grounds, the two remaining links, the Crown and a common nationality, were once again scrutinized.[72] In analysing the concept of India's 'common nationality' and Britain's 'Commonwealth citizenship', this section hopes to show that Commonwealth citizenship, unlike 'common nationality', only worked as a 'common denominator' and had a far more limited connotation than 'common nationality'.

An Indian republic and its Commonwealth membership

Those governmental officials who were involved in Indian affairs had been determined that India should remain friendly to Britain and stay within the Commonwealth after its independence.[73] At the outset, there was some disagreement among them over the method: whether it should be on the basis of a treaty or of Commonwealth membership.[74] A thorough examination of the economic, political and military field was subsequently conducted by the Treasury, the Board of Trade, the Colonial Office and the Foreign Office. The government eventually concluded that the advantages of including India as a republic within the Commonwealth would outweigh the disadvantages, dismissing the option of forming a relationship with India on the basis of a treaty.

Militarily, India, with its vast population, was the main source of manpower for the imperial army. For example, four-fifths of the British defence effort east of Suez during the Second World War was provided by Indians.[75] With India's strategic position in Asia, furthermore, it was inevitable that Britain should maintain a friendly relationship with India under any circumstances. Nonetheless, the establishment of a central machinery for Commonwealth defence policy had already been abandoned in 1946. From the military perspective, therefore, whether or not India remained within the Commonwealth mattered little as long as India remained friendly with the Commonwealth.[76]

The economic consequences of India leaving the Commonwealth were greater than the military ones. Of greatest concern was that the 'most-favoured-nation' agreement between India and Britain would have to be abolished, were it not for India's membership of the Commonwealth.[77] Without preferential treatment, British industry was likely to lose to competition with other industrial countries a vast Indian market for exports in areas such as manufacturing (worth about £27 million in 1947, that is, about 30 per cent of Britain's total exports) and cotton piece goods (worth about £3 million in 1949).[78]

The highest costs by far would be political, especially with regard to the existing tension between Pakistan and India. If India left the Commonwealth and Pakistan remained inside it, the British government would find it imperative to support Pakistan in the event of threatened aggression from India. Furthermore, in the face of nationalist movements in south-east Asia and the communist influence in Asia, the Foreign Office feared that India might embark on a 'frankly anti-Western policy' after its departure from the Commonwealth. India might then come under communist domination.[79] With a communist-dominated China already in the area, the Foreign Office paper warned that India's secession from the Commonwealth might well lead to the total extinction of Western influence in Asia. On the other hand, it was also aware that India's main concerns and interests lay in Asian affairs and with the Non-Aligned Movement. The divergence of foreign policy interests between India and other members was therefore widening.[80] India's presence within the Commonwealth could thus become detrimental to the unity of the Commonwealth. In spite of these negative points, the Foreign Office paper was still in favour of India's membership of the Commonwealth. It argued that provided an Indian republic decided to stay inside the Commonwealth, the Commonwealth might be able to influence India's policies as well as preserve its size and power 'in the eyes of the world, and particularly of potential aggressors'.[81] Such a constitutional change which enabled an Indian republic to remain a member would also be regarded as 'a further tribute to the Anglo-Saxon genius for compromise'.[82] In sum, a committee on Commonwealth relations concluded that India's secession from the Commonwealth would be politically disadvantageous and had to be avoided.

In the end, the British government decided to follow the recommendations of the committee.[83] In a final communiqué of the prime ministers' meeting in 1949, India's membership was confirmed on the basis of (i) its desire to continue as a full member of the Commonwealth of Nations, and (ii) its acceptance of 'the King as the symbol of free association of its independent member nations and as such the Head of the Commonwealth'.[84] In order to avoid making India's case a precedent, furthermore, it was also agreed in the 1949 conference that it was special and 'would not affect in any way the constitutional relations of those Commonwealth countries which desired to retain unimpaired their allegiance to the Crown'.[85]

'Common citizenship' and Commonwealth citizenship

Before this declaration was finalized, the governments of Britain and India had explored several options. Until the last minute, India tried to claim its membership on the basis of 'common citizenship', refusing to accept the link with the Crown. On the one hand, the British government wanted to maintain some sort of acknowledgement of the Crown among the member countries but at the same time feared that, if India seceded from the Commonwealth, other newly independent countries might follow India's example and desert it, thereby weakening Britain's position in the international arena. In order to make the Commonwealth accessible to as many as possible, the Attlee government eventually came up with the idea of creating a wider framework of the Commonwealth with a two-tier grouping: those which honoured the link with the Crown stayed member countries of the Commonwealth, while those which did not accept the Crown but wanted to keep close links with the Commonwealth became 'associated states'.[86]

From the Indian perspective, on the other hand, full independence had always been associated with republicanism, as the Crown was targeted as 'a symbol of oppression' during the movement for independence.[87] All major political parties other than the Indian National Congress (Congress) were therefore against continued membership of the Commonwealth.[88] Even within Congress, quite a few were, or appeared to be, opposed to the idea of staying in the Commonwealth. Their opposition was based on various reasons, such as India's non-alignment policy, resentment against the discriminatory treatment by some Commonwealth countries of Indians overseas, and the fear of Commonwealth constraints being placed on its foreign policies.[89] Moreover, they simply thought that it would be impossible to explain to the people why they wanted to retain a link with the Crown after a long and hard struggle for independence. As a result, those policy-makers in India who were in favour of continued membership of the Commonwealth had to find a new formula, according to which India did not need to accept allegiance to the Crown but could remain a member.[90] Surprisingly, the breakthrough came from Jawarhalal Nehru, who had appeared to be one of the adamant advocates of withdrawal from the Commonwealth. He suggested in March 1947 in a conversation with Lord Mountbatten, the new Viceroy, that India's membership should be acknowledged on the grounds of 'some form of common nationality'.[91]

Only a month previously the 1947 experts' conference on nationality and citizenship had been held to discuss the common status. India's presence there was very insignificant: the High Commissioner was allowed to attend only as an observer, and left straight after the formal opening ceremony. Furthermore, it was obvious that all the participants, except the British delegates, were eager to make the common status as limited as possible. After all, all the participants at the 1947 conference accepted that the common status had a secondary status in comparison to their own citizenship. The common status, unlike in the pre-Second World War period, was simply an outward, nominal sign of their membership of the Commonwealth.

For Nehru, however, the common status among member countries seemed to be the expedient choice. Policy-makers in India were, around that time, beginning to see the advantages of keeping India inside the Commonwealth. According to some scholars, the change of attitude towards Commonwealth membership was due to Pakistan's declared commitment to the Commonwealth and to the mounting tension between the two superpowers. In addition, others point out that Indian leaders were worried that the plight of overseas Indians in some Commonwealth countries, especially in South Africa, might be worsened if India left the Commonwealth.[92] Nehru did not then specify what exactly he meant by a 'common nationality', that is, the mode of granting it and its status, and how it differed from what other Commonwealth member countries claimed to be a 'common status'. However, Krishna Menon, soon to be India's High Commissioner in London, stressed to Mountbatten 'India's desire for common citizenship' on the basis of 'reciprocity', based on Nehru's idea of 'common nationality'.[93] Menon suggested that the Indian government should be able to prevent its South African counterpart from taking discriminatory measures one-sidedly, as the common status was given on the basis of reciprocity. His argument however stopped there, the details of the plan for 'common citizenship' being left unclear.

From the beginning, British officials with legal expertise were cautious about India's plan for 'common citizenship' because of the difficulties involved, especially with regard to the way in which 'reciprocity' was established. For example, they were sceptical as to whether the OCW countries would grant common status to Indians on the basis of reciprocity.[94] More importantly, the idea of 'common citizenship' seemed to be developed so as to provide that a citizen of the Indian Union would owe allegiance first of all to India and further to the monarch as head of the Commonwealth. In order for reciprocity to stand, therefore, a citizen of the United Kingdom would have to owe allegiance, while in India, to the Indian Union. British officials could not see on what basis this would be possible.

The potential of 'common citizenship' and Commonwealth membership was nonetheless further investigated by Sir B. N. Rau, constitutional adviser to the Constituent Assembly. Between October and December 1947, during the preparations for drawing up India's constitution, he was dispatched to the United States, Canada, Éire and Britain for discussions with leading constitutional experts. On his return, Rau tried to apply to India the Irish example of reciprocal citizenship. According to his first plan, its population would enter the contract of reciprocal citizenship on the grounds of sharing common ideals such as the supremacy of law and freedom of speech.[95] He gradually realized, however, that some of the OCW countries, such as South Africa and Canada, were not willing to form the type of 'common citizenship' which Rau imagined. From their perspective, their ability to form a national citizenship of their own might be limited if they committed their citizenship to shared ideals. Rau, therefore, shifted the emphasis in his version of 'common citizenship' to a multilateral agreement, under which the common status was acknowledged in all the member countries. Eventually, his view on 'common citizenship' increasingly converged with that underlying the Canadian scheme and consequently with the Commonwealth citizenship which was created by the CCA 1946 and the BNA 1948.[96] As far as policy-makers in Britain could see, it was also never clear how far the Indian government itself would give preferential treatment to Commonwealth citizens from other member countries over foreigners in terms of right of entry and deportation.[97]

In the end, the question came down to what kind of citizenship Commonwealth citizenship was, that is, whether or not it could be proved that its holders formed a distinctive group which could be differentiated from others. An official committee finally concluded in February 1949 that Commonwealth citizenship within the scheme of the BNA 1948 was not a genuine form of 'common citizenship' after all.[98] The real value of Commonwealth citizenship was summarized as follows:

> The conception of Commonwealth citizenship is not ... at present supported by any comprehensive system of equal and compensating citizenship rights and obligations applying evenly throughout the Commonwealth. And in the absence of such a system of substantial reciprocity, the Commonwealth citizenship could not alone and in itself be regarded as a sufficient constitutional link to justify the claim that the Commonwealth countries are not foreign to one another.[99]

Commonwealth citizenship was only considered to be 'a secondary or supporting argument in general case based mainly on the historical continuity of the Commonwealth connection'.[100] By this official statement, the British government admitted that Commonwealth citizenship, at least outside Britain, possessed neither citizenship-as-rights nor citizenship-as-desirable-activity, and the holders of Commonwealth citizenship did not need to share a sense of belonging to the Commonwealth. Their status of Commonwealth citizenship was simply given to them from above as a result of a contract between member countries.

Existing works on India's membership of the Commonwealth tend to focus on the constitutional relationship whereby republican India was accommodated with the other members which recognized the Crown. What has been overlooked in such studies is the debate between policy-makers in India and Britain on the nature of Commonwealth citizenship, which was carried out in parallel with constitutional debate over the Commonwealth. In going through major constitutional changes, the Commonwealth had at the same time to adjust its rules for the formal membership of its population.

In the end, as all the participants in the 1947 conference other than Britain wanted, Commonwealth citizenship ended up simply being the outward nominal proof that member countries formed one combined unit as the Commonwealth. Whereas the common status prior to the Second World War – British subjecthood – granted its holders citizenship rights and obligations, Commonwealth citizenship was declared as 'no more than a name' and 'not ... [a] sufficient reality'.[101] Unlike British subjecthood, furthermore, Commonwealth citizenship did not on its own provide its holders with links with the Commonwealth and with each other. Although the common code system was established on a statutory basis, the British government's assumption – that all the Dominions with the exception of Éire valued their special relationship with Britain more than any other bilateral relationship – was probably right. Immediately after the Second World War, the British government still wanted to maintain the close relationship between Commonwealth member countries, and consequently kept Commonwealth citizenship much in line with British subjecthood.[102] To some extent, other countries went along with its plan. When the Indian republic tried to maintain its Commonwealth membership on the basis of establishing 'common citizenship', however, the exact features of Commonwealth citizenship were again examined, only for the conclusion to be reached that it would work only as a nominal citizenship status.[103]

In the late 1940s and 1950s, it was the British government this time that began to withdraw the substantive aspects of citizenship from Commonwealth citizenship, reducing it to a nominal status just as in other countries.

THE COMMONWEALTH IMMIGRANTS ACT 1962

Until the enactment of the CIA 1962, Commonwealth citizenship was the basis of citizenship rights and privileges inside the United Kingdom. Yet, as was discussed earlier, it was never the intention of the British government that those citizenship rights and privileges should be enforced freely by Commonwealth citizens outside the United Kingdom. Commonwealth citizenship under the BNA 1948 continued to grant substantive aspects of citizenship in the United Kingdom simply because Commonwealth citizenship replaced British subjecthood, which had substantive aspects of citizenship. In the face of the NCW immigration in the 1950s, therefore, the Macmillan government had to decide whether the NCW citizens should be nominal citizens only, or whether they were entitled to enjoy citizenship rights and privileges alongside those born in the United Kingdom and their descendants.

NCW immigration into Britain after the Second World War

In the area of immigration after the Second World War, the focus of argument had been exclusively on immigration from NCW countries, mainly in the Caribbean and south Asia. It was, however, neither the only nor the first inflow to Britain after the war. Manpower shortages, especially in industries key to post-war recovery and reconstruction – coal mining, textiles and construction – and in the health service, were one of the biggest concerns for the Attlee government. Unlike other countries in Europe, there were also few surplus labourers left in the agricultural sector in Britain who could be transferred to the industrial sector.[104] Such unpopular sectors as construction and coal-mining were, therefore, compelled to rely heavily on foreign labour sources. As a result, quite a few Europeans came to Britain as labourers immediately after the war, such as the so-called European Volunteer Workers (EVWs) from the war-torn Continent, and the Irish.[105] Britain, for example, received as EVWs 77,000 displaced persons from eastern Europe between 1946 and 1950, and 8,000 Ukrainian prisoners of war brought from Italy in 1947 were later also included in this category. The EVWs were admitted under strict conditions and assigned by the Ministry of Labour and National Service to work in undermanned industries.[106]

The Irish, who had always been the largest immigrant group in Britain, continued to enter in large numbers even during the war. Indeed, the period immediately after the war saw the second-largest wave in the history of their emigration to Britain. Although the precise number is unknown, a scholar places the range at between 70,000 and 100,000 during the period between 1946 and 1951.[107] This high level of immigration continued until the mid-1960s, Irish labourers being employed in the areas which could not attract sufficient native recruits due to poor working conditions and low wages, namely building, metal manufacturing and transport.[108]

Compared with these two groups of European immigrants, the arrival of 417 Jamaicans in 1948 was insignificant. Moreover, they were Commonwealth citizens who were, just like Londoners, entitled to reside in the United Kingdom with full access to citizenship rights and privileges. During the month of their arrival, however, the Minister of Labour, George Isaacs, stated, 'I hope no encouragement is given to others [Jamaicans] to follow their example.'[109] An interdepartmental working party was established in the same year, which later recommended that Britain should reduce the immigration flow from the colonies with collaboration from the colonial governments.[110]

Responding to the recommendation, the British government asked its colonial counterparts to make it known that jobs and accommodation in the United Kingdom were not easily found, and to restrict the issue of passports. Although the NCW citizens were equally as entitled as those from the OCW to enter Britain by right, Westminster did not hesitate to put pressure on the colonial governments. Nonetheless, the number of immigrants from the Caribbean rose sharply in 1954, mainly owing to the favourable labour situation in Britain and the restrictive US immigration legislation established in 1952.[111] The first draft of an immigration bill had already been written at this time by an interdepartmental working party based in the Home Office.[112] In spite of a decrease in immigration between 1957 and 1959, 1960 saw a marked increase in the number of immigrants from the NCW countries. In addition, two anti-black 'riots', one in Nottingham and the other in Notting Hill, had broken out in 1958, drawing much public attention to NCW immigration. The Commonwealth Immigrants Bill was finally presented to Parliament in November 1961, to become the CIA 1962.

The Commonwealth Immigrants Act 1962: the method of control and its justification

The CIA 1962 was the first statutory attempt in Britain to restrict the freedom of movement of Commonwealth immigrants. The Conservative government claimed that the bill was introduced 'after a long and anxious consideration and considerable reluctance'.[113] The Home Secretary, R. A. Butler, explained that it was necessary to combat the situation 'for a temporary period', and that it '[would] apply to all Commonwealth immigrants and [was] more liberally conceived than the present power of control of aliens'.[114] In spite of this explanation, the government's real intentions for introducing immigration control were different. The CIA 1962, according to a memorandum by the Home Office, was needed primarily on two grounds: the 'strain imposed by coloured immigration on the housing resources of certain local authorities', and the 'dangers of social tension inherent in the existence of large unassimilated coloured communities'.[115] These two reasons were not made public, as the government was afraid that it would give rise to criticism in Commonwealth countries and controversy in Parliament.[116] Furthermore, the British government had not totally given up the idea that the Commonwealth could uphold its prestige and position in the international arena. It thus still intended to maintain Commonwealth citizenship and its citizenship structure, under which all the citizens of the member countries held Commonwealth citizenship. As a result, it could neither abolish Commonwealth citizenship by amending the BNA 1948, nor impose immigration control exclusively on NCW citizens.

The government instead concentrated on the increase in the number of immigrants, and introduced a piece of immigration legislation which would supposedly control it. In order to present the immigration issue as if it were purely an economic and labour problem, furthermore, the government chose a method of control based on employment. With the problem of labour shortages still unsolved, however, the politicians and officials were aware that the inflow of immigrants was not in itself a problem.[117] For example, an annual average of 23,000 work permits was issued for aliens between 1946 and 1950.[118] Even after the enactment of the CIA 1962, annual figures continued to show an upward trend, reaching a peak in 1969, when the number of permits issued to aliens reached 68,000,[119] showing that the labour market had been in need of labourers during the period under discussion. In short, on the basis that the system of employment vouchers was operated strictly in accordance with the needs of the labour market, there should have been no need to control inflows of immigrants. Regardless of the government's comments, which emphasized the number of the NCW immigrants, its objective in passing the CIA 1962 could not have been to prevent the inflow of immigrant labourers but to select their sources.

The CIA 1962 controlled the immigration of Commonwealth citizens in the following way.[120] First, the act acknowledged those born in the United Kingdom, those holding a passport issued in the United Kingdom or the Republic of Ireland, or dependants included in these passports as 'in common parlance belong[ing] to the UK' (s. 1).[121] On that ground, they were guaranteed 'the absolute right to come here [the United Kingdom] and remain here even if diseased, or with a criminal record, or if they were security risks'.[122] Only those Commonwealth citizens under section 1 were 'native to this country [the United Kingdom]', and were guaranteed an absolute right of free access, and consequently could enforce full citizenship rights whenever they wished.[123] Second, the other CUKCs, who (i) were ordinary residents in the UK, their wives and children under 16 accompanying or joining their husbands or parents; (ii) had a voucher issued by the Ministry of Labour; or (iii) were students, and those in possession of independent means with no need for employment in the

United Kingdom, had to fulfil the conditions set by section 2 before being allowed to enter the United Kingdom. Unlike those Commonwealth citizens under section 1, they were granted entry into the United Kingdom only under the scrutiny of immigration officers (s. 2(1)–(3)).

There were three different categories of employment voucher, issued by the Ministry of Labour. Voucher 'A' was for applicants who could satisfy the Ministry of Labour that they had jobs to come to; voucher 'B' was for those who possessed training, skills or technical qualifications likely to be useful in the United Kingdom; and voucher 'C' was for those who fell into neither of the above categories and was issued on a first-come-first-served basis. Of the three categories only the number of the 'C' vouchers was controlled by the government in accordance with 'all the factors which [bear] on [the] capacity to absorb further immigrants without undue stress or strain'.[124] According to the explanation by the then Minister of Labour, John Hare, the vast majority of immigrants would be expected to come under category 'C', thus there was no need to place a limit on the number of vouchers 'A' and 'B'.[125] It was, nonetheless, not the real reason behind this arrangement. In theory, the voucher system should have applied without reference to colour or race. Judging from previous figures, however, the government expected that the voucher system under the CIA 1962 'in practice ... would interfere to the minimum extent with the entry of persons from the Old Commonwealth'.[126] The OCW immigrants should fall in the 'A' and 'B' categories, so that their entries would not be restricted by the CIA 1962.

Had the real purpose of introducing the CIA 1962 been not to prevent the 'coloured' NCW immigrants from entering Britain, but to restrict the number of immigrants, and consequently to improve housing conditions and to avoid job competition, the choice of control method would have been different.[127] First of all, a tight labour situation had been one of the government's concerns since the end of the Second World War. The unemployment rate remained low in the 1950s, and some scholars attributed the recurrent economic cycles of 'stop–go' during that period to a 'lack of spare capacity, both labour and capital'.[128] The Treasury had, therefore, been hesitant over introducing immigration control up to the last minute, as it was anxious about the possibility of losing a beneficial supply of supplementary labour for economic growth.[129] In short, the fear of job competition and a rise in unemployment were exaggerated or even unfounded.

Second, in spite of the repeated expression of concern, there was no concrete evidence that racial tension was mounting, except in a few areas where the population of immigrants was concentrated. A report published after several 'riots' in 1958 concluded, for example, that there was 'still no evidence of any significant increase of racial tension outside London'.[130] An interdepartmental committee had also admitted, as late as October 1961, that it could not justify the introduction of immigration control on the grounds of public order.[131] Housing problems had always been put forward as one of the main reasons for introducing immigration control. However, serious doubts were expressed during parliamentary debates as to whether these would be solved by the method which the government proposed. A method of controlling immigration on the basis of a check on accommodation had been examined and rejected, because it involved intolerable supervision and regimentation.[132] While admitting that there were housing shortages and racial tension, Patrick Gordon Walker, Labour's Foreign Secretary designate, proposed that they would be better solved by dispersing the immigrant population and combating racial prejudice.[133] He concluded that the introduction of immigration control would only 'divert anger in the cities from the Government and its policies' rather than remedying it.[134]

In short, the introduction of the CIA 1962 and the method of control it employed could not be justified on the grounds the government put forward. From the perspective of the economic and labour situation, moreover, a voucher system (where the control method was based on the 'economic situation' of the time) would have had an overall negative effect on Britain's economy. It would also have targeted the kind of labourers whom its economy most needed. The government was able to consider four potential sources of labour in order to alleviate labour shortages. Those were: the Irish workers, those from the OCW, those from the NCW and aliens.[135] The relative immobility of native workers in terms of geography and occupation was one of the reasons for labour shortages in certain sectors and regions. It was therefore advantageous for the government to be able to admit those labourers who could take up jobs where there was a shortfall and who could be restricted to these economic sectors and geographic areas. Furthermore, in order to reduce the pressures on housing and the potential for social conflict, the more the government could do to control immigrant workers' jobs and where they settled, the better for the alleviation of those problems.

Considering their likely contributions to the labour market, the choice should have been between NCW immigrants and Irish and alien workers. In terms of their small incoming numbers and their likely sectors of employment, the introduction of OCW workers was not the answer to filling the labour gap. Regarding the Irish, NCW and the alien workers, the government had never intended to impose immigration control on the Irish workers. As was discussed earlier, the British government had already accepted at the time of the enactment of the BNA 1948 that the Irish and British shared a common heritage and were members of a common, if extended, family.[136] The same rhetoric was repeated during the debate about the CIA 1962. The Earl of Huntingdon, for example, commented in the House of Lords that Ireland was and would be an anomaly because of 'a very unhappy history of this country [Britain]'.[137] Even if the inflow of the Irish labourers was to continue, however, the government was aware that it could not fulfil all its labour needs.

The Macmillan government, therefore, had to allow either NCW or alien immigrants to enter the United Kingdom and its labour market. As a result, the number of work permits issued to aliens after the CIA 1962 continued to increase until 1970, while those issued to the NCW workers decreased.[138] This suggests that the government chose aliens in preference to NCW workers and let in aliens outside the framework established by the CIA 1962. By separating immigration control for Commonwealth citizens from that for aliens, the government could limit the entry of the NCW workers while labour needs were being filled by aliens. In order to achieve that purpose, the voucher system was chosen and operated in the way described earlier. Control of NCW immigrants was more important than that of aliens, because the former, on the basis of their Commonwealth citizenship, were entitled to claim all citizenship rights once inside the United Kingdom, and to be treated on an equal basis to those British people who were born in the United Kingdom. However, at the same time, in order to maintain the Commonwealth citizenship structure, the British government could not show its real intention. Instead, it had to emphasize the argument about the potential number of immigrants, state publicly that immigration control for Commonwealth citizens would be more generous than that for aliens, and finally choose a control method which was supposed to be linked to the 'economic situation' in Britain.

Commonwealth citizenship: citizenship without substance

The CIA 1962 was after all the final stage of long-standing governmental efforts to allow a national citizenship of a constituent political unit of the British Empire (later, the Commonwealth) to emerge while maintaining the citizenship structure of multiple citizenships. Following the tradition of using immigration control to enable multiple citizenships – citizenship of constituent political units and that of the British Empire (later, Commonwealth) – to co-exist, the British government enacted the CIA 1962, and not a new nationality act. It was concerned that creating British citizenship by passing a new nationality act would 'weaken [the] ties with [the colonies and the members of the Commonwealth] at the time when the control of immigration would itself be causing strain'.[139] With the BNA 1948 intact, the Macmillan government could not only promote the unity of the Commonwealth but also avoid granting all the holders of Commonwealth citizenship the substantive aspects of citizenship.

The debates on the enactment of the CIA 1962 showed that the British government's understanding of citizenship had not adjusted to the national type of citizenship. As was discussed earlier, citizenships introduced by the BNA 1948 did not reflect nationhood in Britain, nor were they intended to do so, and were completely ignored by immigration control in the 1960s and 1970s. For the British government, citizenship after the Second World War continued to be more of a symbol which was handed down from above to maintain the Commonwealth. The government was aware that its holders were theoretically entitled to the substantive rights and privileges of citizenship in the country of citizenship, but saw this as secondary. It simply did not think then that Commonwealth citizens outside the United Kingdom would actually take up their citizenship rights and privileges.

In the 1960s and 1970s, the meaning and role of citizenship were completely muddled in Britain. Citizenship rights and obligations in theory granted through Commonwealth citizenship were in practice conferred by immigration control. Within the framework of Commonwealth citizenship, immigration control took over the functional aspect of granting citizenship in the 1960s and 1970s and prepared for the creation of British citizenship in 1981.

NOTES

1. The Balfour Report in 1926 declared that the Dominions were 'autonomous Communities within the British Empire, equal in status, in no way subordinate one to another in any aspect of their domestic or external affairs, though united by a common allegiance to the Crown, and freely associated as members of the British Commonwealth of Nations'. *Imperial Conference 1926. Summary of Proceedings*, Cmd 2768, HMSO, 1926. The Statute of Westminster was enacted in 1931 to enforce the resolutions in the Balfour Report, for which see Ch. 3.
2. During the war the British government was forced to amass sizeable debts in order to finance its war efforts and liquidate a great part of its foreign assets. By the end

of the war it admitted that Britain was 'no longer the "primary" global power, and the United States was the ultimate bulwark of western security against the USSR'. PRO, DEFE 4/8. COS Joint Planning Staff Paper. Strategic Summary. 16 October 1947.

3. United Nations Charter, Article 1(2). The attitude of the UN towards the colonized peoples and territories immediately after the war was, to say the least, ambivalent, mainly because of conflicts of opinion among the Permanent Members. See Catherine L. Burke, 'The Great Debate: The Decolonization Issue at the United Nations, 1945–1980', D.Phil. thesis, Oxford University, 1986.

4. Although it is correct to say that immigration control after the Second World War applied to all Commonwealth citizens, whether they were from the OCW or the NCW countries, a number of primary papers in relevant ministries showed that the real target of immigration control was the NCW immigrants. Nonetheless, I find it too simplistic and unsustainable to regard the British people or society as being predominantly more racially discriminatory than others. Even if they were so proved, the racially discriminatory attitudes of British people or society would not solve the question of why a new nationality law was not enacted but immigration control tightened instead.

5. It is not the purpose of this section to present a comprehensive view of international relations after the war. Nor is it possible to do so in the field of British foreign policy. This section, instead, only looks at the period immediately after the war in order to provide the context for a discussion of the Commonwealth and later Commonwealth citizenship. For British foreign policy after the war, see, for example, John Darwin, *Britain and Decolonisation: The Retreat from Empire in the Post-War World* (Macmillan, London, 1988); David Sanders, *Losing an Empire, Finding a Role: British Foreign Policy since 1945* (Macmillan, London, 1990); David Reynolds, *Britannia Overruled: British Policy and World Power in the 20th Century* (Longman, London, 1991), Chs 6–10.

6. A Colonial Office circular explained that Britain's position had changed from being one of the major creditor countries to being the world's principal debtor. For more detail see PRO, CO 852/555/4, no. 9. Financial Results of the War in the United Kingdom. CO Circular Telegram to Governors. 27 September 1945.

7. In 1945 alone, for example, financial assistance from overseas amounted to £2,100 million. Substantial aid from the United States on reasonable terms was therefore imperative. PRO, CAB 129/1. Our Overseas Financial Prospects. Cabinet Memorandum by Lord Keynes. 13 August 1945.

8. As the archival documents on the bilateral relationship between the United States and the United Kingdom during the war became available, so numerous works started to question whether the bilateral relationship was really 'special'. See, for example, William Roger Louis, *Imperialism at Bay: The United States and the Decolonization of the British Empire, 1941–1945* (Clarendon Press, Oxford, 1977); William Roger Louis and Hedley Bull (eds), *The 'Special Relationship': Anglo-American Relations since 1945* (Clarendon Press, Oxford, 1986).

9. In March 1941, Congress decided that the United States would provide the leasing or lending of defence articles to the countries whose defence the president deemed vital to its security.

10. Reynolds for example describes the wartime alliance between two countries as 'abnormally close ... the temporary response to a temporary world crisis'. David Reynolds, 'The Wartime Anglo-American Alliance', in Louis and Bull, *'Special Relationship'*, p. 40.

11. PRO, FO 371/50912, no. 5471. Stocktaking after VE-Day. Memorandum by Sir O. Sargent. August 1945.

12. Ibid.
13. PRO, CAB 131/2. Cabinet Defence Committee. Memorandum by the Secretary of State for Foreign Affairs. 13 March 1946. With regard to Britain's position in the Mediterranean, Bevin was most concerned that Soviet influence would expand should Britain's position be weakened. For Britain's Middle East policy up to the Suez Crisis see, for example, Elizabeth Monroe, *Britain's Moment in the Middle East: 1914–1956* (Chatto & Windus, London, 1963).
14. PRO, FO 800/444, ff. 29–31. Trade Relations with Europe, America and the Empire. Minute from Bevin to Attlee. 16 September 1947.
15. Darwin, *Britain and Decolonization*, p. 72. The Colonial Office took a lead in promoting the plan to increase production of foodstuffs and raw materials in the colonies. For example, see PRO, CAB 129/19. Development of Colonial Resources. Memorandum by Creech Jones. 6 June 1947.
16. The principle of national self-determination and its interpretation in practice remain one of the major causes of today's conflicts, both domestic and international, and voices demanding its review have been rising. See, for example, Adam Roberts, 'Beyond the Flawed Principle of National Self-Determination', in Edward Mortimer and Robert Fine (eds), *People, Nation and State: The Meaning of Ethnicity and Nationalism* (I. B. Tauris, London, 1999), Ch. 8.
17. Cobban, *Nation-State and National Self-Determination*, p. 39.
18. Ibid., pp. 62–6. Naoko Shimazu, *Japan, Race and Equality: The Racial Equality Proposal of 1919* (Routledge, London, 1998), pp. 186–7. Shimazu argues that, at the time of the Peace Conference, a handful of the elite in the great powers could determine which principle should be applied and to what extent it should prevail in the world. The principle of national self-determination was one typical example, which was imposed from above with the intention of limited applicability.
19. Cobban, *Nation-State and National Self-Determination*, p. 66.
20. For details of the mandate system, see, for example, William Roger Louis, 'The Era of the Mandates System and the Non-European World', in Hedley Bull and Adam Watson (eds), *The Expansion of International Society* (Clarendon Press, Oxford, 1984), pp. 201–13; James N. Murray, *The United Nations Trusteeship System* (University of Illinois Press, Urbana, IL, 1957), Ch. 1; and Burke, 'The Great Debate', Ch. 1.
21. The League of Nations Covenant, article 22.
22. The Atlantic Charter, section 3: 'they respect the right of all peoples to choose the form of government under which they will live; and they wish to see sovereign rights and self-government restored to those who have been forcibly deprived of them'. However, it carefully avoided binding its signatories to any specific commitments.
23. Parliamentary Debates, House of Commons, vol. 374, cols 68–9, 9 September 1941.
24. For details of this episode see Nicholas Mansergh, *Survey of British Commonwealth Affairs: Problems of Wartime Co-operation and Post-War Change 1939–1952* (Oxford University Press, London, 1958), pp. 191–4.
25. The Statute of Westminster, 22 Geo. 5., c. 4.
26. For details of the debates on the trusteeship system see, for example, Murray, *Trusteeship System*, and Burke, 'Great Debate', Ch. 1.
27. UN Charter, article 76.
28. The degree of support for the Commonwealth differed country by country, Australia and New Zealand being most enthusiastic and Éire the least, and issue by issue, economic co-operation being supported far more than military.
29. PRO, PREM 8/726. Ceylon Constitution. Cabinet. Colonial Affairs Committee. Ceylon Constitution. Memorandum by the Secretary of State for the Colonies. 29 April 1947.

30. The movement for legislating Canadian citizenship existed prior to the Second World War. The Canadian Nationals Act was first introduced to Parliament in 1931, but failed on its second reading.

31. Parliamentary Debates, House of Commons, Dominion of Canada, 2nd Session 1945, vol. II., col., 1337, 22 October 1945 (Paul Martin, Secretary of State of Canada). This motion did not go further than the first reading, but a similar bill was introduced in April 1946, which later became the Canadian Citizenship Act 1946 (CCA 1946). For details of the CCA 1946 see Parry, *Nationality and Citizenship Laws*, pp. 464–71.

32. The Canadian government made it clear that 'as far as Canada is concerned the dominant fact will be that of being a Canadian citizen. With it, as a correlative, and important in the Commonwealth as a whole, each will also have the status of British subject.' See Parliamentary Debates, House of Commons, Dominion of Canada, 2nd Session 1945, vol. II, col. 1336, 22 October 1945. After creating Canadian citizenship, the Canadian government declared that a Canadian citizen continued to be a British subject. Canadian Citizenship Act 1946, section 21.

33. According to Torpey, passports and identification cards of various kinds allowed states to distinguish between their own peoples and foreigners and to monopolize the legitimate means to control their movements, resulting in 'an essential aspect of the "state-ness" of states'. He points to the First World War as the turning point in immigration control. Henceforward, a passport system became the central institutional tool for immigration control. Torpey, *Invention of the Passport*, p. 3.

34. The Canadian government did not intend to deny the existence of the common status. Several MPs were concerned that the creation of Canadian citizenship might lead to the abolition of British subjecthood itself. Some even opposed the creation of Canadian citizenship, insisting that they valued British subjecthood. Martin had repeatedly to assure them that the status of British subjecthood would be maintained under the new Canadian citizenship scheme. See, for example, Parliamentary Debates, House of Commons, Dominion of Canada, 1st Session 1946, vol. I, col. 598, 5 April 1946 and col. 1018, 29 April 1946.

35. PRO, PREM 8/851. Canadian Citizenship Bill. Memorandum by the Home Secretary, November 1945. CAB 130/13. GENs. 141–54. Committee on British Nationality. 1st Meeting. 7 August 1946.

36. For details see Ch. 3.

37. PRO, DO 35/104/2. Inter-departmental Committee on Inter-Imperial Relations. Legal Sub-Committee. The issue of maintaining the common status was debated after the Report of the Operation of Dominion Legislation in 1929, and for the preparation of the imperial conference 1930. A similar plan was also raised by General Hertzog just before the imperial conference 1937. For Hertzog's proposals see Ch. 3.

38. An interdepartmental working party was formed to prepare for the draft scheme. PRO, DO 35/1159/P201/19. BN & SA Act. Draft Scheme of the British Nationality, Citizenship and Status of Aliens Bill. Meeting of Experts.

39. Because Éire remained neutral during the Second World War, the government of Éire was not invited to the 1944 prime ministers' conference and neither was it present in 1946.

40. PRO, CAB 133/87. Meeting of Prime Ministers. Committee of Officials on Nationality Question.

41. Mr Beckett, a legal adviser attending from the Foreign Office, represented the typical view of the meeting. He agreed that uniformity with regard to the form of the common clause and on the question of Éire would 'seem to be particularly desirable', but on other points divergence would 'probably be inevitable'. One of

the major disagreements among the participants was the treatment of dual nationality of member countries. In relation to this issue, each delegation differed on the extent to which the holders of British subjecthood would be treated advantageously in comparison to aliens, when applying for citizenship of other member countries. PRO, CAB 133/87. Committee of Officials on Nationality Question.

42. For the details of the conference, see PRO, CAB 133/6. British Commonwealth Conference on Nationality and Citizenship. The earlier draft scheme and the final version can be found in the same Cabinet paper.

43. PRO, CAB 133/6. Minutes of the First Meeting of the British Commonwealth Conference on Nationality and Citizenship. 3 February 1947.

44. There are a number of works that deal with the BNA 1948 in detail. See, for example, Parry, *Nationality and Citizenship Laws*, pp. 90–144; Fransman, *Fransman's British Nationality Law*, Chs 4–6.

45. The debate regarding the creation of British citizenship will be dealt with in Ch. 5.

46. At the time of enactment of the BNA 1948, only nine countries were ready to enact their own citizenship laws: Canada, Australia, New Zealand, the Union of South Africa, Newfoundland, India, Pakistan, Southern Rhodesia and Ceylon. Many countries subsequently passed citizenship laws of their own as they became independent.

47. Lord Altrincham, for example, insisted on the need to create British citizenship in order to denote 'the people of this Island'. But he was in a minority in Parliament. Parliamentary Debates, House of Lords, vol. 155, col. 787, 11 May 1948.

48. Ibid., cols 755 and 763 (the then Lord Chancellor, Lord Jowitt).

49. For example, the Attorney General explained that the government was responsible for the colonial peoples until all the colonies became independent. Parliamentary Debates, House of Commons, vol. 453, col. 503, 7 July 1948. With regard to the creation of CUKC by the BNA 1948, see also Ch. 5.

50. Although BPPs were not defined as aliens, they were not given the status of Commonwealth citizenship either. The British Nationality Act, s. 32(1).

51. Sir David Maxwell-Fyfe, for example, criticized it as 'only a verbal residue to cover what is left when we have subtracted the citizens of each of the Dominions', and moreover, citizenship rights and obligations in Britain were granted on the basis of holding Commonwealth citizenship. Thus, he concluded that the CUKC did not have any relevance. Parliamentary Debates, House of Commons, vol. 453, col. 1027, 13 July 1948.

52. For example, see the statement by Viscount Simon, Parliamentary Debates, House of Lords, vol. 155, col. 766, 11 May 1948.

53. Ede uses the analogy of the relationship between the mother country and the colonies to justify the creation of the CUKC. Parliamentary Debates, House of Commons, vol. 453, col. 394, 7 July 1948. In the same line, for example, one MP clearly states that 'We are the Mother Country of this great Commonwealth, and it is quite common for mothers to give to their children benefits which they do not themselves receive.' House of Commons, vol. 453, col. 415, 7 July 1948.

54. Debates over NCW immigration in the 1950s and 1960s are dealt with later in this chapter.

55. The Union of South Africa put forward a proposal prior to the 1937 imperial conference to change the title of British subjecthood. However, it was turned down at that time. PRO, CAB 32/127. Imperial Conference 1937, Nationality: Memorandum by the Inter-departmental Committee on Intra-Imperial Relations. April 1937.

56. For the details of the legal development of Irish citizenship, see R. F. V. Heuston,

'British Nationality and Irish Citizenship', *International Affairs*, 26, 1 (November 1949), pp. 77–90.

57. My book relies on the existing pieces of work which have been devoted to the Anglo-Irish relationship, such as those by Lyons and Jackson, and only touches on issues of Irish citizenship. F. S. L. Lyons, *Ireland since the Famine* (Weidenfeld & Nicolson, London, 1971); J. A. Jackson, *The Irish in Britain* (Routledge, London, 1963).

58. PRO, DO 35/1159/P201/19. Draft Scheme of the British Nationality, Citizenship and Status of Aliens Bill. Observations on the Foreign Office Legal Advisers' Draft Scheme for the UK Legislation Necessary to Implement the Proposed New Commonwealth Citizenship System. For example, Irish citizens were not included as British subjects when the Foreign Office submitted a draft scheme on as early as 1 May 1946.

59. Attlee described the Commonwealth as such. Parliamentary Debates, House of Commons, vol. 443, col. 1837, 5 November 1947.

60. PRO, FO 372/5011. L. S. Brass to Beckett. 11 January 1947.

61. In return for the BNA 1948, the Irish government enacted Citizens of United Kingdom and Colonies (Irish Citizenship Rights) Orders, 1949, (S.I. No. 1 of 1949), s. 2. It states that 'citizens of the United Kingdom and Colonies shall, subject to law, enjoy in Ireland similar rights and privileges to those enjoyed by Irish citizens in the United Kingdom and Colonies by virtue of the British Nationality Act 1948'.

62. The composite type of citizenship is discussed in detail in Ch. 1.

63. The British government enacted the Ireland Act 1949 (12 & 13, Geo. 6., c. 41), in which it was declared that 'the Republic of Ireland is not a foreign country for the purpose of any law in force in any part of the United Kingdom or in any colony, protectorate or United Kingdom trust territory, whether by virtue of a rule of law or of an Act of Parliament or any other enactment or instrument whatsoever … and references in any Act of Parliament, other enactment or instrument whatsoever … to foreigners, aliens, foreign countries, and foreign or foreign-built ships or aircraft shall be construed accordingly' (s. 2(1)).

64. Dummett and Nicol, *Subjects, Citizens, Aliens and Others*, p. 134. It is true that the Secretary of State for the Home Department, Mr Ede, described the British Nationality Bill as 'of the utmost constitutional importance'. Yet his emphasis was on the change in the method of keeping the common status, not on the consequences of the change. He was therefore not then aware of the possibility that holders of Commonwealth citizenship outside Britain could come and enjoy their citizenship rights in Britain. Parliamentary Debates, House of Commons, vol. 453, col. 385, 7 July 1948.

65. For details of national citizenship see Ch. 1.

66. For the debates preceding the enactment of the BNA 1948, see the earlier part of this section.

67. During the parliamentary debates, the Lord Chancellor repeated that all Commonwealth citizens, whether from the OCW or the NCW countries, could come to the United Kingdom and exercise their full citizenship rights. See, for example, Parliamentary Debates, House of Lords, vol. 155, col. 785, 11 May 1948.

68. Parliamentary Debates, House of Commons, Dominion of Canada, 1st Session 1946, vol. I, col. 509, 2 April 1946.

69. Unlike other countries, successive British governments argued that there is no right to be issued with a passport. The practice of issuing passports in Britain after the Second World War is discussed in Ch. 5 in relation to the CIA 1968 and the IA 1971.

70. For a summary of the way in which Asian membership of the Commonwealth developed, see, for example, Mansergh, *Problems of Wartime Co-operation*, 1958,

pp. 239–61. For details of Indian membership, see R. J. Moore, *Making the New Commonwealth* (Clarendon Press, Oxford, 1987).

71. PRO, CAB 32/69. Conference on the Operation of Dominion Legislation, 1929. Minutes of Meetings and Reports of Committees. 8 October 1929.

72. There are a number of valuable works on India's membership of the Commonwealth and the way in which India's republicanism was accommodated with the status of the crown. For the last days of British rule in India, see, for example, Michael Edwardes, *The Last Years of British India* (Cassell, London, 1963). For a detailed examination of India's membership of the Commonwealth after the end of the Second World War, see Moore, *New Commonwealth*. Mansergh examines the conflict between republicanism and the status of the Crown by looking at both the Irish and Indian cases. Mansergh, 'Constitutional Transformation, Irish Republican Secession, Indian Republican Accession and the Changing Position of the Crown', *The Commonwealth Experience*, Ch. 12. The focus of this section is more limited than these works.

73. PRO, PREM 4/46/12. Cripps to Churchill. 29 November 1944.

74. Some policy-makers in Britain feared that the NCW countries, including India, would be unreliable without formal organization and treaties, arguing that their membership of the Commonwealth was insufficient. For example, see 'Record of Meeting', 11 March 1947, Nicholas Mansergh and Penderel Moon *et al.* (eds), *Constitutional Relations between Britain and India: The Transfer of Power 1942–7*, IX, 522 (HMSO, London, 1981).

75. PRO, CAB 134/117. Cabinet Official Committee on Commonwealth Relations. 8 August 1947. The Attlee government was gravely concerned with the likely loss of India's contributions in the field of military operations after its independence. Anita Inder Singh, 'Imperial Defence and the Transfer of Power in India', *International History Review*, 4 (November 1982), pp. 570–6.

76. *Central Organization for Defence*, Cmd. 6923, HMSO, 1946. PRO, DEFE 4/20. Chiefs of Staff, 31st Meeting. 21 February 1949.

77. PRO, CAB 130/45. Official Committee on Commonwealth Relations. The Financial Consequences of a Change in India's Constitutional Position. Memorandum by the Board of Trade. 16 February 1949.

78. In contrast to the Board of Trade, which feared the loss of most-favoured-nation clauses, the attitude of the Treasury regarding India's membership of the Commonwealth was more flexible. It concluded that as long as India remained inside the sterling area, which it expected that it would, India's membership of the Commonwealth would not have any immediate direct effect. PRO, CAB 130/45. Memorandum by the Treasury. 16 February 1949. The Treasury did not expect India to leave the sterling area, as it would be more damaging to India than Britain because of, for example, its hard currency deficit.

79. PRO, CAB 130/45. Memorandum by Foreign Office.

80. Ibid., India's Future Relations with the Commonwealth. Implications for Commonwealth Country.

81. Ibid.

82. Ibid.

83. PRO, CAB 21/1824. Noel-Baker to Attlee. 20 April, 1949. Noel-Baker wrote that 'the Commonwealth could most profitably seek to mould her views and influence her action and modify the philosophy underlying non-alignment'.

84. Parliamentary Debates, House of Commons, vol. 464, col. 370, 28 April 1949. This statement was read to the House of Commons by the Lord President of the Council, H. Morrison. Before the 1949 conference, the opinions of the Commonwealth prime ministers varied, New Zealand being concerned with the loss of the Crown link,

South Africa anxious about the problem of overseas Indians, and Ceylon and Pakistan sceptical about India's commitment to the Commonwealth. PRO, CAB 133/91. Meeting of Prime Ministers. Informal Meetings with Certain Commonwealth Representatives. April 1949.

85. PRO, CAB 133/89. Meeting of Prime Ministers. Minutes of Meetings and Memoranda. April 1949.

86. PRO, CAB 134/118. Commonwealth Relations Committee. 10 March and 21 July 1948. The 'two-tier' plan of the Commonwealth – 'Commonwealth of British and Associated Nations' – had several versions. Whichever the plan, its essence was the same. Those members which could not accept common allegiance to the Crown would become 'associated states', whereas the existing members of the Commonwealth which were prepared to accept it would form an inner circle. However, the idea of 'associated states' was soon dropped, mainly for two reasons. First, it was considered practically impossible to differentiate between 'associated', Commonwealth and foreign countries, and to treat them differently. Second, the official committee feared that some of the OCW countries, such as Canada and South Africa, might also prefer the status of 'associated states' to that of Commonwealth membership in order to avoid any constraints on their economic and political activities.

87. V. K. Krishna Menon (the Indian High Commissioner to the United Kingdom from 1947) explained to Lord Mountbatten (the last Viceroy in India) that, 'for purely political warfare motives', Congress had been attacking the Crown. 'Record of Interview Between Rear-Admiral Viscount Mountbatten of Burma and Mr Krishna Menon', 17 April 1947, in Mansergh and Moon, *Constitutional Relations*, X, 169.

88. For example, the Commonwealth Relations Official Committee (CRO) reported in as late as September 1948 that India's Congress Working Committee was unanimous that India should leave the Commonwealth. Krishna Menon, however, claimed that a strong section of the Congress Party actually supported the idea of retaining the Commonwealth connection. PRO, PREM 8/1008. J. S. H. Shattock (UK High Commissioner in Delhi) to H. A. F. Rumbold (CRO). 14 September 1948. PREM 8/1008. Acting UK High Commissioner to CRO. 14 September 1948.

89. Michael Brecher, 'India's Decision to Remain in the Commonwealth', *Journal of Commonwealth and Comparative Politics*, 12 (1975), pp. 64–5.

90. Brecher suggests that the British-educated bureaucrats of the foreign service and the British-trained senior officers in the army favoured sustaining the link with Britain. Among the advocates of continued Commonwealth membership, he considers Sir B. N. Rau and V. K. Krishna Menon to be the most influential. Brecher, 'India's Decision', pp. 65–6.

91. 'Record of Interview between Rear-Admiral Viscount Mountbatten of Burma and Pandit Nehru', 24 March 1947, in Mansergh and Moon, *Constitutional Relations*, vol. X, no. 11. Nehru suggested the idea of common nationality to Mountbatten as a new formula for Indian membership. Mountbatten speculated that leaders in Indian politics, including Nehru, could not afford to say that India would stay in the Commonwealth, although they supported the idea.

92. Moore, *New Commonwealth*, pp. 122–5. For a study of India and its attitude towards Indians overseas during the period under discussion see, for example, Tinker, *Separate and Unequal.*

93. Alan Campbell-Johnson, *Mission with Mountbatten* (Robert Hale, London, 1951), p. 50.

94. 'Sir Walter Monckton to Rear-Admiral Viscount Mountbatten of Burma. Mountbatten Papers. Official Correspondence Files: Hyderabad, Part I (a)', 4 May 1947, in Mansergh and Moon, *Constitutional Relations*, X, 308. Sir Walter Monckton

was an adviser to the Government of Hyderabad on constitutional matters. Sir Hartley Shawcross, the then Attorney General, also feared that other Dominions would not join the type of 'common nationality' scheme which was contemplated by Mountbatten and Nehru. PRO, CAB 127/169, Sir H. Shawcross to Sir S. Cripps. 9 May 1947.

95. B. N. Rau (ed.), *India's Constitution in the Making* (Orient Longman, Bombay, 1960), pp. 347–8. After the trip, Rau wrote a paper in January 1948, 'India and the Commonwealth', and submitted it to Mountbatten and Nehru.

96. While negotiations continued between the British and Indian governments, the Irish government in September 1948 declared itself to be in favour of becoming a republic, and that it would leave the Commonwealth. Governments in the member countries decided nevertheless that there should be no change in regard to tariff preferences and the special treatment of citizens even after Éire's secession from the Commonwealth. In contrast to their flexibility towards Éire, British officials were adamant that the Irish case could not apply to India. For one of the early summaries of the agreement between the Commonwealth and Irish governments which were reached in November, see PRO, CAB 21/1836. Outward Telegram from the Commonwealth Relations Office to UK High Commissioners in Canada, Australia, New Zealand, Union of South Africa, India, Pakistan, Ceylon and UK Representative to Éire, No. 106. 19 November 1948.

97. According to the report by the official committee in February 1949, it was unclear in the draft of the Indian Constitution what rights would be given to Commonwealth citizens who were not Indian nationals. The committee was therefore sceptical as to how far India's claim for 'common citizenship' was valid. PRO, CAB 134/119. Committee on Commonwealth Relations. Report by Official Committee. 23 February 1949.

98. PRO, CAB 134/119. The Commonwealth Relationship. 5th Report by Official Committee. 4 February 1949.

99. PRO, CAB 129/33. C. P. (49)58. 14 March 1949.

100. PRO, CAB 129/33. C. P. (49)58. 14 March 1949.

101. PRO, CAB 21/1824. Conference of Commonwealth Prime Ministers London 1949.

102. According to Tinker, for example, the British government acted as if it wished 'to broaden the conception of citizenship so that the Commonwealth became much more of a mutual, reciprocal association'. Tinker, *Separate and Unequal*, p. 363.

103. In accordance with the three types of alternative citizenship outlined in Ch. 1, Commonwealth citizenship, the common status after the Second World War, is similar to a composite type of citizenship, unlike British subjecthood, which shared more features of the imperial type of citizenship.

104. Charles Kindleberger, *Europe's Postwar Growth: The Role of Labour Supply* (Oxford University Press, London, 1967), p. 69.

105. They consisted largely of members of the Polish armed forces, displaced persons from the camps on the Continent, and those recruited from countries with large-scale unemployment, notably Austria and Italy. For more details see J. A. Tannahill, *European Volunteer Workers in Britain* (Manchester University Press, Manchester, 1958).

106. Unit for Manpower Studies, Department of Employment, *The Role of Immigrants in the Labour Market*, Project Report, 1977, pp. 6, 161–2.

107. Jackson, *Irish in Britain*, p. 14.

108. Ibid., pp. 105–7, 198–9.

109. Parliamentary Debates, House of Commons, vol. 451, col. 1851, 8 June 1948.

110. PRO, CO 1006/1. Working Party on Employment in the United Kingdom of Surplus Colonial Labour. October, 1948. LAB 26/226. Report of the Working Party

on the Employment in the United Kingdom of Surplus Colonial Labour. February 1949. The committee originally sought a combined solution to two problems in different areas of the Commonwealth: the labour shortages in Britain and high unemployment in the colonies, especially in the Caribbean. It then rejected that option.

111. Lord Butler pointed to the establishment of the 1952 McCarran-Walter Act in the United States as one of the main reasons for the increase. Both Layton-Henry and Peach, on the other hand, argued that the labour shortage in Britain had the biggest impact on the increase. R. A. Butler, *The Art of the Possible* (Hamish Hamilton, London, 1971), p. 205; Zig Layton-Henry, *The Politics of Race in Britain* (Allen & Unwin, London, 1984), p. 17; Ceri Peach, *West Indian Migration to Britain* (Oxford University Press, London, 1968).

112. Zig Layton-Henry, 'The State and New Commonwealth Immigration: 1951–56', *New Community*, 14, 1/2 (Autumn 1987), pp. 64–75; Rose, *Colour and Citizenship*, pp. 206–31.

113. Parliamentary Debates, House of Commons, vol. 649, col. 687, 16 November 1961.

114. Ibid., col. 688, 26 November 1961.

115. PRO, CAB 129/107. Commonwealth Migrants. Memorandum by the Secretary of State for the Home Department. 6 October 1961.

116. PRO, CAB 129/107. Memorandum by the Secretary of State for the Home Department. 6 October 1961.

117. A Cabinet paper clearly ruled out the possibility of justifying immigration control on the grounds of employment. PRO, CAB 129/107. Commonwealth Migrants.

118. 'Aliens' included, after the enactment of the BNA 1948, the nationals of foreign countries but excluded Commonwealth and Irish citizens.

119. Unit for Manpower Studies, Department of Employment, *Role of Immigrants*, p. 7.

120. A working party, for example, actually rejected the imposition of a labour permit system, as that method severely curtailed the number of immigrants. PRO, LAB 8/2704. Working Party Report on the Social and Economic Problem Arising from the Growing Influx into the UK of Coloured Workers from Other Commonwealth Countries. 28 April 1961.

121. Parliamentary Debates, House of Commons, vol. 649, col. 695, 16 November 1961.

122. Ibid., vol. 650, col. 1296, 5 December 1961 (Mr David Renton, the then Minister of State for the Home Affairs Department).

123. Ibid., vol. 650, col. 1296, 5 December 1961.

124. Ibid., vol. 649, col. 696, 16 November 1961.

125. Ibid., vol. 654, col. 727, 22 February 1962.

126. PRO, LAB 8/2704. Curtailment of Immigration by Employment Control. Note by the Ministry of Labour. 28 April 1961.

127. Parliamentary Debates, House of Commons, vol. 649, col. 687, 16 November 1961. The government explained that the purpose of the CIA 1962 was to tackle problems of 'overcrowding, unemployment and to foster racial harmony'.

128. Rose, *Colour and Citizenship*, p. 78.

129. PRO, LAB 8/2704. Curtailment of Immigration by Employment Control. Report to Ministerial Committee. 27 July 1961.

130. PRO, CO 1032/197. Working Party on Social and Economic Problem. 25 June 1959.

131. PRO, CAB 129/107. Commonwealth Migrants. Memorandum by the Secretary of State for the Home Department. 6 October 1961.

132. Parliamentary Debates, House of Commons, vol. 649, col. 695, 16 November 1961.

133. Gordon Walker lost his Smethwick seat in the 1964 general election to the Conservative candidate, Peter Griffiths, who had fought a racist campaign. Nonetheless, Gordon Walker was made Foreign Secretary without a seat in the

Commons. He fought a by-election in 1965, but lost again. These two election losses convinced the Wilson government that the working-class population was in favour of tight immigration control.

134. Parliamentary Debates, House of Commons, vol. 649, cols 714–6, 16 November 1961.

135. While the enactment of the CIA 1962 was being debated, the Macmillan government was also considering applying to join the Common Market. The Macmillan government made it clear from the start that it would continue giving favourable treatment to Commonwealth workers over those from the Common Market. For the purpose of maintaining the unity of the Commonwealth and the citizenship structure based on it, the British government did not have any choice but to choose workers from the Commonwealth over those from the Common Market. PRO, LAB 8/2701. Common Market Negotiations (Official) Committee Draft Brief on the Free Movement of Workers. Note by the Ministry of Labour. 16 May 1962.

136. PRO, CAB 128/13. 18 November 1948. It was stated that Irish citizens should be treated as if they remained Commonwealth citizens on the grounds of 'ties of blood, history and intermingling of peoples'.

137. Parliamentary Debates, House of Lords, vol. 238, col. 43, 12 March 1962.

138. Unit for Manpower Studies, Department of Employment, *Role of Immigrants*, table 1, p. 12. In 1962 the number of workers admitted to the United Kingdom from NCW and foreign countries (excluding the Common Market countries) were 4,213 and 22,873, respectively. In 1970, those from foreign countries increased to 31,333, while those from the NCW dropped to 3,119. With the enactment of the IA 1971, the two control systems – one for Commonwealth citizens and the other for aliens – were integrated into one.

139. PRO, CAB 134/1469. Commonwealth Migrants Committee, 2nd Meeting. 17 May 1961. The debate on Britain creating its own citizenship is dealt with in Ch. 5.

— 5 —
Emerging National Citizenship through Immigration Control: From the Commonwealth Immigrants Act 1962 to the Immigration Act 1971

AFTER THE enactment of the CIA 1962, immigration law rather than citizenship law was used to define who 'belonged', and consequently what it meant to 'belong', to Britain. The CIA 1962 totally ignored the citizenship statuses created by the BNA 1948, rendering the entitlement to citizenship rights and obligations subject to immigration control, not the other way around as in other countries. For example, within the status of CUKC, those from Hong Kong became subject to immigration control, whereas those born in the United Kingdom did not. The neglect of citizenship statuses continued with the next major immigration law passed in the 1960s, the Commonwealth Immigrants Act 1968 (CIA 1968). The then Attorney General, Sir Elwyn Jones, in introducing it, made it clear that 'the general principle that a person should not be deprived of the right to enter the territory of the state of which he was a national, did not apply when he did not belong in any real sense to the territory in question'.[1] In the absence of British citizenship up to 1981, immigration laws were enacted for the purpose of confining substantial aspects of citizenship to those who 'belonged' to Britain.

Chapter 4 examined the period immediately after the Second World War up to the enactment of the CIA 1962. During that period Commonwealth citizenship, unlike its predecessor, British subjecthood, was reduced to a purely symbolic status in all member counties other than Britain, a status to which no substantive aspects of citizenship were attached. This chapter focuses on the period after the enactment of the CIA 1962 and offers a study of the process of establishing the rules which determined who 'belonged' to Britain within the framework of Commonwealth citizenship. The CIA 1962 used the definition of people who 'in common parlance belong to the UK';[2] the CIA 1968 narrowed it to people with a 'close connection' to the United Kingdom; and finally the Immigration Act 1971 (IA 1971) established the concept of 'patriality' (s. 2(6)).[3] In analysing this series of immigration controls as a means of consolidating the rules about who 'belonged' and what it meant to 'belong' to Britain, this chapter takes a different course from existing works that simply perceive each immigration act during this period as a racially discriminatory measure.

First, this chapter aims to examine the way in which political leaders in Britain during the period under discussion perceived the role and meaning of citizenship. In the face of a long history of British subjecthood, they failed to foresee the importance of national citizenship in other parts of the world after the Second World War. For them, citizenship was still a legal status and neither an entitlement to citizenship rights and obligations nor the embodiment of nationhood. The framework of Commonwealth citizenship created by the BNA 1948 did not envisage that citizenship in newly independent countries in the Commonwealth would be used as a means to exclude a group of residents who would not fit into their definition of 'nation', whatever this was. Misunderstandings over citizenship between Britain and the other member countries of the Commonwealth were therefore inevitable, leading to institutional changes in Britain's immigration and citizenship policies.

Second, this chapter also tries to demonstrate that the development of national citizenship in Britain did not result from either careful planning by successive governments or strong demands by the public. None of the immigration acts of the 1960s and 1970s was deliberately enacted for the purpose of defining Britishness. Most of the politicians and the public who supported those immigration acts were not aware of the broader consequences of immigration control on the concept of citizenship. As a result, the creation of national citizenship in 1981 was inadvertently preceded in Britain by increasingly sophisticated methods of immigration control which, although they applied in theory to all Commonwealth citizens, were intended to target the 'coloured' NCW immigrants.

The chapter ends by analysing the concept of 'patriality' found in the IA 1971, by which British citizenship was defined in 1981. It concludes that the accumulation of the exclusive effects of each immigration act, whose real purpose was to prohibit NCW immigration within the framework of Commonwealth citizenship, ultimately determined British citizenship.

CREATION OF CITIZENSHIPS WITHOUT NATIONAL CITIZENSHIP

Previous works have concentrated exclusively on immigration policy, overlooking the emergence of a prototype of national citizenship through immigration control in the 1960s and the early 1970s. It is, however, this development that left a lasting impact on the definition of Britain's national citizenship in 1981. This section will first examine the reasons why successive governments after the Second World War repeatedly decided not to create the national type of citizenship in Britain. It then analyses the way in which citizenship was understood by political leaders during the period immediately after the war, within the framework of Commonwealth citizenship.

The first attempt to create national citizenship

After the Second World War the British government had at least two opportunities before the enactment of the CIA 1962 to create a citizenship of its own. The first chance arose with the preparation of the British nationality bill, enacted as the BNA 1948. In preparation for a conference of legal experts in 1947, the Attlee government set up an interdepartmental working party of the Home Office (in the chair) and the Dominion, Foreign, India and Colonial offices. The issue there was the nature of the citizenship to be conferred on the peoples in overseas territories. The working party neither intended to examine the necessity of creating British citizenship, nor planned to confine the citizenship status only to those people who were deemed to 'belong' to Britain. For example, Dummett rightly points out in her work that Sir David Maxwell-Fyfe (the then Shadow Home Secretary) was one of the few Conservatives who argued that citizenship was 'the common enjoyment of civic rights and the acceptance of civic responsibilities', on which basis he condemned the bill.[4] However, Maxwell-Fyfe's opposition derived from the creation and naming of CUKC, as he was in favour of keeping the term British *subjecthood*. He therefore did not intend to demand that British citizenship be established on the basis of Britishness, however it was defined. On the contrary, he was against the creation of a distinctive citizenship for Britain and the colonies. Accepting that other parts of the Commonwealth could enact their own citizenship laws, he insisted that Britain should not do so, in order to 'maintain our [British] great metropolitan tradition of hospitality to everyone from every part of our [British] empire'.[5] The issue of citizenship was therefore discussed inside the working party only in relation to how to deal with colonial subjects.

With regard to the position of colonial subjects, the opinion of the Foreign Office and the Colonial Office was divided from the start. The draft prepared by the Foreign Office first requested the creation of a separate citizenship for the United Kingdom and for every colony.[6] In the draft, all those in these two categories of citizenship – citizens of the United Kingdom and of every colony – in combination with citizens of Dominions would be British subjects. With the addition of British Protected Persons (BPP), they were all deemed nationals of Her Majesty. Participants at the working party, although admitting the clarity of the logic behind the Foreign Office draft, found the use of three different terms, 'UK citizens', 'British subject' and 'national of Her Majesty', confusing.[7]

Kenneth Roberts-Wray (the Colonial Office) was strongly opposed to the draft's conferment of a separate citizenship on every colony.[8] He preferred the British government to abstain from the whole scheme. If it could not, he suggested that a few of the larger and more advanced colonies could be granted separate citizenship, such as a West Indies citizenship, by grouping them together. The remainder of the colonies, he said, should then fall into 'a residue which would either bear the UK label or such other terms as could be evolved'.[9] As a representative of the Colonial Office, he insisted that one of the fundamental principles of colonial policies had been to strengthen the ties between the United Kingdom and the colonies, and the common status had always been one of the strongest and most important ties. By creating a separate local citizenship, he argued, one of the most direct links would be cut, and it would appear to the colonial peoples that they were being put in an inferior position to UK citizens. He accepted the clarity of the rules behind the Foreign Office draft, but claimed that the common status was 'much more than a mere vehicle for conferring privileges or imposing obligations', symbolizing 'common loyalty and equal status'.[10] Sir Oscar Dowson (Home Office), although sympathizing with Roberts-Wray's dislike of a separate citizenship for the colonies, found the Colonial Office's plan of differentiating colonies difficult and that of conferring UK citizenship on inhabitants of a remote islands thousands of miles away from the UK unrealistic. This Colonial Office plan was thus soon rejected.

Later, the working party decided on four options: (i) the creation of a UK citizenship and the citizenship of each colony; (ii) no citizenships of the United Kingdom or any of the colonies, but continuation of British subjecthood; (iii) the creation of a combined citizenship for the United Kingdom and the colonies; and (iv) the creation of a citizenship for the United Kingdom and of a colonial citizenship of all the colonies.[11] The working party later added a fifth option, which created a UK citizenship and simply conferred British subjecthood on the inhabitants of the colonies.[12] In the course of the meetings of the working party the Colonial Office supported either the second or third option, and the Foreign Office favoured the first. The fourth option was rejected as politically impossible, because a general colonial citizenship, separate from that of the United Kingdom, would be considered as inferior by all the colonies. The third option, although it in the end became the basis of the BNA 1948, was, at this stage, described as too artificial and dropped. The first option would preserve the unity of the Commonwealth by allowing Britain to join the Canadian scheme in full with other members, although it departed from traditional colonial policies. However, if the second option were chosen, the coherence of the Canadian scheme would be broken and the maintenance of the common status would eventually fail. As a compromise between the interests of the Colonial and the Foreign Offices, the fifth option was preferred at this stage.[13]

Sir Alexander Maxwell (Home Office), however, was opposed to this conclusion, claiming that, without UK citizenship, the inhabitants of the colonies would feel inferior to UK citizens.[14] He made a counterproposal to reconsider option three, which had been rejected earlier. This time, the option of creating a combined citizenship for the United Kingdom and colonies (CUKC) rapidly gained support from all sections. The officials at the Dominion Office thought that, under such a solution, Britain could fully participate in the new scheme for common status, and those at the Colonial Office were satisfied as long as the option of a separate colonial citizenship was avoided. In the end, the view of the Colonial Office prevailed over that of the Foreign Office.[15]

As is explained in Chapter 4, the existence of the Canadian citizenship bill was considered by the Attlee government to offer a good opportunity to replace the common code system. The government accepted that 'UK legislation should create some form of citizenship which would be the gateway through which the status of British subject would be conferred on the inhabitants of the UK'.[16] Its emphasis was placed on creating 'the gateway', not a separate national citizenship in Britain on the basis of Britishness. Lord Altrincham was in the minority when he insisted that a 'national citizenship ... for the people of this Island' be created and 'the title of "British" which is ours by every right of blood and soil' conferred on it.[17] The British government deliberately chose to create a citizenship which would apply to both the United Kingdom and the colonies, emphasizing the importance of the unity between them.

The second attempt to create national citizenship

Thirteen years after the enactment of the BNA 1948, a Conservative government this time had the chance to establish national citizenship, when it was preparing for an immigration law to deal with the increased NCW immigration into Britain. This time, the suggestion to create a national citizenship was made with regard to the special position of Irish citizens in British immigration policy. Citizens of the Republic of Ireland, although they were no longer Commonwealth citizens after the BNA 1948, had the unconditional right to enter the United Kingdom, and were given all the citizenship rights and accompanying obligations if they became residents.[18] The Macmillan government wanted to retain their exemption from immigration control, because of Ireland's special and entangled relationship with Britain and Britain's labour shortage at that time. Irish workers had not only historically taken unpopular jobs as well as seasonal work in Britain, which few of the native workers wished to do, but because of their proximity the supply was flexible.[19] However, the government feared that it might be accused of racism if Irish citizens were not subject to immigration control, while coloured NCW immigrants were. It therefore tried to justify the exemption of Irish citizens from immigration control by emphasizing economic as well as other practical grounds: the heavy passenger traffic, likely delays at the ports, the probable introduction of identity documents for the people of Northern Ireland, and the additional enormous costs.[20] It also insisted that wartime experience had already proved that control of the land border between the republic and Northern Ireland was hard to enforce.[21]

Of the five categories which the BNA 1948 created – the CUKC, citizens of independent Commonwealth countries, British subject without citizenship (BSWC), BPP and aliens – only those in the first three had the status of the Commonwealth citizenship and were exempt from immigration control.[22] Irish citizens, although not included among Commonwealth citizens, were also not subject to immigration control. The Commonwealth Migrants Committee was unanimous at the outset over keeping them outside immigration control. In order to do so, it explored several options, among which was the possibility of establishing a new 'UK citizenship' – 'citizenship of the British Islands' – which was defined so as to include citizenship of the Irish Republic.[23] The committee in 1961 considered that it might be time to amend the BNA 1948 and reorganize immigration control according to the holding of relevant citizenship. In this way, immigration control in Britain could have come in line with all other countries.

The committee proposed two changes to the BNA 1948.[24] First, a new citizenship, 'citizenship of the British Islands', would be established in place of the CUKC. This citizenship would embrace all citizens of the Irish Republic as well as all those existing CUKCs whose citizenship depended on their connection with the United Kingdom. Second, the rest of the CUKCs, who had been given that status in connection with a colony, would be excluded from the new 'citizenship of the British Islands'. After careful scrutiny over nearly three months, the plan was dropped for several reasons, both political and practical.

First, two political objections were raised, with regard to the inclusion of Irish citizens and the separation of colonial citizenship from 'citizenship of the British Islands'. It was never the purpose of the committee to define Britishness and create citizenship of the British Islands on the basis of it. Its only purpose was to consider a way of restricting the movement of certain citizens from the Commonwealth, namely those from the NCW, without being accused of racial discrimination.[25] The committee was nonetheless concerned that the Irish government would regard the conferment of citizenship of the British Islands on Irish citizens as interference in its domestic affairs. After all, one of the main reasons for enacting the BNA 1948 was to release Irish citizens from the status of Commonwealth citizenship while continuing to treat them as if they retained it. The proposal on citizenship of the British Islands therefore had to be changed, so that Irish citizens were not included in a new 'United Kingdom citizenship', but continued to receive the benefits of UK citizenship.[26]

The committee also did not know what kind of citizenship should be created for the remaining colonies. Again, considerable time was devoted to the issue that the BNA 1948 also addressed, that is, whether a separate citizenship for each colony or a joint citizenship of all the colonies should be created. Whichever option was to be selected, the British government could not have avoided the objection that they were bestowing on the colonial citizens an inferior citizenship.[27] The Colonial Office, which had always been sensitive towards colonial demands, was especially concerned with this criticism.[28] Furthermore, the British government could not be seen to treat colonial citizens unfavourably in comparison with Irish citizens. After all, it was still responsible for the remaining colonies until they became independent, whereas the Irish Republic had long since left the Commonwealth. Considering the likely objection from colonies, therefore, it was difficult for the government to create a citizenship which was specifically attached to the United Kingdom and left out colonial peoples.

Second, the committee was also aware that the plan to create UK citizenship had not only political but also practical difficulties. After a long history of generous common law rule on nationality, the committee pointed out that even immigration control on the basis of citizenship could not prevent all those people whom it wanted to control from entering Britain. For example, a person born in Jamaica whose father happened to have been born in the United Kingdom would be granted a new UK citizenship by descent, and would thus be exempt from immigration control.

In the end, the plan to create UK citizenship was once again abandoned. The committee admitted, however, that, had it been implemented, it could have brought British nationality law in line with that of other countries. Furthermore, UK citizenship would finally have conferred on its holders both citizenship-as-rights and citizenship-as-desirable-activity. However, it came to the conclusion that anomalous cases were bound to happen whether or not the criterion of holding citizenship was to be applied.[29] A working party thus recommended that the status of CUKC should be retained, while only 'persons belonging to the UK' should be exempted from immigration control. According to one of its papers, 'freedom of entry is only one aspect of citizenship rights', and thus did not need to correspond to possession of citizenship.[30] For policy-makers in Britain, the substantive and nominal aspects of citizenship did not need to match each other. They did not think that citizenship needed to be granted on the basis of nationhood. As a result, the creation of a UK citizenship was suggested only as one method of immigration control, as the committee saw 'presentational advantages in making the right of free entry to the United Kingdom a privilege restricted to those who enjoy particular citizenship'.[31] So long as citizenship was perceived by policy-makers as a legal status with no reference to the nationhood which it should give to its holders, it was possible for Irish citizens to be given British citizenship. Neither did the British government hesitate to deprive NCW citizens of the right to enter and reside in Britain.

New Commonwealth immigrants, Old Commonwealth citizens and Commonwealth citizens

So far, this section has explained that successive British governments did not intend to create British national citizenship and instead maintained Commonwealth citizenship. Legally, therefore, all the holders of Commonwealth citizenship, whether they were from the OCW or the NCW countries, received citizenship rights and privileges. It was thus accurate in law to describe the Commonwealth citizenship which the BNA 1948 had created as 'made up of the aggregate of the separately defined citizens of all Commonwealth countries'.[32] Nonetheless, there was always in Britain a special attachment to the British descendants in the OCW countries. As has been shown in the previous chapters, citizenship laws had already been increasingly inclusive towards this group in the way in which they had expanded the rule of acquisition by descent since the First World War.[33] Furthermore, since 1914, British subjecthood in the Dominions and the United Kingdom had been defined jointly by their governments under the common code system, whereas that in the colonies continued to be laid down by the imperial government.[34] The common code system thus provided the division between British subjects in Britain and the Dominions on the one hand and the colonies on the other with an institutional basis in addition to the long-standing ancestral link.

As a result, within the framework of Commonwealth citizenship, there was a division between those of British descent and those who were not. In spite of the government's efforts to deny its intention, the CIA 1962 was enacted on the premise of two distinctive groupings of Commonwealth citizens – OCW *citizens* and NCW *immigrants* – and aimed to prevent the latter from entering Britain.[35] With the links with OCW citizens still very much valued, the government opted not to create a British citizenship based on distinctive 'Britishness' in order to keep the effect of immigration control on OCW citizens to a minimum.[36] For the then policy-makers, citizenship was simply a legal status and they could decide what it meant and who owned it. The enactment of the CIA 1962 and the immigration control which it imposed on Commonwealth citizens therefore did not affect the citizenship statuses created by the BNA 1948.

Unlike the other anti-immigration MPs in Britain, Enoch Powell quickly became aware of the change in the concept of citizenship in the post-Second World War era, and demanded the creation of national citizenship in Britain as early as the late 1950s.[37] Although Powell was later accused of triggering anti-immigration resentment, he was in a way pressing for a more fundamental challenge than others.[38] While anti-immigration advocates concentrated on imposing immigration control on NCW immigrants, he went further and tried to define 'a citizenship of the people of this country [Great Britain]'.[39] He was one of the first people to warn of the danger of the British government persisting with Commonwealth citizenship and neglecting the importance of national citizenship,[40] but his view remained that of the minority, and his attempt to create national citizenship at the time of the passage of the CIA 1962 failed.

Powell's view on citizenship was well expressed in the following comment in April 1961, which he made at one of the meetings of the Commonwealth Migrants Committee. Powell, the then Minister of Health, pointed out that

> the necessary step is to proceed to divide the citizenship of the United Kingdom and colonies into a 'citizenship of the United Kingdom' and a 'citizenship of the Colonies' ... Indeed, from the beginning the 'citizenship of the United Kingdom and Colonies' was an artificial and rather absurd entity, being merely a residuum left in the course of transition from subjecthood based on allegiance to citizenship based on statute. The recognition of a United Kingdom citizenship is a natural further development.[41]

For Powell, the concept of citizenship should reflect that of the political unit, and it was time for the transitional period represented by citizenship statuses such as CUKC to come to an end. Consequently, he claimed that a UK citizenship should be created to mark it. In contrast to Powell's support for creating national citizenship, most of the anti-immigration MPs were content with prohibiting NCW immigrants from entering Britain.[42]

In fact, Commonwealth citizenship and its citizenship structure could not have been sustained for a period of time unless member countries of the Commonwealth supported it, or at least acquiesced in it. For example, there was no demand within the British Empire at the end of the Second World War to demolish the common status itself. The hesitancy of successive British governments to create national citizenship was, to some extent, compounded by the fact that the other member countries did not want Britain to do so either. Even in the late 1960s, the OCW governments expected their citizens to be preferentially treated by Britain's immigration control. Some of them even opposed the British government imposing immigration control on their citizens. For example, when Harold Wilson's government tightened up the system of 'working holidays' in 1965, both governments and individuals in the OCW countries immediately criticized it.[43] It was pointed out several times in governmental papers that the OCW citizens, especially those of Canada, Australia and New Zealand, were offended, not because of unfair treatment, but simply because of the fact that they were subject to immigration control in Britain.[44] Officials also observed that these reactions were 'echoed in the UK itself and strengthened by the belief that these countries suffer because of the need of the UK government to erect a barrier to a flood of coloured immigrants seeking permanent settlement in the UK'.[45]

The sense of affinity between people in Britain and the OCW countries lingered on, long after the special relationship between Britain and the OCW countries was weakened in the areas of economy and defence.[46] Even after the enactment of the CIA 1962, therefore, the British government remained reluctant to impose immigration control on OCW immigrants. When it faced inflows of immigrants from east African countries, it was thus not surprising that, regardless of their citizenship status, the government did everything it could to keep those of British descent from immigration control, while imposing it on those of Asian origin.[47]

INDEPENDENCE IN EAST AFRICA AND THE COMMONWEALTH IMMIGRANTS ACTS

Independence and citizenship in east Africa

Almost as soon as the CIA 1962 was enacted, it became apparent to government officials that it was not successful in reducing the number of immigrants. Already in 1963 the Commonwealth Immigration Committee signalled a warning about 'the upward trend of immigration in the third quarter of that year'.[48] It was particularly concerned about 'the many more Indian and Pakistani dependants arriving'.[49] These were exactly the immigrant groups which the act had originally targeted. As a result, amendments to the voucher system were already being discussed at committee level in July 1963.[50] In the end, a White Paper was published in August 1965 on examining future policy on immigration to Britain from the Commonwealth.[51] The core methods of immigration control created by the CIA 1962 had to undergo significant changes within less than three years.[52]

The defects of the CIA 1962, however, went deeper than the voucher system and its failings, as the 1965 White Paper suggested. They also derived from clashes between Britain and the east African countries which became independent in the 1960s over the concepts of citizenship. Under the BNA 1948, the working citizenship act in Britain at that time, all the newly independent countries would establish citizenship of their own in a way which would include all the residents of the territory at the time of independence. Given that they remained in the Commonwealth, their citizens were to be granted Commonwealth citizenship on the basis of holding the citizenship of each country. Because those citizens would receive a passport issued by their own governments, their entry to Britain should have been subject to the CIA 1962 (s. 1(2)).[53] However, new governments in east Africa established citizenship in such a way as to exclude non-African residents there, forcing those people who were not granted citizenship in these countries to turn to Britain on the grounds of their status of Commonwealth citizenship.[54] The British government was therefore soon forced to introduce a new measure in the face of another immigration flow from the new Commonwealth countries, this time from Africa, particularly Kenya.

It appears natural to us today that the concepts of citizenship of the former African colonies did not match with those in Britain, taking into account the concept's historical origin and development. As is discussed in Chapter 1, the concept of citizenship had its origin in Europe and developed in response to social and political events in Europe. Under today's national citizenship, citizenship has to be both a political and national membership of the political unit. In that sense, national citizenship implicitly presupposes the existence of a 'common culture' within the political unit, however it is defined.[55] The unilaterally delineated boundaries during the colonial period might have suited the economic and political interests of the imperial powers, but augmented the ethnic and cultural diversities in each African colony. As a result, post-independence leaders in Africa were left with the hard task of building unity among peoples who were diverse in language, ethnicity and religion.

Britain's east African colonies, when they became independent, were not exceptional for the ethnic and cultural diversities among their populations. Under the common law principle of allegiance, the status of British subjecthood had been given to all the colonized, irrespective of their cultural and ethnic backgrounds.[56] The imperial government did not concern itself with ethnic and cultural division within its colonies, as long as its rule over them was not hampered. In the case of east Africa, furthermore, the imperial government even encouraged the division by introducing immigrants from other parts of the Empire, namely the Indian sub-continent.[57] In addition to ethnic division, populations in east Africa had also been divided by the difference between the colonized and the colonizing.

In the 1960s, African colonies successively gained independence from Britain, joining the Commonwealth citizenship structure by enacting citizenship laws of their own.[58] Kenya's negotiations for independence took place after 1960. In the process, the creation of Kenyan citizenship and the way in which it would deal with the 'non-native' European and Asian communities was one of the thorny issues which attracted much attention within the British government. During the colonial period the Kenyan population, made up of Africans, Europeans and Asians, with a smaller number of Arabs, was socially and economically stratified.[59] Among the three largest racial groups, the Europeans held the most prominent places, the Asians predominated at the middle level and the Africans were locked into the bottom layer of the society. One scholar therefore described Kenya as being, in short, 'racially compartmentalised and functionally stratified, that is, malintegrated'.[60] With a colonial bureaucracy as the only link, a sense of community embracing the whole population barely existed in Kenya. Still, new African leaders had to create some basis on which national citizenship could be established. After a long period of suffering under imperial rule, furthermore, the African community felt bitter towards non-African communities and sceptical about their commitment towards the new African-ruled Kenya. Therefore it was not surprising that post-independent leaders stressed their 'African' roots and considered it as one of the crucial qualifying criteria for citizenship.[61] In order to sever links with the colonial past and mark its independence, moreover, they demanded that non-Africans (of both Asian and European origin) should show respect to the members of the host community on every occasion. The demand, however, was sometimes taken to extremes, and invoked punitive measures such as the deportation of non-Africans whom the new government considered to have shown disrespect to Africans or the government.[62]

The British government had been aware that the creation of a citizenship which was exclusively based on African roots might lead to a large exodus of non-African populations from Kenya to the United Kingdom. Nonetheless, there was not much the British government could do to prevent it from happening. It had become an international customary rule by then that each government, whose authority was based on 'the will of the people', had the absolute right to establish citizenship of its own.[63] Furthermore, in 1960 the Declaration on the Granting of Independence to Colonial Countries and People was adopted, supporting the view that national self-determination is a legal principle for colonial independence.[64] It urged the smooth transfer of powers 'without any conditions or reservations, in accordance with their [the peoples in the colonies] freely expressed will and desire ... in order to enable them to enjoy complete independence and freedom'(s. 5). Under these international circumstances, the Kenyan government assumed full responsibility for creating a citizenship of its own. What the British government could do during the constitutional conference was therefore limited to two things: recommending Kenyan political leaders to make generous provisions for the automatic acquisition of Kenyan citizenship, and amending legislation on nationality and immigration in Britain in order to absorb those who were excluded from Kenyan citizenship.[65]

Even at the stage of drafting the Kenyan constitution it had been decided that the new Kenyan citizenship would be chiefly granted by birth or descent, thus a majority of those of Asian and European descent (totalling 170,000 and 45,000, respectively) would be left ineligible for it.[66] Those who had not automatically acquired Kenyan citizenship were given two years' grace after independence in which to apply for it, on condition that they renounced all other citizenships including that of the CUKC.[67] The non-African population, in applying for Kenyan citizenship, was therefore expected to give total dedication to the new country. A prominent politician, Tom Mboya, for example, argued during the debate on the citizenship bill:

> we are demanding the maximum from a non-African: that before he becomes a part of the Kenya nation, he must do one most important thing. He must be able to say that he renounces his original nationality, his country, his people. He will only give one loyalty to Kenya and Kenya only.[68]

As is clear in Mboya's speech, membership of the Kenyan 'nation' was the basis of citizenship of the newly independent Kenyan 'country'. Non-African people who were not members of the 'nation' therefore had to prove their commitment to, and involvement with, the 'country', otherwise they remained outside the 'country', let alone the 'nation'. Ironically, however, the more Kenyan citizenship stressed African traditions, or supposed traditions, in reaction against its colonial past, the less likely it was that the non-African population would be able to receive it, and also the more suspicious Africans became about the real motives of those non-Africans who applied for Kenyan citizenship. As a result, those non-Africans who did not apply for Kenyan citizenship were considered disloyal and forced to leave Kenya. On the other hand, those considering applying for Kenyan citizenship feared that they would be accused of opportunism and have their application refused, ending up being forced to leave Kenya just the same.

From the outset the British government was determined to help the European (mostly British) community, and it thus offered three remedies: (i) special compensation for Europeans in the Kenya civil service; (ii) a £50 million land purchase fund to enable European settlers to sell their lands, if they wished; and (iii) the British Nationality Act (No. 1) 1964 (BNA 1964).[69] Under this act, a CUKC who had renounced that citizenship was entitled to reacquire it on two conditions. First, the only reason for the renunciation had been that it was necessary to retain or acquire citizenship of a Commonwealth country. Second, this act applied only to a person who had a 'qualifying connection' with the United Kingdom and colonies, a protectorate or Protected State, either by way of birth, naturalization or registration in a place which on the date of application was within the United Kingdom and colonies, or of having such a father or paternal grandfather. A woman married to a person with a qualifying connection was also qualified.[70] Introduction of this amendment to the BNA 1948 was decided on as early as October 1963 during the preparatory talks for Kenyan independence. The intention was apparently to protect the British settlers and their descendants in case of future troubles.

Unlike the European community, the Asians in Kenya did not receive such sympathy from the British government. Those of Asian origin considered that whether they acquired Kenyan citizenship or not they would be exposed to discrimination in the economic field, face deportations, and have their citizenship taken away by the government.[71] The Indian government had made it clear in as early as 1963 that it would accept no responsibility for people of Indian origin who were not Indian citizens.[72] For the Kenyan Asians, therefore, the status of CUKC became the only insurance that they had against the uncertain future in Kenya.

The BNA 1964 fitted in very well with the government's view on the various groups which constituted Commonwealth citizens: British descendants should hold Commonwealth citizenship with citizenship rights and privileges, while other Commonwealth citizens should be satisfied with having the nominal status. Once again, the nationality act in Britain was amended without any debate on Britishness, but for the purpose of enabling British descendants to enjoy the substantive aspects of citizenship, while keeping the framework of the Commonwealth intact.

The new Kenyan citizenship and the Commonwealth Immigrants Act 1968

It had become clear by now that Britain's policy-makers after the Second World War, like those before the war, still regarded citizenship as simply a legal status. As a result, the Macmillan and Wilson governments could easily ignore the 'citizenships' conferred by the BNA 1948 on peoples in the NCW, depriving them of the right to enter and reside in Britain.[73] For most politicians and civil servants, the decoupling of the formal and substantive aspects of citizenship by the CIA 1962 was possible and even logical, if it were to serve the purposes of immigration control. Furthermore, as was pointed out earlier, the framework of Commonwealth citizenship remained in spite of the enactment of the CIA 1962, as the conditions and substances of its entitlement were at each member country's discretion. At the time of Kenyan independence in 1963, as a result, colonial citizens in Kenya, under the CIA 1962, did not have the right freely to enter and reside in Britain. Had all the people living in Kenya become Kenyan citizens, they would have received a passport issued by the Kenyan government and thus remained subject to immigration control in Britain.

Here lay the need for the British government to introduce immigration control for the Asian population in Kenya. Without Kenyan citizenship, they would remain CUKCs and be able to obtain passports not from the Kenyan government, but from the British High Commissioner; these passports were, under the CIA 1962, regarded as UK passports which conferred on their holders exemption from immigration control. In short, if they had not applied for Kenyan citizenship they would once again become free from immigration control in Britain as had been the case prior to the act. As a result, according to one government paper, 'the Asians are showing no inclination to acquire local citizenship and the majority are likely to remain our [Britain's] liability at least for an initial period'.[74] Government officials repeatedly pointed out that under the current nationality and immigration laws the British government could not prevent Kenyan Asians from enjoying the right to enter and reside in Britain.[75]

The Wilson government was hesitant, in the face of its international commitment, to refuse entry outright to Kenyan Asian immigrants. It was acknowledged, for example, in the Universal Declaration of Human Rights that to be able to leave and return to one's country of citizenship was a human right which could not be denied.[76] More specifically for Britain, Protocol No. 4 to the 1950 European Convention for the Protection of Human Rights and Fundamental Freedoms, article 3(2), states that 'No one shall be deprived of the right to enter the territory of the State of which he is a national.' Although Britain had not yet ratified Protocol No. 4, it was a signatory of the Convention. In the case of the Kenyan Asians without Kenyan citizenship, the status of CUKC was the only citizenship status that they had. They therefore would have become stateless had Britain refused them entry, and the Foreign Office admitted that Britain had at least a moral responsibility for them. However, it argued that the Convention presupposed that citizens 'belonged' to the country of citizenship. In line with that understanding, the Foreign Office accepted that the Convention guaranteed to persons who 'belonged' to Britain the right of entry into Britain and Britain had to abide by it, but it simultaneously insisted that it could refuse the right of entry into Britain to Commonwealth citizens who 'belonged' to a Commonwealth country other than Britain.[77] Also, it had been a Commonwealth policy not to impose immigration control on a specific group of Commonwealth citizens, so that the Kenyan Asians could not be excluded as a group from entering Britain. The government, in the end, decided to postpone taking any measures against the Kenyan Asians until the number of their immigrants rose further.

As was explained earlier, the Kenyan constitution gave a two-year grace period to those who were not automatically granted Kenyan citizenship, during which they could apply for it. As the British government feared, the pace of applications was initially slow, only 3,911 Asians and Europeans registering as citizens during the first year.[78] Just before the end of the period of grace, the bulk of approximately 10,000 applications was finally made. Looking at this process, African government leaders were convinced that the European and Asian communities were not fully committed to the African Kenya. Even among the applicants, therefore, the Kenyan government was sceptical about their loyalty. As a result, there were quite a number whose applications were not processed. Alarmed by the situation, one prominent legislator asked in parliament, 'Are we [African citizens] accusing them [Asians and Europeans] for being disloyal in not applying, or are we accusing them for applying and saying that we do not want to give it [Kenyan citizenship] to them?'[79] In these circumstances Kenyan Asians' mistrust of the Kenyan government grew, and was confirmed by its mishandling of applications.

In 1967 the Immigration Act and the Trade Licensing Act were passed in Kenya, through which the Kenyan government started to promote its 'Africanization'[80] programme in a more systematic way. For example, the Immigration Act withdrew all existing residents' certificates, forcing non-citizens to apply for one of the 12 new classes of entry permits. It then became illegal for non-citizens to work without obtaining a permit, and employers were also to be prosecuted for hiring non-citizens without the appropriate permit. Non-citizens were, under this new law, deprived of the freedom to move from job to job, as work permits were issued for a particular position. Any change of occupation had to be authorized by the Immigration Department, which had the power to deport non-citizens. In this way, the Ministry of Home Affairs, which controlled the entry and removal of immigrants, could allocate the post to Africans as soon as skilled Africans became available. In addition to the restrictions imposed by the Immigration Act, under the Trade Licensing Act non-citizen traders required a licence do business in certain areas of the country, such as central Nairobi, and were banned from dealing in specified goods, including both agricultural and non-agricultural products. With these two acts on the statute book, the outflow of Kenyan Asians, both citizens and non-citizens, increased dramatically.[81]

As the number of immigrants from Kenya grew, the issues of immigration and deportation of Kenyan Asians and Europeans came to receive more and more attention in the United Kingdom, both in Parliament and from the press in 1967. The debate on whether or not immigration controls should be introduced for them was further fuelled by Enoch Powell's speech in which he claimed that, in Kenya alone, there were about 200,000 CUKCs of Indian origin who were entitled to come to Britain and they were about to come all at once.[82] At a meeting of the Commonwealth immigration committee following his speech, the then Home Secretary, James Callaghan, recommended that the government should introduce a new piece of legislation to control the immigration of Kenyan Asians.[83] He also suggested that it should be introduced very quickly in order to beat the last-minute rush.[84] A representative of the Commonwealth Relations Office (George Thomas) was the only one in the committee who was against the proposal, arguing that 'it was a calculated decision of the British government of the time to offer these people [Kenyan Asians] the security of a British passport'.[85] Renouncing their right to enter Britain by enacting a new immigration act, he continued, would turn them into stateless persons, thereby violating international law. In spite of their previous hesitancy, however, the majority of the committee had by then been convinced that the introduction of immigration control was inevitable.

Wilson himself confessed: 'Few problems could have presented more difficult issues for the Cabinet or a greater issue of conscience for liberal-minded people throughout the country. The Bill created agony for our back-benchers, as earlier it had for the Cabinet.'[86] The main reason for the 'agony' was clearly summarized by David Steel, then a Liberal MP, in his comment during the second reading stage:

All I am saying is that in 1963 we should have made it clear if we intended that their option [of either becoming a Kenyan citizen or retaining the status of CUKC] was not a real option and that they would not have British citizenship status if they did not opt in favour of Kenya citizenship status ... We never made that clear. Now that the two-year period [of choosing citizenship] has expired and a number of people have decided to retain the status of 'British citizen', we are saying in the Bill, 'having given you [the] option, we are now taking away the choice which you decided to make at that time'. That is what I regard as indefensible as the basis for this legislation.[87]

The bill split both the Conservative and the Labour party during parliamentary debates, but was still passed by a comfortable margin, receiving the royal assent on 1 March, less than a week after its introduction.[88]

Although the government made a deliberate choice to introduce immigration controls for Kenyan Asians in spite of the promise which it had made in 1963, it seemed to have forgotten the promise which had been made at the time of Indian independence.[89] During those negotiations the Colonial Office had stressed that Indian settlers within the Empire remained British subjects, owing allegiance to the Crown, and that they should therefore look only to Britain, not India.[90] In the end, the CIA 1968 exempted from immigration control only those CUKCs who not only held UK passports but were also themselves or had at least one of their parents or grandparents, born, adopted, registered or naturalized in the United Kingdom.[91] The criterion for exemption from immigration control was changed from the holding of a relevant passport under the CIA 1962 to the 'qualifying connection' with the United Kingdom which showed that the holder 'belonged' to the United Kingdom. Without any ancestral links, the Kenyan Asians and other east African Asians, in spite of holding the status of CUKC in addition to UK passports, had to go through immigration control before entering their country of citizenship. Once again, 'citizenships' established by the BNA 1948 were only, as one scholar describes it, given a 'featherweight' value.[92]

The CIA 1968 was criticized categorically by the press as a racist act.[93] *The Times*, for example, described it as 'probably the most shameful measure that the Labour members have ever been asked by their whip to support'.[94] Such accusations, however, took little account of the fact it had always been the case within the British Empire that the nominal and substantive aspects of citizenship could be separated by immigration control. Under the CIA 1962, the same theory was applied to Britain itself, and Commonwealth citizenship lost any weight, whether substantive, such as citizenship rights and privileges, or psychological, such as allegiance. Once the introduction of immigration control for Commonwealth citizens was justified in Britain, the contentious issues came down to defining the targets of immigration control and the method to be used. Once the inflow of Kenyan Asians was more than political leaders considered Britain could absorb, they had to be subject to immigration control. The CIA 1968 could make the Kenyan Asians subject to control, ignoring the fact that they held UK passports.[95] For the government, the issuing of a UK passport did not itself confer any rights on its holders,[96] given that politicians at that time still refused to accept the national type of citizenship.

Through previous experiences with other NCW countries which had enacted citizenship laws of their own, the British government could foresee that the Kenyan conception of citizenship would be formed on the basis of African 'tradition' and a full commitment to the state and government. It also rightly predicted the exodus of Kenyan Asians to Britain. Yet, it could not impose immigration control exclusively on NCW citizens, this time Kenyan Asians, and leave the OCW citizens out of it for fear of harming the unity of the Commonwealth. As a result, the CIA 1968 simply added another condition – 'a close connection to the UK' – to those laid down by the CIA 1962, if a person was to be exempted from immigration control. Furthermore, the core of the problem inside and outside Parliament at that time was the way to prevent the Kenyan Asians from entering Britain. The Wilson government in 1968 did not therefore need to reorganize immigration control as a whole to meet that particular need. The CIA 1968 was established in line with the CIA 1962; the BNA 1948 was kept intact. As a result, while the nominal citizenships of the BNA 1948 continued to be maintained, the criterion for free entry to Britain and subsequently citizenship rights and privileges was further narrowed, to entitle only those with ancestral links with Britain.

The general review of immigration control finally began, within each party and the government, after the line of immigration restriction first established by the CIA 1962 had been pursued to its full extent.

'PATRIALITY': THE BASIS OF BRITISH NATIONAL CITIZENSHIP

The Immigration Act 1971

The Conservatives were returned to power by the 1970 general election, having fought it on a manifesto which pledged to stop large-scale permanent immigration.[97] Although Edward Heath, the then Conservative leader, tried to keep a distance from Powell and his extravagant language such as that of the 'river of blood' speech, the latter's influence on the party policies was obvious.[98] After all, only the Conservatives promised tougher immigration control in their manifesto. The Liberals did not touch on the issue of immigration at all, and the Labour Party had since 1964 adopted a bipartisan policy with regard to immigration control, excluding it from electoral issues,[99] and in its manifesto only referred to its past immigration policy with the words: 'the rate of immigration [was] under firm control and much lower than in past years'.[100] It preferred to focus instead on race relations.

The following year the Heath government introduced the Immigration Bill which later became the Immigration Act 1971 (IA 1971). During its second reading the then Home Secretary, Reginald Maudling, began his speech by stressing the need to 'bring more order into our rather confused legislation' and to 'place control of immigration on a logical basis and ... on a definitive basis'.[101] In order for this to be done, for the first time in British history the control systems for aliens and Commonwealth citizens were consolidated into one statutory form. In addition, the bill created the right of abode, by which it '[defined] people who have a right of abode, who can come and go and stay here as much as they like, totally free of control'.[102] The term 'patrial' was used to describe them, and 'patriality' became the basis of the new system of immigration control, under which 'there will be no further large-scale permanent immigration'.[103]

Under the IA 1971, even citizens of Commonwealth countries were termed 'patrial' if one of their natural or adoptive parents was at the time of their birth or adoption a CUKC by reason of birth in the United Kingdom or in any of its Islands (the Channel Islands and Isle of Man). The group of patrials therefore came to include those Commonwealth citizens whom the two Commonwealth Immigrants acts in the 1960s had prevented from entering Britain. In the case of citizens of Commonwealth countries, however, the ancestral link was limited to only one generation, and moreover, the relevant parent had to be born rather than naturalized or registered or adopted in the United

Kingdom.[104] Nonetheless a substantial number of OCW citizens were, as patrials, removed from the immigration control to which they had been subject since the enactment of the CIA 1962.

In the end, the purpose of the IA 1971 never became clear during parliamentary debates, except that the Conservative government wished to fulfil an election pledge. With several million Commonwealth citizens now being freed from immigration control, its purpose could not be seen as reducing the number of immigrants. For example, James Callaghan, immediately after Maudling's opening speech at the second reading, declared that he would oppose the Immigration Bill because 'the new single system of control is not an improvement on the existing system ... It [the bill] is not about controlling numbers, whatever else it may be said to be about.'[105] During the third reading David Steel summarized the whole debate by saying that 'The saddest conclusion I have reached at the end of our discussion is that, regrettably, this was a thoroughly unnecessary measure .... This Bill does nothing about numbers.'[106] Given that the complicated situation of immigration control should be clarified, those MPs who opposed the bill demanded a new citizenship law, not another immigration law. As a result, the supporters of the creation of British citizenship consisted of a strange coalition between liberal-minded MPs and Enoch Powell. Although their definition of British citizenship differed, they were in agreement on the need for its creation. The former wished to extend citizenship to the east African Asians, while the latter wanted to create an exclusive citizenship on the basis of the ancestral link. More than two decades after the enactment of the BNA 1948, the creation of British citizenship finally became a topic of parliamentary debate.

Britain's understanding on citizenship and the Immigration Act 1971

At this time Britain's application to join the European Communities (EC) was being negotiated. It was finally accepted in 1971, after two previous failures under the Macmillan and Wilson governments. Article 48(1) of the Treaty of Rome which stipulates the right of free movement of workers would thus apply to Britain after 1 January 1973.[107] In terms of immigration and citizenship laws this was significant in two ways. First, Britain would have to accept freedom of movement for 'nationals' of EC member states, when under the IA 1971 virtually all the NCW immigrants had lost it. Second, the government would also have to define who were 'nationals' of the United Kingdom with freedom of movement to other EC member states.

For those of us looking at the debate on the IA 1971 nearly 30 years later, a big puzzle is why the government, once again, let the chance of creating British citizenship slip away.[108] Peter Shore, a prominent Labour MP, pointed out that EC matters were not being addressed, and warned that the bill, even if passed, would soon have to be amended.[109] Only a few MPs, however, linked the two issues – accession to the EC and enactment of the IA 1971 – during debates on the bill. When accession to the EC was debated at Westminster, there was again no debate about creating British citizenship. With regard to the impact on the Commonwealth, policy-makers were mostly concerned with Caribbean sugar and New Zealand dairy produce, not immigration control.[110] Without any parliamentary debate the government unilaterally declared that the term 'nationals' meant

> (a) persons who are citizens of the United Kingdom and Colonies or British subjects not possessing that citizenship or the citizenship of any other Commonwealth country or territory, who, in either case, have the right of abode in the United Kingdom, and are therefore exempt from UK immigration control;
> (b) persons who are citizens of the United Kingdom and Colonies by birth or by registration or naturalization in Gibraltar, or whose father was so born, registered or naturalized.[111]

Although documents on the IA 1971 and on accession to the EC have begun to be made available, at the time of writing it cannot be demonstrated that there was a direct relationship between them. The concern of the politicians in other EC member countries was the possibility of large inflows of colonial and Commonwealth citizens when Britain joined the Common Market. Regardless of the way in which it had been reached, they were prepared to accept Britain's unilateral declaration, so long as the definition of British 'nationals' was exclusive towards Commonwealth citizens outside the United Kingdom.[112] Nonetheless, why did the Heath government not take the opportunity to create British citizenship at the time of the enactment of the IA 1971 or the Treaty of Accession?

One of the recent works on immigration policy after the Second World War argues, on the basis of Conservative Party archival materials, that the Heath government was concerned with the likely hostility of Commonwealth governments incurred by the redefinition of various citizenships under the BNA 1948.[113] Rather than amend the BNA 1948, therefore, the government took the decision to repeal the Aliens Restriction acts and the Commonwealth Immigrants acts and introduce the IA 1971. This might explain the external reasons why the Conservative government did not want to create national citizenship. However, were these enough for Parliament to approve the surrender of one of the most important aspects of sovereignty – the unconditional ability to establish citizenship of its own – which governments after the Second World War had secured? How could Parliament have justified the fact that, unlike other Commonwealth and Common Market members, Britain was the only country that did not have its own citizenship and deprived its citizenship holders by way of immigration control of their citizenship rights?[114]

By that time, the government had acknowledged that the unity of the Commonwealth, and Commonwealth citizenship as its symbol, were not as important as in the immediate aftermath of the Second World War. There were also only a handful of colonies left, thus their complaints over amending the BNA 1948 would not have amounted to as much as ten years previously when the CIA 1962 was enacted. Despite strong mutual attachment between Britain and the OCW countries, the OCW governments could not expect the British government to postpone forever the creation of British citizenship, something they had done for themselves nearly 30 years previously. It was also strange that those MPs who opposed the Immigration Bill in 1971 did not after all push their demand for creating British citizenship, one of the most controversial issues during parliamentary debates being a slight adjustment to the definition of 'patrials'.[115] There must have been other reasons, in addition to external pressure from the Commonwealth countries, for not creating British citizenship.

What is important here, therefore, is the fact that the government in 1971 could still choose not to create British citizenship and to maintain the framework which the CIA 1962 had established: decoupling the nominal and substantive aspects of citizenship. From the government's point of view, there was no need to create British citizenship, both because the concept of national citizenship had not taken root yet and because the existing legislation already excluded those the government wanted to keep out. Furthermore, there was confusion at that time as to what Britishness should be based on, so that it might not have been possible to establish national citizenship with confidence, even if it had been attempted. For successive British governments the ideas of citizenship based on nationhood and of citizenship confined to the territory of the United Kingdom were still new in comparison to the long history of subjecthood based on allegiance.[116] The government did not therefore really acknowledge the importance of national citizenship. It was also apparent in the way in which the definition of British 'nationals' was unilaterally decided on that citizenship was still considered by political leaders to be simply a nominal status – citizenship-as-status – which the government could give and also take away at its discretion. As far as the legal framework was concerned, furthermore, what was important to the British government was to decide who enjoyed the substantive aspects of citizenship: citizenship-as-rights and citizenship-as-desirable-activity. Here the definition of who 'belonged' to Britain had been consolidated through a series of immigration acts since the enactment of the BNA 1948. As long as the government had a firm grip on immigration control, therefore, it could decide to maintain the citizenship statuses which the BNA 1948 had created.

In other words, it had historically been the case in Britain until the end of the Second World War that citizenship-as-status had been granted by the imperial government, either unilaterally or jointly with the Dominion governments, in the form of alternative types of citizenship.[117] The imperial government had also always accepted that the colonial or Dominion governments were entitled to separate the nominal and substantive aspects of citizenship and to control the latter by local immigration laws. As a result, citizenship-as-status had never been perceived by successive governments to denote Britishness as such, citizenship-as-rights and as-desirable-activity being controlled by local immigration laws. With this historical background which persisted without interruption up to 1948, most of the policy-makers and politicians in the 1950s and 1960s did not find it necessary to amend Britain's anomalous situation of not having a citizenship of its own.

As a recently published work demonstrates, furthermore, the Conservatives in the 1960s and the early 1970s did not have the foundations on which Britain's nationhood could be based.[118] Although the Conservatives always predominated in the politics of nationhood prior to the Second World War, they understood Britain's nationhood on the basis of state patriotism, social cohesion, the territorial integrity of the United Kingdom and the Empire, all of which seemed to be losing importance in the eyes of the public after the end of the war. As a result, among Conservative MPs only Enoch Powell expressed clearly defined concepts of Britishness at that time.[119] It is true that, during the debate on the IA 1971, Labour and Liberal MPs argued for the creation of British citizenship, but neither party offered a concrete basis on which it should be formed.[120] The Labour Party, for example, frankly admitted in 1972 that it was 'not adequately equipped to engage in a full examination of all the legal and constitutional aspects' of British citizenship, urging a governmental enquiry.[121] In the end, therefore, even if the government had wished to create British citizenship, it would appear that no one could have offered the basic premise on which it should be established.

After all, as long as the government could accept the presupposition that citizenship did not necessarily take the form of national citizenship, which should possess all the nominal, substantive and functional aspects, it was much more convenient to enact another immigration law within the framework of the CIAs. First, in this way, Commonwealth citizenship and its citizenship structure would remain intact. A special link between Britain and Commonwealth countries was supposed to be embodied in Commonwealth citizenship, and its holders were still given all the citizenship rights and privileges once they entered Britain. For those politicians in Britain who wished to maintain the ties with the Commonwealth, it would be wholly inappropriate to scrap Commonwealth citizenship and establish British citizenship when accession to the EC was being prepared for. Second, entry was strictly controlled by immigration legislation, with only the 'patrials', who predominantly consisted of OCW citizens with European origins, being let in. Consequently, granting Commonwealth citizenship to NCW citizens did not involve any real costs to the British government, while the special attachment between people in Britain and their descendants in the OCW countries was unharmed. Just before the IA 1971 became effective Heath clarified this point when he said that 'it has never been our purpose to erect fresh barriers against people coming to this country from Australia, New Zealand and Canada. Nor is that what our legislation did. We welcome them to our shores not just as friends but as members of our own family.'[122] As a result, the enactment of another immigration law rather than a new nationality law delivered what successive British governments had wanted since the end of the Second World War.

In conclusion, successive British governments in the 1960s narrowed down, through immigration control rather than citizenship laws, the definition of who 'belonged' to the United Kingdom by excluding NCW citizens from the group of citizens who held the substantive aspects of citizenship. By choosing this route, the government could focus on deciding who had a right to enter Britain and how it should implement the necessary controls. The main issue therefore became a technical one. The government searched for the best way in which to include OCW citizens as much as possible within the definition of who belonged to Britain without being seen as 'racist'.

Had a citizenship law been proposed, the debates on the legislation would have been more focused on Britishness and nationhood. However, debates on those matters were theoretically settled as long as the citizenships of the BNA 1948 remained in place. As a result, the traditional understanding of citizenship in an imperial period – a formal membership established on the basis of the Empire and substantive aspects of citizenship dealt with locally – persisted in the 1960s. The definition of who 'belonged' to Britain was consolidated within the domain of immigration control, as had been the case for the local identity of the self-governing and non-self-governing colonies prior to the Second World War. After nearly two decades of the divergence of immigration and citizenship laws in Britain, the gap between those who held the nominal status of citizenship and the substantive aspects of citizenship continued to widen. This way of understanding citizenship thus became a source of constant misunderstanding and social friction both with other countries and within Britain, its disadvantages outweighing the advantages.[123] The need to create British citizenship thus became increasingly urgent after the mid-1970s, and the talk about a new nationality law louder. When British citizenship was finally established in 1981, it was defined in such a way as to correspond with the 'patriality' status set out in the IA 1971.

NOTES

1. PRO, CAB 134/2637. Commonwealth Immigration Committee. 2nd Meeting. 13 February 1968.
2. Parliamentary Debates, House of Commons, vol. 649, col. 695, 16 November 1961.
3. Under the IA 1971, 'patriality' was given only to those people who were free from immigration control. Details of the act are discussed later in this chapter.
4. Parliamentary Debates, House of Commons, vol. 453, col. 410, 7 July 1948.
5. Ibid., col. 411, 7 July 1948.
6. PRO, HO 213/200. Nationality. Proposed Commonwealth Citizenship. British Nationality, Citizenship and Status of Alien Bill. 24 April 1946. This is a Foreign Office draft which was submitted to the Home Office.
7. PRO, HO 213/200. Observations on the Foreign Office Legal Advisers' Draft Scheme for the UK Legislation Necessary to Implement the Proposed New Commonwealth Citizenship System. 1 May 1946.
8. PRO, HO 213/200. 3rd Inter-Departmental Meetings. 17 May 1946.
9. Ibid.
10. Ibid. Proposals for Change in the Law.
11. PRO, HO 213/202. Treatment of Colonies under Proposed Scheme. Changes in British Nationality Law. The Question of UK and Colonial Citizenship Prepared by the Foreign Office. 5 July 1946.
12. Ibid. Note of 5th Inter-Departmental Meeting. 10 July 1946.
13. PRO, DO 35/1159/P201/19. Draft Scheme of the British Nationality. Citizenship

and Status of Aliens Bill. Meetings of Experts. Changes in British Nationality Law – Part III, the Question of UK and Colonial Citizenship. 13 July 1946.

14. Ibid. Note of the 6th Meeting. 15 July 1946.
15. The conclusion reached at the working party became the basis for the scheme proposed by the UK representatives at the 1947 conference of experts. PRO, CAB 133/6. British Commonwealth Conference on Nationality and Citizenship. British Nationality, Citizenship of the UK and Colonies and Status of Alien. January 1947.
16. PRO, CAB 130/13. GENs. 141 – 154. Committee on British Nationality. 1st Meeting.
17. Parliamentary Debates, House of Lords, vol. 155, col. 787, 11 May 1948.
18. See Ch. 4 for details of the BNA 1948.
19. PRO, HO 213/2331. Letter from J. Chadwick (Commonwealth Relations Office) to J. M. Ross (Home Office). 23 March 1961.
20. For example, see PRO, CAB 129/107. Part I. Cabinet. Commonwealth Immigrants Bill: Application to the Irish Republic. Memorandum by the Secretary of State for the Home Department. 8 November 1961.
21. PRO, CAB 129/84. Colonial Immigrants. Supplementary Report of the Committee of Ministers. 14 November 1956.
22. Although BPP were not defined as aliens, they were not granted the status of Commonwealth citizenship, and were thus subject to immigration control. BNA 1948, s. 32(1). See Appendix III.
23. PRO, HO 213/2331. Working Party to Report on the Social and Economic Problems Arising from the Joint Influx into the UK of Coloured Workers from Other Commonwealth Countries. Citizenship in Relation to the Commonwealth Immigrants Bill. 8 March 1961.
24. Ibid.
25. For details of the CIA 1962 see Ch. 4.
26. PRO, LAB 8/2704. Working Party to Report on the Social and Economic Problem Arising from the Growing Influx into the UK of Coloured Workers from Other Commonwealth Countries. Report to Ministerial Committee. Appendix C. 25 July 1961.
27. PRO, CAB 134/1469. Commonwealth Migrants Committee. 2nd Meeting. 17 May 1961.
28. The Colonial Office was finally merged with the Commonwealth Relations Office in 1966.
29. PRO, HO 344/14. Working Party on Coloured Immigrants, Ministerial Committee etc. 10 July 1961.
30. At one of the meetings a working party argued that 'the mere fact that a person is free to enter and reside in a country does not make him a citizen of that country'. See PRO, HO 344/14. Working Party on Coloured Immigrants. 10 July 1961.
31. Ibid.
32. In the face of these two changes, Gordon Walker compares Commonwealth citizens with British subjects, and explains that 'the recasting of the concept of citizenship was wholly in accord with the idea of a Commonwealth of equal nations. No relic was left in it of the doctrine of "common allegiance".' Patrick Gordon Walker, *The Commonwealth* (Secker & Warburg, London, 1962), p. 168.
33. Acquisition of the status of British subjecthood became increasingly extended towards British descendants abroad by means of inheritance after the enactment of the BN & SA act 1918. See Ch. 3.
34. Those studies which deal with immigration and nationality laws in Britain prior to the Second World War, such as that by Clive Parry, pay attention to the differences between the common status before and after the Second World War. Yet they remain silent about the different grounds on which British subjecthood

was granted to people in the colonies on the one hand, and those in the Dominions and Britain on the other. Parry, *Nationality and Citizenship Laws*, Ch. 3.

35. For details of post-Second World War immigration in general and the CIA 1962 in particular see Ch. 4.

36. As is explained in detail in the previous chapter, the CIA 1962 was enacted in the face of 'the existence of large unassimilated coloured communities' and introduced the voucher system which would in practice 'interfere to the minimum extent with the entry of persons from the Old Commonwealth'. PRO, CAB 129/107. Commonwealth Migrants. Memorandum by the Secretary of State for the Home Department. 6 October 1961. LAB8/2704. Curtailment of Immigration by Employment Control. Note by the Ministry of Labour. 28 April 1961.

37. Foot describes the way in which Powell became involved with the issue of immigration and citizenship, especially after the mid-1950s. Paul Foot, *The Rise of Enoch Powell: An Examination of Enoch Powell's Attitude to Immigration and Race* (Penguin, Harmondsworth), pp. 53–4.

38. It has not been stressed as much as it should by other scholars that Powell took a step further than other anti-immigration MPs and sought to reconstruct Britishness. One of the few references on this point is made by Miles, who, in defining the concept of racism, points out that the controversial speeches by Enoch Powell are 'as much, if not more, nationalist than racist'. Robert Miles, *Racism* (Routledge, London, 1995 [1989]), pp. 119–20.

39. Parliamentary Debates, House of Commons, vol. 813, col. 76, 8 March 1971.

40. His anti-immigration speeches, including that made in Birmingham on 20 April 1968, were fully cited and analysed. See Bill Smithies and Peter Fiddick, *Enoch Powell on Immigration* (Sphere, London, 1969).

41. PRO, HO 213/2331. Commonwealth Migrants Committee. 14 April 1961.

42. Although politicians were careful not to make an explicit comment in Parliament, they were more open about their racially discriminatory attitudes outside Parliament. For example, Cyril Osborne, one of the stoutest anti-immigration MPs, once famously said: 'Britain is a white man's country and [I] want it to remain so.' *Daily Mail*, 7 February 1961. As was clear in his comment, Osborne's goal was not to define 'Britishness' and create national citizenship on its basis, but to prevent non-white immigrants from entering Britain.

43. In 1966, the system of working holidays changed. Any Commonwealth citizens who intended to come to Britain for an extended working holiday, unlike under the previous system, had to prove to an immigration officer that (i) their intention was to return home; and (ii) they could support themselves even if they failed to find a job. Sheila Patterson, *Immigration and Race Relations in Britain 1960–1967* (Oxford University Press, London, 1969, pp. 65–7. See also PRO, CAB 134/2637. Commonwealth Immigration Committee. 4th Meeting, 24 November 1966.

44. See, for example, PRO, CAB 134/2637. Commonwealth Immigration Committee. Australians and the Immigration Control. Memorandum by the Secretary of State for the Home Department. 29 March 1967; CAB 134/2460. Official Committee on Commonwealth Immigration. The Special Considerations Applying to Canada, Australia and New Zealand. Memorandum by the Commonwealth Office. 20 July 1967, and 2nd Meeting, 3 August 1967.

45. PRO, CAB 134/2460. The Special Considerations Applying to Canada, Australia and New Zealand. 20 July 1967.

46. J. D. B. Miller argues that while disillusionment over the Commonwealth developed in the 1960s mainly due to 'dissatisfaction with economic and military policies', emotional attachments still remained strong. He points to 1961 and South Africa's subsequent withdrawal from the Commonwealth as a starting

point of the decline of many Conservatives' faith in the Commonwealth, and accession to the EC as a further blow. J. D. B. Miller, *Survey of Commonwealth Affairs: Problem of Expansion and Attrition 1953–69* (Oxford University Press, London, 1974), Ch. 15. A White Paper published by the Conservative government in 1971 also made it clear that the Commonwealth did not 'offer us [Britain], or indeed wish to offer us alternative and comparable opportunities to membership of the European Community'. *The United Kingdom and the European Communities*. Cmnd. 4715, July 1971.

47. The issue of 'who is British' finally became the central topic in the 1970s, especially because of an upsurge of nationalist sentiment in Scotland and Wales. Scottish and Welsh nationalism aside, there were a number of nationalistic movements in western Europe in the 1970s. See, for example, Milton J. Esman (ed.), *Ethnic Conflict in the Western World* (Cornell University Press, Ithaca, 1977); Rokkan Stein, and Derek Urwin (eds), *The Politics of Territorial Identity: Studies in European Regions* (Sage, London, 1982).

48. PRO, CAB 134/1468. Commonwealth Immigration Committee. Minutes of a Meeting of the Committee. Rate of Issue of Vouchers. 6 November 1963.

49. Ibid.

50. Ibid. The committee singled out two defects of the voucher system. First, it proved impossible to tell the total number of arriving immigrants solely by reviewing the number of vouchers issued. Second, two types of immigrants – dependants and students – were subject to no control and contributed to the increase in numbers.

51. In 1965 the Wilson government sent a mission headed by Lord Mountbatten of Burma to several Commonwealth countries to discuss with their governments what they could do to regulate the flow of immigrants to Britain. A minute by Lord Mountbatten suggested that Commonwealth citizens should be treated more favourably than aliens, lest Commonwealth relations should be damaged permanently. However, his report had little influence on future immigration policies, and immigration restrictions on Commonwealth citizens continued. PRO, PREM 13/1572. Copy of a minute from Lord Mountbatten of Burma to the Prime Minister. 13 June 1965.

52. The White Paper introduced two changes in the methods of immigration control under the 1962 act. First, 'C' vouchers (vouchers issued on a first-come-first-served basis), whose number had become smaller by then, were to be discontinued. Second, definitions of 'dependants' and 'students' were tightened in response to recommendations made by the White Paper. After the publication of the 1965 White Paper, for example, entry of dependants over the age of 16 was strictly limited even to join parents already settled in Britain. *Immigration from the Commonwealth*, Cmnd. 2739, HMSO, 1965. For the details of recommendations of the 1965 White Paper, see, for example, Patterson, *Race Relations*, pp. 42–5, 48–52.

53. Under the CIA 1962, 'UK passport' means 'a passport issued to the holder by the Government of the United Kingdom, *not being a passport so issued on behalf of the Government of any part of the Commonwealth outside the United Kingdom'* (emphasis added).

54. PRO, DO 175/92. Immigration of Asians from East Africa. A letter to Commonwealth Relations Office from Home Office. East Africa here includes Uganda, Tanganyika and Kenya.

55. Marshall talks of 'common culture' as a 'common possession and heritage' of citizens. T. H. Marshall, *Class, Citizenship and Social Development* (Anchor, New York, 1965), pp. 101–2.

56. As an imperial type of citizenship, British subjecthood does not require national membership from the holders.

57. R. Emerson, *From Empire to Nation* (Harvard University Press, Cambridge, MA, 1967). For the case of introduction of Indian labourers in east Africa, see, for example, J. S. Mangat, *A History of the Asians in East Africa, 1886 to 1945*, Clarendon Press, Oxford, 1969), esp. Chs 1 and 2.

58. For Britain's withdrawal from Africa between the late 1950s and the mid-1960s, see Darwin, *Britain and Decolonization*, pp. 244–78. For the case of Kenya, see Keith Kyle, *The Politics of the Independence of Kenya* (Macmillan, London, 1999).

59. Rothchild argues that Kenyan society had a three-tiered racial structure. Donald Rothchild, 'Citizenship and National Integration: The Non-African Crisis in Kenya', *Studies in Race and Nations* (Center of International Race Relations, Graduate School of International Studies, University of Denver), 1, 3 (1969–70), p. 8. Maxon points out that, in addition to three racial communities – African, European and Asian – there also existed the sizeable Arab population. Furthermore, he argued that each community was far from unified and homogeneous but was divided by, for example, economic class, religion, tribe and language. Robert M. Maxon, 'Social and Cultural Changes', in B. A. Ogot and W. R. Ochieng (eds), *Decolonization and Independence in Kenya 1940–93* (James Currey, London, 1995), pp. 110–22.

60. Donald Rothchild, *Racial Bargaining in Independent Kenya: A Study of Minorities and Decolonization* (Oxford University Press, London, 1973), p. 317.

61. In 1962, Europeans comprised 0.7 per cent of the Kenya's total population and Asians 2 per cent. Rothchild, *Racial Bargaining*, p. 31.

62. The deportation of a Kenyan Asian and a European was discussed in Parliament. During the debate a statement made in Nairobi by Daniel Arap Moi, then Kenya's Vice-President, was quoted to explain that the cause of deportation was an insult and disrespect to the African people and the Kenyan government. Parliamentary Debates, House of Commons, vol. 751, col. 1184, 28 July 1967.

63. For example, the Universal Declaration of Human Rights, article 21(3), which declares that 'The will of the people shall be the basis of the authority of government.'

64. Declaration on the Granting of Independence to Colonial Countries and Peoples, 1960. It was adopted by the UN General Assembly in Resolution 1514 (XV) with nine abstentions, one being that of the United Kingdom.

65. PRO, DO 168/47. Official Brief for the Kenya Constitutional Conference. Draft Brief No. 9. Citizenship.

66. PRO, DO 168/48. EGA 27/42/4. Kenya Independence Conference. 14 November 1963. According to Section 1 of the Constitution of Kenya, citizenship was automatically granted to those born in Kenya to at least one parent born there.

67. The Constitution of Kenya, Section 2(5). At the time of independence, most of the inhabitants of Kenya were either CUKC or BPP.

68. Cited by Rothchild, *Racial Bargaining*, p. 187.

69. Dummett and Nicol, *Subjects, Citizens, Aliens and Others*, p. 198.

70. British Nationality Act 1964, section 1(1)(a) and (b).

71. Rothchild, *Racial Bargaining*, p. 327.

72. PRO, DO 175/92. Immigration of Asians from East Africa. Inward Telegram to the Commonwealth Relations Office. No. 211. 28 October 1963. According to the memoir of James Callaghan, Home Secretary in 1968, however, the Indian government later seemed to have changed its attitude with regard to Kenyan Asians of Indian origin, and Prime Minister Indira Gandhi secretly promised that India would accept them if they were deported by the Kenyan government. James Callaghan, *Time and Change* (Collins, London, 1987), p. 265.

73. This book emphasizes here again that it was the Commonwealth citizenship

structure established by the BNA 1948, and the unity of the Commonwealth which it was supposed to represent, that successive British governments acknowledged and tried to maintain. 'Citizenships' and 'citizenship' statuses under the BNA 1948 were, for them, not meant to grant citizenship rights and privileges or assume obligation to the holders, as is the case with national citizenship.

74. PRO, DO 168/48. EGA 27/32/3. Kenya Independence Conference. 14 November 1963.
75. For example, see PRO, DO 175/92. Immigration of Asians from East Africa. Letter from the Home Office to the Commonwealth Relations Office. 15 October 1963. Letter from the Foreign Office to the Home Office, 22 October 1963. CIA Renewal Brief. No. 32. Asians in Kenya. 1963.
76. Universal Declaration of Human Rights, article 13(2).
77. PRO, CAB 134/2639. Official Committee on Commonwealth Immigration. Cabinet. Commonwealth Immigration (Official) Committee. Immigration into the UK of CUKC Having No Close Connection with the UK. Memorandum by the FO. 12 May 1966.
78. Rothchild, *Racial Bargaining*, p. 188.
79. This statement by Fitzval de Souza is cited in Rothchild, *Racial Bargaining*, pp. 188–9.
80. The term 'Africanization' was used in several different senses. Africanization, for some, implied a pan-African sense, while for others, it emphasized the employment of Kenya Africans in preference to all others. In the most common usage, however, it meant 'the process of replacing non-Africans by Africans'. Rothchild, *Racial Bargaining*, pp. 226–31.
81. The first signs of immigration by Kenyan Asians were discerned at the beginning of 1965. Since they were exempt from immigration control, the exact annual rate was hard to establish and only speculated to be around 5,000. At the turn of 1967, however, the numbers grew dramatically and reached around 13,600. PRO, CAB 129/121/93. Immigration of Asians from East Africa. Memorandum by the Secretary of State for the Home Department. 6 July 1965; and CAB 134/2637. Commonwealth Immigration Committee. Asian Immigration from East Africa. Memorandum by the Secretary of State for the Home Department. 8 February 1968.
82. The exact number of Kenyan Asians who had an absolute right to enter Britain was never known. Foot, for example, estimates about half the number claimed by Powell. Foot, *Rise of Enoch Powell*, p. 110. For the published extract of a speech, see Smithies and Fiddick, *Enoch Powell*, pp. 19–22. Callaghan, the then Home Secretary, said at one of the Commonwealth immigration committee meetings that there were about 270,000 people in the whole of east Africa who had the right to come to Britain. PRO, CAB 134/2637. Commonwealth Immigration Committee. 2nd Meeting. 13 February 1968.
83. PRO, CAB 134/2637. Commonwealth Immigration Committee. 2nd Meeting. 13 February 1968.
84. He also suggested that the new immigration act should be pressed ahead along with the new race relations act in order to balance the restrictions against an assurance of equal treatment once immigrants were let in.
85. PRO, CAB 134/2637. Commonwealth Immigration Committee. 2nd Meeting. 13 February 1968.
86. Harold Wilson, *The Labour Government, 1964–1970: A Personal Record* (Weidenfeld & Nicolson, London, 1971), pp. 502–3.
87. Parliamentary Debates, House of Commons, vol. 811, col. 1288, 27 February 1968.

88. Iain Macleod and 12 other Tories as well as the Liberals opposed the bill. Rose, *Colour and Citizenship*, p. 612.
89. There was argument at that time, especially between Duncan Sandys (the Commonwealth and Colonial Secretary at the time of independence in Kenya) and Iain Macleod (the Chancellor of the Duchy of Lancaster), as to whether the Conservative government in 1963 had actually agreed that it would receive Kenyan Asians if they were forced to leave Kenya. A number of official documents which are now open show that the Macmillan government and its successor, the Wilson government, had unwillingly conceded that it would have to accept immigration of Kenyan Asians, as they held no citizenship other than CUKC. For details of debates between Sandys and Macleod, see Hansen, *Citizenship and Immigration in Post-War Britain*, pp. 169–76.
90. PRO, CO 537/1910. Draft Cabinet Paper. Question of Nationality in relation to the Proposed Treaty with India providing for Matters Arising out of the Transfer of Power. Memorandum by the Secretary of State for India and Burma.
91. The CIA 1968 accepted that the right of entry into Britain should be derived from a female parent or grandparent, too.
92. Dummett, and Nicol, *Subjects, Citizens, Aliens and Others*, p. 188.
93. Callaghan seemed to try to avoid the criticism of the 1968 Commonwealth Immigration Bill as racially discriminatory by asking Parliament to consider it alongside the proposed race relations bill, soon to be introduced. He claimed that these bills together were 'parts of a fair and balanced policy on this matter of race relations'. The Race Relations Act 1968, the second of its kind, was passed seven months after the CIA 1968 but did not ease the criticism of the CIA 1968. Parliamentary Debates, House of Commons, vol. 759, col. 1242, 27 February 1968.
94. *The Times*, 27 February 1968.
95. In Britain it is officially the case that no citizen has a legal right to a passport. A House of Lords official report in 1955 made it clear that 'the grant of UK passports is a Royal prerogative exercised through Her Majesty's Ministers and in particular the Foreign Secretary … in theory the Foreign Secretary has the power to withhold or withdraw a passport at this discretion'. PRO, DO 176/2. Law and Practice regarding the UK Passport. Extract from House of Lords Official Report. 1 November 1955. For more details on the practice of issuing passports in the United Kingdom see Justice, *Going Abroad: A Report on Passports* (Barry Rose, London, 1974). Vincenzi also examines the practice of issuing passports in relation to a Royal prerogative. Christopher Vincenzi, *Crown Powers, Subjects and Citizens* (Pinter, London, 1998), pp. 94–5.
96. Even in as late as 1972, the government claimed that 'a United Kingdom passport does not in itself confer a citizenship or other status on the holder. It recognizes the status which he already has and is accepted internationally for travel purposes.' Parliamentary Debates, House of Commons, vol. 843, col. 172 (Written Answer), 23 October 1972.
97. F. W. S. Craig (ed.), *British General Election Manifestos 1900–1974* (Macmillan, London, 1975), pp. 329, 339.
98. Powell made his infamous 'river of blood' speech at the Midland Hotel, Birmingham, on 20 April 1968, two days before the second Race Relations Bill was introduced. He was then sacked from the Shadow Cabinet. For the entire speech see Smithies and Fiddick, *Enoch Powell*, pp. 35–43. Some give the 'Powell effect' as the biggest reason for the Conservative victory in the 1970 election. See, for example, *The Times*, 6 September 1972; D. T. Studlar, ' Policy Voting in Britain: The Coloured Immigration Issue in the 1964, 1966 and 1970 General Elections', *American Political Science Review*, 72 (1978), pp. 46–72.

99. Despite its strong opposition to the CIA 1962, the Labour Party, which had taken office in 1964, also switched its policy in favour of immigration control. The two main parties were thus agreed on promoting immigration control over NCW immigrants in the second half of the 1960s. Although there was no written agreement between the two parties, a bipartisan consensus emerged under the Wilson government on the control of NCW immigration. See, for example, Zig Layton-Henry, *The Politics of Immigration: Immigration, 'Race' and 'Race' Relations in Post-War Britain* (Blackwell, Oxford, 1992), Ch. 4; Paul Foot, *Immigration and Race in British Politics* (Penguin, Harmondsworth, 1965), Ch. 8.

100. Craig, *Manifestos*, p. 362.

101. Parliamentary Debates, House of Commons, vol. 813, cols 42–43, 8 March 1971.

102. Ibid., col. 45.

103. Ibid., col. 56.

104. IA 1971, s. 2(1)(d). In the case of CUKCs, the ancestral link was extended to two generations, and the parent or grandparent could be born, adopted, registered or naturalized in the United Kingdom. In the original bill, Commonwealth citizens with a grandparent who had been born in the United Kingdom were also classified as patrials, but during the committee stage this clause was amended to apply only to those with a United Kingdom-born parent. However, its effect was reinstated in the immigration rules of 1973. *Statement of Immigration Rules for Control on Entry: Commonwealth Citizens*, HC. 79, January 1973, para. 27. For details of the process of establishing the IA 1971 and the immigration rules of 1973, see Hannan Rose, 'The Immigration Act 1971: A Case Study in the Work of Parliament', *Parliamentary Affairs*, 26 (1973), pp. 69–91; Philip Norton, 'Intra-Party Dissent in the House of Commons: A Case Study. The Immigration Rules 1972', *Parliamentary Affairs*, 29 (1976), pp. 404–20.

105. Parliamentary Debates, House of Commons, vol. 813, cols 58–9, 8 March 1971.

106. Ibid., vol. 819, col. 757, 17 June 1971.

107. There was no definition of 'workers' in the Treaty of Rome. But in accordance with administrative and judicial practice, it was understood that the term 'workers' referred to nationals of one of the member states, excluding non-citizens.

108. To the surprise of one researcher, the Heath government's Immigration Bill of 1971 'ignored the EC completely' and the immigration rules issued under it were 'phrased as though the Community had nothing to do with control over immigration into the United Kingdom'. Dummett and Nicol, *Subject, Citizens, Aliens and Others*, p. 215.

109. Parliamentary Debates, House of Commons, vol. 813, col. 108, 8 March 1971.

110. Stephen George, *An Awkward Partner: Britain in the European Community* (Oxford University Press, Oxford, 1998 [1990]), pp. 50–2. A recently opened document showed that the two subjects of discussion raised by Commonwealth representatives were with regard to agricultural goods, that is, pigmeat, liquid milk and eggs, and, additionally, the Common External Tariff. PRO, FCO 30/780. Consultation with the Commonwealth about Entry of the UK into the EEC. Enlargement Negotiations: Meeting of Deputies. Commonwealth Briefing. 16 September 1970.

111. *Treaty concerning the Accession of the Kingdom of Denmark, Ireland, the Kingdom of Norway and the United Kingdom of Great Britain and Northern Ireland to the EEC and the European Atomic Energy Community (with Final Act) Decision of the Council of the European Communities Concerning the Accession of the Said States to the European Coal and Steel Community*, Cmnd. 4862-I, HMSO, 22 January 1972.

112. W. R. Böhning, *The Migration of Workers in the United Kingdom and the European Community* (Oxford University Press, London, 1972), p. 132.

113. Hansen, *Citizenship and Immigration in Post-War Britain*, p. 193. See also CPA, CRD 3/16/4, 'Integration of the Law Relating to Aliens and Commonwealth Immigrants', undated.

114. It is true that debate on the creation of British citizenship had been under way among policy-makers behind the scenes. For example, the then Home Secretary, Robert Carr, admitted in the House of Commons in 1972 that the government had been reviewing the BNA 1948. Parliamentary Debates, House of Commons, vol. 847, cols 1660–1, 7 December 1972. This study stresses that it took another ten years, however, for the BNA 1948 to be abolished, in 1981.

115. There were a large number of amendments, in addition to the definition of 'patriality', which were introduced into the bill at committee stage and also in the House of Lords. They included one which confirmed that Commonwealth immigrants would have the right to bring in their wives and children. The government also dropped the provision that non-patrial Commonwealth citizens would have to register with the police.

116. As is discussed further in the Epilogue, a meticulous study on citizenship found that even today the historical conception of subjecthood based on allegiance remains influential in the understanding of British citizenship law. Gardner, *White Paper*, pp. 184–5.

117. For the characteristics of alternative types of citizenship see Appendix II.

118. Philip Lynch, *The Politics of Nationhood: Sovereignty, Britishness and Conservative Politics* (Macmillan, London, 1999).

119. Dummett and Nicol, *Subjects, Citizens, Aliens and Others*, pp. 224–7.

120. Detailed studies on the creation of British national citizenship really began in the 1970s. One of the earliest works was by the Labour Party. LPA, *Citizenship, Immigration and Integration: A Policy for the Seventies*, 1972.

121. Ibid., p. 32.

122. This speech, made by Heath on 30 November 1972, is cited in CPA, ACP 73/78. The Control of Immigration.

123. In 1975 the referendum on membership of the EC demonstrated substantial support among the public. By then, the preparation for the creation of British citizenship had been well under way in both the Conservative and the Labour parties. For example, the study group on race relations and immigration which was established within the Conservative Parliamentary Home Affairs Committee issued a report in 1976, in which it acknowledged the entry to the EC as a watershed. It continued: 'Now it is the time to end constitutional anomalies which are no longer justified by reality. The concept of a citizenship common to the whole Commonwealth has become a serious disadvantage for Britain, promoting misunderstanding and social friction. It should be ended.' CPA. CRD 3/16/3. Immigration (General). Report of the Study Group on Race Relations and Immigration, June 1976.

Epilogue:
An Appraisal of the
British Nationality Act 1981

THE BRITISH Nationality Act (BNA) 1981 finally established 'British citizenship' in the statute book. In general, scholars of migration commented that the BNA 1981 represented a thorough 'overhaul',[1] needed since the Second World War, of British immigration and citizenship policies. However, the way in which the BNA 1981 is interpreted differs greatly from scholar to scholar. The majority of the previous works on the BNA 1981 have criticized it as the logical result of the racist policies followed since the Second World War.[2] However, a recently published book has challenged those criticisms as unjust and even absurd, and instead has credited the act with being a 'massive effort at rationalization and clarification' of British citizenship on the basis of the territorial unit of the United Kindom.[3]

Since the Public Record Office documents on the BNA 1981 have not yet been made available, it is not possible to provide an authoritative account of its enactment. This epilogue will therefore examine the citizenship plans submitted by Conservative and Labour parties in the 1970s. In so doing, it concentrates on the three aspects of citizenship explained in Chapter 1,[4] and clarifies what kind of citizenship the BNA 1981 really established with regard to them.

THE BRITISH NATIONALITY ACT 1981

The creation of British citizenship came to receive serious attention from all the major political parties during the 1970s. The Labour Party, moving earlier than the Conservative Party, included in its 1970 general election manifesto a proposal to review the citizenship law. Two years later, as is pointed out in Chapter 5, the study group on immigration set up by its national executive committee had published a Green Paper. In admitting a lack of preparation, it nonetheless called for a new UK citizenship with 'a positive content, with specified rights and obligations'.[5] The Conservative Party also mentioned in its 1974 general election manifesto that it had set in motion a review of British nationality law and might table the relevant motion in the next Parliament.[6] By the mid-1970s, therefore, there was no longer any disagreement in principle among politicians in the two major parties that British citizenship should be created in Britain. What remained unclear was what kind of citizenship both parties wanted.

In introducing the bill which became the BNA 1981, the Home Secretary, William Whitelaw, pointed out during the second reading that 'the citizenship created by the British Nationality Act 1948 no longer gives any clear indication of who has the right to enter the United Kingdom'.[7] He maintained that citizenship and the right of abode had been parted over the years and that the main reason for the enactment of the new nationality law was to relate each to the other. The BNA 1981 thus finally merged the holding of British citizenship and the right of abode by conferring British citizenship exclusively on patrial CUKCs.

Nonetheless, even after the BNA 1981, there are six citizenship statuses, namely British citizenship, British Dependent Territories citizenship (BDTC), British Overseas citizenship (BOC), British subject (BS), British National (Overseas) (BN(O)), and BPP.[8] According to the intentions underlying the BNA 1981, however, five statuses – all except British citizenship – will eventually disappear, either by natural loss of the status in the case of BDTC and BOC or by acquisition of citizenship of any other country in the case of BS and BPP.[9] Since patrial Commonwealth citizens are only allowed to keep their right of abode for their lifetime (s. 39(2)), British citizenship will slowly but eventually become the sole basis of immigration control.

Major controversy erupted during the parliamentary debate over the abandonment of *jus soli*. Under the rule of acquisition by birth, the BNA 1981 confers British citizenship on those born in the United Kingdom only if either parent is: (a) a British citizen; or (b) is 'settled' in the United Kingdom (s. 1). 'Settled' is defined as 'being ordinarily resident in the United Kingdom without being subject under the immigration laws to any restriction on the period for which he may remain'(s. 50). In this way, the new act no longer allowed those who should not have been residing in the United Kingdom – illegal entrants and overstayers – or those who were only temporary residents – short-term visitors and students – to secure British citizenship for their children born in the United Kindom.[10] The government claimed that, provided that the traditional *jus soli*, which had originated from the notion of allegiance to the sovereign of the territory of one's birth, continued, 'British Citizens so created ... would form a pool of considerable size, and they would have little or no real connection with the United Kingdom.'[11] By adding the principle of *jus sanguinis*, therefore, the act was supposed to link British citizenship with having a 'close connection' with the United Kindom.[12] In the end, at the time of enactment, approximately 60–80 million persons, mostly in the United Kingdom, acquired the status of British citizenship.[13]

In contrast to the procedures for determining the legal status of British citizenship, the substantive aspects of citizenship – its entitlements and obligations – were of little concern to either party. According to its three election manifestos brought out during the 1970s, Labour's official position was that immigration policies, especially since the enactment of the IA 1971, had been based on 'colour', and that a new British citizenship was needed to provide a rational and non-racial basis for immigration control. From Labour's point of view, winning the support of Afro-Caribbean and south Asian voters was the crucial issue at that time. The significance of those voters had begun to be apparent to all the major political parties in the 1970s, and their steady support for Labour could not be taken for granted.[14] The party's main interests therefore lay in the removal of the racial aspects of immigration control, not in the creation of national citizenship itself.[15]

However, in its 1972 paper Labour asserted that it was 'of the utmost importance' that the new British citizenship should have full civil and political rights, including the right to free movement in and out of the United Kingdom without immigration control.[16] Yet, as a number of scholars have pointed out, Labour's policies on immigration during the period under discussion were often incoherent, and those it held while in government and in opposition tended to be contradictory.[17] The party's position with regard to the substantive aspects of British citizenship also fluctuated from time to time. In contrast to the 1972 paper, published while the party was in opposition, the Green Paper published in 1977, when Labour was in office, expressed no enthusiasm for the full incorporation of citizenship rights into the status of British citizenship. Instead, it used the term 'privilege' rather than 'right', and claimed that civic privileges 'do not stem directly from the law of nationality and so are not dealt with in this document'.[18] During the parliamentary debates on the British Nationality Bill Whitelaw cited this passage from Labour's 1977 paper, using it to justify the Conservative government's omission from the bill of substantive aspects of British citizenship.[19]

The Conservative Party, in contrast, was rather more consistent about separating citizenship status and citizenship rights. After its election losses in 1974, however, its policies on citizenship were lost for a short while in the search for a fine balance between two of its election pledges: stricter measures against future immigration from the NCW and the promotion of good race relations in Britain.[20] For its first two years in opposition, the party was weighing up so-called 'immigrant voters', trying to soften the public impression it had given of being tough on immigration and race relations.[21] However, by 1976 its restrictive polices on both issues were on the verge of being revived. Clearly, Margaret Thatcher, who had become party leader in 1975, was not as sympathetic towards ethnic communities as had been her predecessor, Edward Heath.[22] For her, the emphasis should be on individual self-help and not on the recognition and protection of the rights of ethnic communities by legislation. She was not the only one reluctant to accept the Race Relations Bill in 1976 until the last minute; a substantial number of Conservative MPs were against the bill and some of them even voted against it on the third reading.[23] Moreover, the popularity of the far-right National Front was at its peak around that time, gaining the support of those Conservative supporters who wanted a firmer stand on immigration control and who were sceptical about the way in which race relations were being dealt with.

To Thatcher, therefore, the policy on race and immigration obviously needed readjustment. The party statement, 'The Right Approach', which was published just before the enactment of the 1976 Race Relations Act, clarified what was to be the party's position under her leadership, putting a priority on an immediate reduction in immigration as the pre-condition for racial harmony.[24] Accordingly, also in 1976, a paper prepared by the Conservatives' study group on race relations and immigration publicly renounced Commonwealth citizenship, claiming that citizenship at that time needed to go with the right of entry.[25] It then recommended that a new British citizenship should be 'defined along the lines of the existing concept of patriality', and that the right of entry and abode be restricted exclusively to the holders of this new citizenship status.[26] Her famous Granada television interview in 1978[27] confirmed the Conservatives' attitude towards immigration, and in consequence, the new nationality act. Referring in the interview to British fear of being 'rather swamped by people with a different culture', Thatcher made it clear to the electorate once again that her party should, and was ready to, have a tight grip on NCW immigration.[28] In the search for a means of immigration control which would not be seen as racially discriminatory, therefore, the right of entry and abode was linked to the status of British citizenship. Since favourable treatment of the holders of citizenship by their own government was by then justifiable, the new British citizenship, equivalent to patriality, would absolve the government of accusations of operating racist immigration controls. In the end, the BNA 1981 would continue the same immigration practices as the IA 1971 but under a different name. Citizenship rights, except the right of entry and abode, were not an issue at all.

AN UNANSWERED QUESTION

During the second reading of the British Nationality Bill in 1981, Whitelaw condemned the opposition's criticism of the government's silence over citizenship rights as 'unfair', claiming that the government was only doing what had always been done in Britain.[29] Vincenzi, in his work on prerogative powers, explains that the negative aspects of subjecthood continue today, and that citizenship rights, apart from those of entry and abode, are identified only by legislation which excludes specific rights from non-citizens.[30] As is described above, therefore, the BNA 1981 simply followed the precedents in not defining the substantive aspects of citizenship on the statute book. How did the BNA 1981 conclude the third aspect of citizenship, citizenship-as-social-enclosure?

The 1972 and 1977 Labour Party papers on immigration and race relations both recommended the creation of British citizenship, but did not provide a consistent statement defining Britishness. The 1972 paper intended to include people in the remaining colonies as the holders of British citizenship and extend to them citizenship rights including the right of free entry and abode. The 1977 paper, on the other hand, dropped the idea of extending British citizenship to colonial people, and instead emphasized that British citizenship was linked with 'those who belong to this country [the United Kingdom]'.[31] During the parliamentary debate on the 1981 bill, the Shadow Home Secretary, Roy Hattersley, demanded 'a positive statement of nationality based on objectively defined principles', yet the only principle he came up with was that of being 'clean of all racial considerations'.[32] In the end, the Conservative government claimed that its bill took over the basic principles of Labour's 1977 Green Paper.[33] Despite the vigorous attack by Hattersley, therefore, Labour's opposition to the bill lacked credibility. Furthermore, although the bill had already been through its committee stage, the Labour Party conference in 1981 was unable to come up with an alternative basis for British citizenship. It thus accused the 1981 bill of being 'deliberately ambiguous in its definition of citizenship', but could only decide to bring forward to the next year's conference a proposal which would form 'the basis for a future White Paper on the issue of nationality and lead to the scrapping of the Tory Nationality Bill'.[34] Although the 1983 election manifesto proposed to repeal the IA 1971 and review the BNA 1981, the contents of the new legislation suggested by the Labour were quite similar to the existing ones.[35]

As is discussed in Chapter 5, the Conservatives were also struggling to find new foundations for Britishness after the Second World War. Some party members insisted that Britishness should be defined by the homogeneity and unity of the people and their shared historical experiences, but the majority remained unclear about what Britishness consisted of, much less how it could be defined without damaging fragile race relations.[36]

Chapter 5 addressed Powell's consistent demands for the definition of Britishness and the creation of British citizenship on that basis. Although his ideas never became mainstream party policy, those who sympathized with him did not disappear. A committee of the Society of Conservative Lawyers, for example, prepared a report in 1975 which insisted:

> In most countries in the world, the basis of citizenship law is that of homeland. By and large, citizens are members of families whose homes are within or main links are with their country of citizenship. Citizenship so based is a natural homogeneous bond. This is the correct basis for citizenship law, and it is possible today to break away from the previous historical foundation of our citizenship. [37]

Some other right-wing Conservative Party members went even further, emphasizing the rule of 'blood' and allegiance to the Crown as the basis for British citizenship.[38]

Officially, however, Britishness was not elaborated on in detail, any more than was the linking British citizenship to patriality 'so as to restrict it to those having a real and close relationship with the country and its inhabitants'.[39] Despite the alleged link between the ascent of Thatcher and that of the concept of nationhood and the nation-state, even the 1980 White Paper only mentioned 'a close personal connection with the United Kingdom' as the basis for eligibility for British citizenship.[40] After all, the BNA 1981 was an 'immigration measure' to fulfil the 1979 election manifesto pledges, no matter how strenuously Timothy Raison denied it.[41] The introduction of a new British Nationality Act, in order to define entitlement to British citizenship and to the right of abode in Britain, was, for example, the first of eight pledges in the section significantly entitled 'Immigration and race relations' in the 1979 election manifesto.[42] However, British citizenship under the BNA 1981 came only with the right of abode, and did not clarify what Britishness was, however it was then understood. Again, just as the IA 1971 took no account of the citizenships created by the BNA 1948, so the BNA 1981 did not assume that the holding of citizenship should carry with it all three aspects of citizenship.[43] The Institute for Citizenship Studies even today concludes that British citizenship is 'wholly a creature of statute' and 'a mere infant in a legal history' and that the 'old historical relationship between subject and sovereign based on the duty of allegiance still remains "crucial"'.[44] Citizenship in Britain has never historically meant national citizenship; the entitlements of citizenship were not related to its legal status. In the case of the British citizenship under the BNA 1981, the definition of Britishness was not pursued since it was not the issue at stake.

In sum, this epilogue emphasizes that British citizenship under the BNA 1981 was only a legal status, that no interest was shown in the BNA 1981 in defining the holders of the substantive aspects of citizenship, and that it remained silent about what 'Britishness' means. In a limited sense, it might be right to claim that neither the BNA 1981 nor the British citizenship it created were ethnically exclusive. The main purpose of the act itself was only to link the legal status of British citizenship with the right of entry and abode. The job of discarding the NCW citizens and saving the OCW citizens with UK ancestry had already been done by the enactment of the IA 1971. Nonetheless, an examination of the processes preceding the enactment of the BNA 1981 shows that the act cannot be completely freed from inferences of racist inclinations. After all, British citizenship under the BNA 1981 was conferred on the basis of the concept of patriality, which was introduced by the IA 1971 to exempt kith and kin OCW citizens from immigration control while coloured NCW citizens remained subject to it.[45] Again in 1981, the discrepancy between those who exemplified 'Britishness', whatever this meant, and those with citizenship status remained. There has been a resurgence in the late 1990s in arguments over what it means to be British, to pursue what the BNA 1981 had left unanswered.

NOTES

1. Juss, *Immigration, Nationality and Citizenship*, p. 55.
2. For example, Macdonald and Blake argued that the BNA 1981 'merely enshrines the existing racially discriminatory provisions of immigration law under the new clothing of British citizenship'. I. Macdonald and N. Blake, *Immigration Law and Practice in the United Kingdom*, 4th edn (Butterworth, London, 1995), p. 144.
3. Hansen, *Citizenship and Immigration in Post-War Britain*, p. 207.
4. Appendix II sets out the three aspects of citizenship.
5. LPA, *Citizenship, Immigration and Integration*, 1972.
6. Iain Dale (ed.), *Conservative Party: General Election Manifestos, 1900–1997* (Routledge, London, 2000), p. 222. The Heath government had already admitted in an Oral Answer in 1972 that the 1948 act had become anomalous, and that they were 'reviewing [the nationality act], and the technical studies involved are well in hand'. Parliamentary Debates, House of Commons, vol. 847, col. 1661, 7 December 1972.
7. Parliamentary Debates, House of Commons, vol. 997, col. 935, 28 January 1981.
8. For details of the BNA 1981 see, for example, Fransman, *Fransman's British Nationality Law*, Section B. See also Appendix III. CUKC was divided into three statuses, that is, British citizenship, BDTC and BOC. BDTC was granted to those CUKC who had a connection with a colony, whereas those CUKC who fell into neither of the first two categories were given BOC. Neither BDTC nor BOC were given the right of free entry to Britain. BSWC under the BNA 1948 was confusingly renamed 'British subject'. BDTCs in Hong Kong were given the opportunity to acquire another new status, BN(O), in 1985. BN(O) remained in existence even after the return of Hong Kong to China in 1997, but it did not carry the right of free entry to Britain.
9. BOC is not transmissible and thus is designed to disappear eventually. The number of BDTC also dwindles, as the remaining colonies become independent. For the BN(O), a child of the BN(O) of Chinese origin will become Chinese, while that of non Chinese origin will become BOC. For the BN(O), see Robin M. White, 'Hong Kong: Nationality, Immigration and the Agreement with China', *International and Comparative Law Quarterly*, 36, 3 (July 1987), pp. 483–503.
10. Raison (the Minister of State for the Home Department) admitted that the changes of the principle of *jus soli* had 'immigration implications'. He insisted that those who were in the United Kingdom temporarily or had remained in breach of conditions of entry or who had entered illegally should not have British citizenship conferred on their children. Parliamentary Debates, House of Commons, vol. 5, col. 980, 3 June 1981.
11. *British Nationality Law: Outline of Proposed Legislation*, Cmd 7987, HMSO, 1980, para. 43.
12. In two specific cases, those who are born in the United Kingdom but do not acquire British citizenship by birth can become British citizens at a later stage: first, if either of their parents subsequently becomes a British citizen or settles in the United Kingdom; second, if the child remains in the United Kingdom for ten years after its date of birth without an absence of more than 90 days in any one year. In either case, an applicant while still a minor can register as a British citizen (s. 1(3)&(4)). There is also a special provision to prevent statelessness (schedule 2).
13. Fransman, *Fransman's British Nationality Law*, p. 271.
14. Community Relations Commission, *The Participation of Ethnic Minorities in the General Election, October 1974* (CRC, London, 1975).
15. According to Layton-Henry, Labour's policies became more appealing to Afro-Caribbean and Asian voters and more antagonistic towards racism in the 1970s a

result of a growing awareness of their pro-Labour sympathies and the party's internal leftward swing. Layton-Henry, *Politics of Immigration*, pp. 155–6.

16. See, for example, LPA, *Citizenship, Immigration and Integration*.

17. See, for example, Layton-Henry, *The Politics of Immigration*, Ch. 7.

18. *British Nationality Law: Discussion of Possible Changes*, Cmd 6795, HMSO, 1977, para. 66.

19. Parliamentary Debates, House of Commons, vol. 997, col. 939, 28 January 1981.

20. For example, Dale, *Conservative Party*, p. 222.

21. See, for example, CPA, CRD4/9/34. Immigration Voters. Community Relations at Constituency Level, 5 July 1974. The paper recommended that the party's image regarding immigrant communities should be changed. For Thatcher's attitudes on race and immigration, see, for example, Zig Layton-Henry, 'Race and the Thatcher Government' in Layton-Henry and Rich, *Race, Government and Politics in Britain*, Ch. 3, and Lynch, *Politics of Nationhood*, Ch. 3.

22. Rather, she shared the concern of Powell about the level of the NCW immigration. Margaret Thatcher, *The Path to Power* (HarperCollins, London, 1995), p. 146.

23. The Race Relations Act 1976, the third act in this field, widened the scope of the previous race relations legislation in 1965 and 1968 by extending the concept of unlawful racial discrimination to include not only direct discrimination on racial grounds but also indirect discrimination. There are numerous works on race-related legislation in Britain. This book is especially indebted to the following works. Favell, *Philosophies of Integration*; Tessa Blackstone, Bhikhu Parekh and Peter Sanders (eds), *Race Relations in Britain: A Developing Agenda* (Routledge, London, 1998); Muhammad Anwar, Patrick Roach and Ranjit Sodhi (eds), *From Legislation to Integration? Race Relations in Britain* (Macmillan, London, 2000).

24. CPA, *The Right Approach: A Statement of Conservative Aims* (Conservative Central Office, London, 1976).

25. CPA, CRD3/16/3. Report of the Study Group on Race Relations and Immigration. The Conservative Parliamentary Home Affairs Committee. June 1976. This paper even suggested that the right to vote in elections should also be limited to holders of British citizenship.

26. CPA, CRD3/16/3. Report of the Study Group on Race Relations and Immigration.

27. In the current affairs programme *World in Action*, 30 January 1978.

28. Layton-Henry, *Politics of Immigration*, pp. 184–7. The Conservative Party was well aware that the levels of NCW immigration had not been on the increase, as the Labour pointed out. The Conservatives, nonetheless, were convinced that the Labour government had made a mistake in being seen as soft on immigration control, and so remained silent about the statistical facts in order to win maximum support for its new immigration policies. CPA, CRD57. Ministerial Briefing: Home Affairs, 20 October 1978.

29. Parliamentary Debates, House of Commons, vol. 997, col. 939, 28 January 1981.

30. Vincenzi, *Crown Powers, Subjects and Citizens*, Ch. 11. Also, the Institute for Citizenship Studies claimed that 'the language of rights, while not foreign, is not central to the vocabulary of English law', concluding that the status of British citizen is 'increasingly redundant as a status necessary for the enjoyment or imposition of hallmark rights and duties'. Gardner, *White Paper*, pp. 7, 184.

31. *British Nationality Law: Discussion of Possible Changes*, Preface.

32. Parliamentary Debates, House of Commons, vol. 997, col. 946, 28 January 1981.

33. Ibid., col. 935, 28 January 1981 (Home Secretary, W. Whitelaw).

34. F. W. S. Craig (ed.), *Conservative and Labour Party Conference Decisions 1945–1981* (Parliamentary Research Service, Chichester, 1982), p. 346.

35. Zig Layton-Henry, 'Opposition Parties and Race Policies, 1979–83', in Layton-Henry

and Rich, *Race, Government and Politics in Britain*, pp. 108–12. The main change included restoration of the principle of *jus soli* but not much more.

36. Previous works have analyzed the Conservatives' struggles in the 1960s and 1970s to find a new foundation for a British national identity by focusing on the debates between Heath and Powell. See, for example, Lynch, *Politics of Nationhood*, Ch. 2.

37. Committee of the Society of Conservative Lawyers, *Towards a New Citizenship* (Conservative Political Centre, London, 1975).

38. Harvey Proctor and John Pinniger, *Immigration, Repatriation and the Commission for Racial Equality* (Monday Club, London, 1981). Some MPs were explicit about their racist intention. John Stoke, for example, said that 'race and racial origin are not mentioned in the Bill, and John Bull becomes a very shadowy figure'. Parliamentary Debates, House of Commons, vol. 997, col. 1004, 28 January 1981.

39. CPA, CRD3/16/3. Report of the Study Group on Race Relations and Immigration. The Conservative Parliamentary Home Affairs Committee. June 1976.

40. *British Nationality Law: Outline of Proposed Legislation*, para. 18. Parekh sees the anxieties about Britishness in the 1960s and 1970s as the debates between the New Right and the liberal. He suggests that the New Right, led by Enoch Powell, Margaret Thatcher, Roger Scruton and others, attacked the cultural diversification of Britain and tried to define Britishness in nationalist and ethnic terms. Bhikhu Parekh, 'National Identity in a Multicultural Society' in Anwar, Roach and Sondhi, *From Legislation to Integration?* pp. 206–11.

41. Parliamentary Debates, House of Commons, vol. 5, col. 980, 3 June 1981 (Minister of State for the Home Department, Mr Timothy Raison).

42. Dale, *Conservative Party*, p. 275.

43. Dummett and Nicol point out that the 'import of the 1948 Act had never sunk into the minds of British people or even of leading politicians'. Dummett and Nicol, *Subjects, Citizens, Aliens and Others*, p. 188.

44. Gardner, *White Paper*, pp. 5 and 185.

45. It is undeniable that patriality has a racial element. Hansen, *Citizenship and Immigration in Post-War Britain*, p. 195. A patrial CUKC under the IA 1971 was granted British citizenship at commencement of the act (s. 11). The term 'patriality' no longer appears on the statute book, but its conception provided the basis of the current British citizenship. For patriality see Ch. 5.

Conclusion

IN THIS book I have sought to explain the immigration and citizenship policies in Britain which repeatedly postponed the creation of British citizenship until 1981 and maintained instead the various alternative types of citizenship. In order to do this, my research went beyond the twentieth century and concentrated on a global institution – first the British Empire and then the Commonwealth – in which Britain was the main political constituent. Existing works highlight domestic aspects and concerns in the development of Britain's immigration and citizenship policies. They analyse the changes from the perspective of Britain's constitutional system and the political manoeuvring that took place between political parties or between policy-makers and the public. This work has offered another perspective, giving an account of the variegated system within a global institution which maintained British subjecthood and later Commonwealth citizenship and enabled a national type of citizenship to emerge alongside them. Complex rules of citizenship and immigration were devised in response to the building and expanding of the British Empire and its transformation into the Commonwealth. Since it took a long time for the concept of national citizenship to insinuate itself into British popular consciousness, it was not until 1981 that British citizenship as a status was created. However, even that citizenship cannot strictly be termed a national type of citizenship and, consequently, the concept of Britishness remains controversial. This final section, after summarizing the arguments of the previous chapters, concludes by reflecting on the contemporary debate over the alternative types of citizenship and the future of national citizenship in Britain.

Today, under the model of national citizenship, immigration and citizenship legislation together determine not only who 'belongs', but also what it means to 'belong', to a political unit. Existing works in the field, however, regard Britain as an exceptional case, because for them the main issue in Britain has been the admission of citizens as immigrants, whereas in other countries it has been the admission of immigrants to citizenship.[1] Furthermore, although scholars assume that the rise and fall of the British Empire and the Commonwealth must have had some impact on its immigration and nationality laws, they do not examine how and to what extent this was so. In contrast, this study has found that immigration policies in Britain after the Second World War developed in the context of the long-held citizenship policy which was to maintain a single status of formal membership within the global institution in the face of the emerging national type of citizenship. Complicated arrangements had developed between citizenship and immigration laws within the framework of (i) British subjecthood based on allegiance, (ii) the common code system, (iii) Commonwealth citizenship up to 1962, and (iv) Commonwealth citizenship after 1962.

From the perspective of nationality and immigration laws in Britain, there has never been any division between British subjects within the British Isles and those outside. There has always been a tension, then, between the concept of formal membership, which had to be shared by all the holders of British subjecthood, and that of Britishness, which was meant to represent a sense of national identity among those who 'belonged' to Britain. Under the national type of citizenship, the division between citizens and non-citizens is drawn by nationality and immigration laws. Any changes in these laws are normally influenced by both domestic and international pressures from political and economic events.[2] Through its examination of nationality and immigration laws in Britain, however, this work demonstrates that successive British governments prior to the Second World War were under a third kind of pressure, that from the constituent political units of the Empire (especially the Dominions) which tried to define local citizenship within the framework of British subjecthood.[3]

Like other countries, Britain had to differentiate between the holders (British subject or Commonwealth citizen) and non-holders of formal membership by responding to pressures both at home and abroad. This task was hard enough – because the distinction between formal members and aliens required continuous adjustments – given that Britain grew into a global institution. However, the task became harder because of an additional pressure which was unique in Britain's case and stemmed from the constituent political units of the Empire and later the Commonwealth. This third pressure derived from the demand in the self-governing colonies (later, the Dominions) for determining who, among all the holders of British subjecthood, would belong to each of them.

In addition to the division between British subjects and aliens, therefore, successive British governments had to allow each colony to differentiate between those subjects who belonged to it and those who did not. At the same time this inner distinction among the holders of British subjecthood had to be maintained at a level which would not break the structure of British subjecthood. Even after the Second World War, the British government sought to maintain a citizenship structure with multiple citizenships: Commonwealth citizenship, citizenship of the Commonwealth member countries, and aliens.[4] For British citizenship to be created on the basis of Britishness, therefore, policy-makers after the war first had to accept that the old imperial links with member countries of the Commonwealth were greatly weakened and had become both politically and economically less significant. As a result, the proposal to create British citizenship did not appear on the parliamentary agenda until as late as the 1970s.[5] Instead, immigration control was tightened in the 1960s, dividing Commonwealth citizens into NCW *immigrants* and OCW *citizens*, and preventing the former from entering Britain. The citizenship status given by the BNA 1948 to peoples in the NCW and colonies was completely ignored by a series of immigration acts in the 1960s, on the grounds that these people did not 'belong' to Britain.[6] Consequently, the majority of NCW citizens, excluding a small number of them who passed through immigration control, lost their citizenship rights in Britain.

In sum, my research has revealed the following four points:

1. Britain's formal membership has always been attached to the global institution, first the British Empire, and then the Commonwealth, which was over-arching and inclusive. The status of British subjecthood and Commonwealth citizenship was a symbol of the unity of the British Empire and the Commonwealth, not of Britain itself. So long as policy-makers in Britain considered it to be beneficial, either politically or economically, to maintain the global institution in some form, the creation of British citizenship was repeatedly rejected as detrimental to this objective.

2. Legislation on immigration and citizenship in Britain was enacted and amended in response to changes in the means by which the constituent political units formed the global institution, be it the British Empire or the Commonwealth. Successive British governments searched for a mechanism by which various groups of people in the global institution could somehow be grouped together as its formal members, although some were more closely linked than others. Unlike in other countries, immigration and citizenship legislation was more than an issue of purely domestic concern, reflecting the relationship between the constituent units within the global institution.

3. Post-Second World War immigration policy was, in practice, a

continuation of pre-war policy, with its all-embracing citizenship law sitting alongside exclusive immigration controls. Furthermore, after the Second World War the internal division remained between citizens in the OCW who shared a sense of affinity with those in Britain, and those in the NCW who did not. Those in the NCW kept the same citizenship-as-status as those in Britain and the OCW, only because the BNA 1948 said so. For policy-makers in Britain, therefore, the status of Commonwealth citizenship held by NCW citizens signified only citizenship-as-status and was devoid of citizenship rights and duties.

4. Successive governments maintained the forms of citizenship structure with which there co-existed an emerging national citizenship in Britain's overseas territories prior to the Second World War, and in Britain itself after the war alongside alternative types of citizenship, that is, British subjecthood and Commonwealth citizenship. Nonetheless, even in Britain a thinning-down process of Commonwealth citizenship, by depriving Commonwealth citizens outside Britain of their citizenship rights and privileges, took place in the 1960s and 1970s through the tightening of immigration control. The enactment of the BNA 1981 was, after all, a belated acknowledgement by the British government that its long-standing efforts to maintain a citizenship structure which enabled the alternative and national type of citizenship to co-exist had been abandoned with the passing of the IA 1971.

RETHINKING CITIZENSHIP IN BRITAIN: ALTERNATIVE AND NATIONAL TYPES

The findings of this book have further implications for the current debate on the limitations of national citizenship and the future of British citizenship. First, this study has expanded the recent argument about 'transnational citizenship' which considers the evolving EU citizenship as its prototype. The core of this argument is that people should receive such rights on the basis not of nationality but of the universality of human rights.[7] According to the advocates of 'transnational citizenship', citizenship will come to refer to 'de-territorialized notions of a person's rights' and no longer to a 'territorialized notion of cultural belonging'.[8] For them, 'transnational citizenship' resulted from 'a profound transformation in the institution of citizenship, both in its institutional logic and in the way it is legitimated'.[9] 'Transnational citizenship' is, therefore, a new type of citizenship, which belongs to a totally different international environment from that of previous periods. In the new era, citizenship will rest on 'the commitment to widen the boundaries of the political community so that insiders and outsiders can be associated as the equal members of a transnational citizenry'.[10]

Instead of going along with the current debate on whether or not 'transnational citizenship' is overtaking national citizenship, I find the arguments for both too simplistic.[11] I agree that national citizenship faces challenges such as globalization and the consequent limits on state sovereignty. To those scholars who dismiss the debates on 'transnational citizenship', my study has made it clear that alternative types of citizenship have historically existed and are too prevalent to be treated as a mere irregularity. However, my acceptance of the concept of 'transnational citizenship' stops here. In response to those who favour 'transnational citizenship', my research finds that it is too premature to claim that national governments have lost control over entry to their borders and their citizenship policies. No matter how broad EU citizenship becomes by passing the authority of granting citizenship rights from the state level to the EU level, it only exists on the basis of holding the citizenship of member countries.[12] Moreover, those advocates of 'transnational citizenship' seem to overlook the fact that alternative types of citizenship were historically created from above through the state's decision. It is still the case in the EU that only state authority can secure and provide citizenship rights and privileges.

Among non-national types of citizenship, therefore, this study classified three forms of alternative types – imperial, composite and cosmopolitan types – of citizenship in order to analyse Britain's experience with various types of citizenship. It then stressed that EU citizenship at present only qualifies as the composite type of citizenship. The cosmopolitan type of citizenship should be totally free from state boundaries and extend to 'like-minded'[13] fellows. With the restrictive nature of the current EU citizenship towards immigrants from non-member countries, it is uncertain how EU citizenship will develop. More importantly, even if the momentum for creating 'transnational citizenship' evolved from below, some kind of contract among the states would be needed to grant citizenship rights and privileges in the transnational setting. My work thus suggests that scholars should pay more attention to the composite type of citizenship if they are to investigate the limitations of national citizenship.

The second point to which my study refers is the future development of national citizenship in Britain after the enactment of the BNA 1981. The Epilogue showed that British citizenship under the BNA 1981 did not fully fit into the national type of citizenship. I have not intended to use this book to claim that the national type of citizenship should be established in Britain, nor to suggest that this type is superior. However, a series of legislation in the field of immigration and citizenship after 1981 seems to imply that intention. As noted in Chapter 1, EU citizenship today remains an aggregate of the citizenship of its member countries, and does not yet generate a shared sense of belonging and loyalty among its holders. Therefore, the existence of EU citizenship is not as damaging to Britishness as the so-called Eurosceptics claim. If anything, the devolution movement within the United Kingdom and the mounting antagonism towards asylum seekers are potentially more damaging to further efforts to consolidate British citizenship.[14]

My argument throughout the book shows that a delicate balance has been kept between Britishness and other regional and ethnic identities within the citizenship structure of multiple citizenships. Recently, however, whether or not 'British identity' needs to be re-created has become a topic of heated debate inside and outside Parliament. The Commission on the Future of Multi-Ethnic Britain, headed by Lord Parekh and sponsored by the Runnymede Trust, issued its report in 2000 and triggered a wave of controversy.[15] It recommended that 'a genuinely multicultural Britain urgently needs to re-imagine itself' and that future polices should reflect, and involve a move towards a greater public awareness of, the diversity of the communities in Britain.[16] For the commission the previous policies were either promoting a single national culture and expecting everyone to assimilate into it, or dividing public and private spheres, in which diversity is only allowed in a private sphere so that unity and cohesiveness of the political culture in the public sphere are maintained.[17] Although the latter policy was more tolerant towards the diversity of communities than the former, the political culture is placed beyond negotiation and a multicultural private realm might be prone to compromise. Instead of a clear distinction between public and private realms, therefore, Parekh and his colleagues envisaged that interdependence within and between the various communities in society at large should result in continual revision of the public realm to accommodate cultural diversity.[18]

I would emphasize that Britishness has never had an exclusive connotation. This book argues that a vagueness over 'Britishness' enabled local identities to co-exist within the multicultural and multinational 'global institution', be it the Empire or the Commonwealth. At the same time successive governments had to separate three elements of citizenship – as a status, as a right, and as a sense of identity – in order to keep some kind of unity among all the residents under the single status of, first, British subjecthood and, later, Commonwealth citizenship. The current debate on Britishness therefore seems to suggest the following options. One requires further devolution, by which not only regional institutions in Scotland and Wales but even large city councils gain more authority to grant rights and duties to local residents. In this way, Britishness remains a catch-all identity for every segment of the country and the creation of British citizenship with all three elements is once again forgone. The other option requires the reinvention of Britishness on the basis of the clear public declaration and acceptance that Britain is a multi-ethnic country.[19]

In conclusion, a passage from a German newspaper of 1938 can help us to understand the circumstances under which Britain's citizenship and immigration policies developed. For a German commentator, the British Empire and the Commonwealth '[give] an impression of unsystematic genius in the Englishman, who has no sense of structural beauty or orderly creation. To him nothing is wrong, however illogical, so long as the machine works.'[20] For successive British governments, the logic behind British subjecthood and Commonwealth citizenship was to give some sort of unity to the multi-racial and multi-ethnic 'global institution' in the face of the increasing challenge of emerging nationhood among its constituent political units. In that sense, its very malleability was the beauty of British subjecthood and Commonwealth citizenship.

NOTES

1. See William Rogers Brubaker, 'Introduction', in Brubaker, *Immigration and the Politics of Citizenship*, p. 11.
2. Dummett and Nicol, *Subjects, Citizens, Aliens and Others*, p. 19.
3. It was at the 1930 imperial conference that the right of Dominion governments to enact their own nationality laws was officially acknowledged. By then Canada and the Union of South Africa had already passed nationality laws. For details of the conference see *Imperial Conference 1930: Summary of Proceedings*, Cmd 3717, HMSO, November 1930.
4. In terms of the substantive aspects of citizenship in Britain, there were two groupings: British subjects and aliens. However, if we focus on the socio-psychological dimension of the functional aspects of citizenship, the holders of British subjecthood (later, Commonwealth citizenship) can be further subdivided into two: citizens of the Dominions and Britain, and citizens of the colonies. This point is elaborated in Chapter 1.
5. The Labour Party national executive committee's study group suggested in 1972 that a non-discriminatory immigration policy should be based on a redefinition of British citizenship. The Conservative Party's 1974 election manifesto stated that 'we have ... set in hand a review of British nationality law, and dependent on its outcome, new legislation to replace the present British Nationality Act may be one of the measures required in the life of the next Parliament'. LPA. Labour Party,

Citizenship, Immigration and Integration: A Policy for the Seventies, 1972. Craig, F. W. S., *British General Election*, p. 393.

6. Criteria for defining who 'belonged' to Britain were slightly changed from the CIA 1962 and 1968 to the IA 1971. The CIA 1962 was based on the kind of passport which each Commonwealth citizen possessed. The CIA 1968 added a 'qualifying connection' with the United Kingdom, which consisted of the birth, registration or naturalization of the applicants, their parent or their grandparent in the United Kingdom. The IA 1971 introduced the concept of 'patriality'. Details of these measures are discussed in Chapter 5.

7. Soysal says that these rights should be granted on the basis of 'personhood'. Soysal, *Limits of Citizenship*, p. 3. Held explains that people would be 'citizens of their immediate political communities, and of the wider regional and global networks which impacted on their lives'. He continues by saying that 'states would no longer be, and would no longer be regarded as, the sole centres of legitimate power within their own border'. David Held, *Democracy and the Global Order: From the Modern State to Cosmopolitan Governance* (Polity, Cambridge, 1995), p. 233.

8. Soysal, *Limits of Citizenship*, p. 3.

9. Ibid., p. 139.

10. Linklater, *Transformation of Political Community*, p. 175.

11. Among those who emphasize the power of the state governments and of national citizenship, see, for example, Christian Joppke, 'Immigration Challenges the Nation-State', in Joppke, *Challenge to the Nation-State*, Ch. 1.

12. For current EU citizenship, see, for example, Sørensen, *Exclusive European Citizenship*.

13. Linklater, *Transformation of Political Community*, p. 167.

14. Lynch points out that the devolution movement is especially threatening to the Conservative understanding of nationhood in Britain which was founded on the idea of 'One Nation'. Philip Lynch, *Politics of Nationhood*, esp. Ch. 5.

15. The report by the Commission on the Future of Multi-Ethnic Britain, headed by Lord Parekh, recently published a controversial report on race relations in Britain. It even claimed that 'Britishness ... has systematic, largely unspoken, racial connotations'. Commission on the Future of Multi-Ethnic Britain, *The Future of Multi-Ethnic Britain* (Profile Books, London, 2000), p. 38.

16. Ibid., p. xiv.

17. Parekh called the former the 'nationalist model' and the latter, the 'liberal model'. Bhikhu Parekh, 'Integrating Minorities', in Blackstone, Parekh and Sanders, *Race Relations in Britain*, Ch. 1. According to Parekh, those philosophers who claim 'constitutional patriotism' support the 'liberal model'. For constitutional patriotism see Margaret Canovan, 'Patriotism is not Enough', *British Journal of Political Science*, 30, 3 (2000), pp. 413–32.

18. Parekh terms it the 'pluralist model'. Commission on the Future of Multi-Ethnic Britain, *Multi-Ethnic Britain*, Ch. 4. The main difference between the pluralist and liberal models is that the former goes beyond the division between public and private domains and demands that the existing national identity is reinvented in line with certain core values such as equality, fairness, dialogue, recognition of and respect for diversity. The latter, however, sticks to the two-domains thesis, replacing national identities rooted in a particularity of the society with the patriotic loyalty to the principles and practices of a free state.

19. Parekh insists that six issues need attention for the future of multi-ethnic Britain: recognition of cultural diversity in the public sphere; public institutions, bodies and services; controversies and disputes; common values; symbols and ceremonies; racism. Commission on the Future of Multi-Ethnic Britain, *Multi-Ethnic Britain*, pp. 48–56.

20. *Berliner Tageblatt*, 20 August 1938, cited in Mansergh, *Problems of Wartime Co-operation*, p. 367.

Appendices

Aspects of Citizenship

Nominal aspect	(citizenship-as-status)
Formal membership of a political unit	
Substantive aspect	(citizenship-as-rights)
	(citizenship-as-desirable-activity)
A bundle of rights and obligations assigned to the holders of citizenship	
Functional aspect	(citizenship-as-social-enclosure)
Functions of inclusion and exclusion on the basis of the holding of citizenship	

APPENDIX II:

Comparison of National and Alternative Types of Citizenship

Attributes	National citizenship	Alternative types of citizenship		
		Imperial	*Composite*	*Cosmopolitan*
Territorial limit	State boundary	Boundaries of combined political unit		Fluid boundaries
Authority for forming a combined political unit		From above (governments of all the constituent political units)		From below (popular consent)
Mode of forming a combined political unit		Unilateral	Bilateral through a contract or an agreement	By shared norm and moral principle (i.e., universal human rights)
Citizenship status	Single status	Unitary (but could be multiple)	Multiple	Multiple (potentially unitary)
Sources of rights/ obligations	State government	Imperial government	Government of constituent political unit	Transnational community
Forms of rights/ obligations	Egalitarian and full	Could be multiple or partial (also possibly hierarchical)	Multiple	Potentially unitary
Basis of membership	Nationhood	Rules (orders) of the metropole	Citizenship of a con-stituent political unit	Shared norm and moral principle (personhood)

Source: Soysal, *Limits of Citizenship*, p. 140, provided the models of national and post-national membership. Her models have been modified and her 'post-national citizenship' has been reclassified into three different forms on the basis of the way in which they were created, that is, from below or from above.

APPENDIX III:

Development of Various Types of Citizenship in Britain

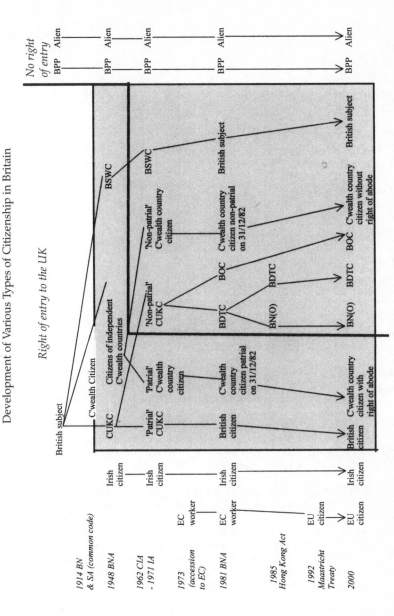

Source: Sue Shutter, *Immigration and Nationality Law Handbook* (Joint Council for the Welfare of Immigrants, London, 1995), p. 275. The period has been extended to 2000 and the section on EU citizens has been added.

Defining British Citizenship

APPENDIX IV:

Entitlement of Citizenship Rights and Privileges in the United Kingdom at the Time
of the Enactment of the British Nationality Act 1981

Citizenship rights and privileges	A: Right to enter and settle in the United Kingdom B: Right to vote C: Right to receive public funds[1] D: Rights acknowledged by the Treaty of Rome			
British nationals*				
British citizens	A	B	C	–
Other types of British nationals (except BPP)	(A)[†]	B	(C)[‡]	–
Citizens of Commonwealth countries*				
Patrials on 1 January 1983	A	B	C	–
Other Commonwealth citizens	(A)[†]	B	(C)[‡]	–
British nationals				
BPP	–	–	–	–
Irish citizens	A	B	C	D
Others				
EC citizens	–	–	–	D
Aliens	–	–	–	–

Source: P. Gordon and F. Klug, *British Immigration Control: A Brief Guide* (Runnymede
Trust, London, 1985), p. 8, as amended.

Notes: [1.] For the purpose of immigration rules, public funds mean: housing, council
tax benefit, income support/job seeker's allowance, housing benefit and
family credit. Under immigration law, people may be admitted to the United
Kingdom on condition that they will not have recourse to public funds.
Statement of Changes in Immigration Rules, HC 395, 1994, para. 6.

    [*] Those in these categories are granted the status of Commonwealth
citizenship under section 37 of the BNA 1981.

    [†] Before the enactment of the CIA 1962, all holders of Commonwealth
citizenship were free to enter and settle in the United Kingdom.

    [‡] All Commonwealth citizens were exempt from immigration control and
consequently entitled to receive public funds without any immigration rule
restrictions. Since 1962, those Commonwealth citizens who are subject to
immigration rules have to be granted an 'Indefinite Leave to Remain' in the
United Kingdom in order to claim public funds.

Chronology

1608   Calvin's Case rationalizes the concept of allegiance and decides that the subject owes allegiance to the Crown and in return receives the Crown's protection.

1700   The Act of Settlement (12 & 13 Will. 3., c. 2) excludes a naturalized subject from political power and place, a natural-born subject enjoying more rights than a naturalized one.

1714   The Naturalization Act 1714 (Geo. 1., c. 4) prescribes that a bill of naturalization should include a clause embodying the disabilities of the Act of Settlement.

1783   The Versailles Treaty ends the American War of Independence.

1800   Act of Union.

1844   The Aliens Act 1844 (7 & 8 Vict., c. 66) removes some of the disabilities on naturalized subjects and introduces a simple, administrative, form of naturalization.

1847   The Act for the Naturalization of Aliens 1847 (10 & 11 Vict., c. 83) lays down that the 1844 act does not apply to the colonies. It confirms local naturalization.

1867   The British North America Act establishes a federal 'Dominion' of Canada.

1870   The Naturalization Act 1870 (33 & 34 Vict., c. 14) repeals the 1844 act and gives the Home Secretary an unambiguous discretion to grant or withhold naturalization. This act determines that voluntary naturalization in other countries leads to a loss of British subjecthood. Indelible allegiance is abandoned.

1887   The First Colonial Conference is held in London.

1901   Australia becomes a Commonwealth Dominion.

1905   The Aliens Act 1905 (5 Edw., c. 13) begins the modern control of immigration into the United Kingdom.

1910   The Union of South Africa is established. The Canadian Immigration Act (9 & 10 Edw. 7, c. 27) establishes 'Canadian citizens' in respect of immigration control.

1914   The First World War begins. The Aliens Restriction Act (4 & 5
            Geo. 5, c. 12) extends the 1905 act in order to deal with
            enemy aliens. The British Nationality and Status of Aliens
            Act (4 & 5 Geo. 5, c. 17) postulates the concept of the
            'common code' throughout the Empire.

1918   The First World War ends.

1919   The Aliens Restriction (Amendment) Act 1919 (9 & 10 Geo. 5,
            c. 92) extends the 1914 act into peacetime and is renewed
            every year until 1971.

1921   A 'Canadian national' is defined by the Canadian
            Nationality Act (11 & 12 Geo. 5, c. 4) as any British subject
            who is a 'Canadian citizen' within the meaning of the
            Immigration Act of 1910. The Anglo-Irish treaty is signed
            and the Irish Free State becomes a Dominion.

1926   The Balfour report provides the meaning of Dominion status.

1927   The Union Nationality and Flag Act is passed in the Union of
            South Africa in order to define the status of Union national.
            This act is restrictive on the principle of *jus soli* and declares
            that the status of Union national is not to be conferred on
            prohibited immigrants and their children.

1931   The Statute of Westminster is enacted.

1935   The Irish Nationality and Citizenship Act (no. 13) repeals the
            BN & SA act 1914.

1938   The Irish Free State changes its name to Éire.

1939–45   The Second World War.

1946   The Canadian Citizenship Act (10 Geo. VI., c. 15) establishes
            'Canadian citizens'. It ends the common code system set up
            under the BN & SA act 1914.

1948   The British Nationality Act is enacted. Ceylon (now Sri
            Lanka) and Burma become independent. Burma leaves the
            Commonwealth. SS *Empire Windrush* arrives from the West
            Indies.

1949   The Ireland Act. Éire becomes a republic and leaves the
            Commonwealth. India's membership of the Commonwealth
            as a republic is approved.

1962   The Commonwealth Immigrants Act, the first statutory
            attempt to restrict Commonwealth immigration, is passed.

1963   Kenya becomes independent.

1965   The first Race Relations Act is passed. A White Paper on
            immigration from the Commonwealth is published.

1968   The Commonwealth Immigrants Act restricts the entry of
            East African Asians. The second Race Relations Act is

enacted, extending the scope of the 1965 act and making racial discrimination unlawful in employment, housing and the provision of goods, facilities and services.

1971   The Immigration Act repeals the Aliens (Amendment) Act 1919 and consolidates the control systems for alien and Commonwealth citizen into one statutory form. This act also introduces the notion of 'patriality' and its holders are given the right of abode.

1973   Britain enters the European Communities.

1976   The third Race Relations Act is enacted and extends the definition of 'discrimination' to include indirect discrimination.

1978   Margaret Thatcher, the Conservative Party leader, is interviewed on Granada television and refers to the fear of being 'rather swamped by people with a different culture'.

1981   The British Nationality Act is passed.

2002   The British Overseas Territories Act is passed, renaming 'British dependent territories citizenship' as 'British overseas territories citizenship' and granting its holders British citizenship.

Select Bibliography

I. DOCUMENTARY SOURCES

1. Official Documents (Public Record Office, Kew Gardens, London)

(1) Cabinet Office
    CAB 21/1824
    CAB 21/1836
    CAB 32/69
    CAB 32/127
    CAB 32/130
    CAB 32/131
    CAB 32/137
    CAB 37/62/113
    CAB 127/169
    CAB 128/13
    CAB 129/1
    CAB 129/19
    CAB 129/33
    CAB 129/84
    CAB 129/107
    CAB 129/121/93
    CAB 130/13
    CAB 130/45
    CAB 131/2
    CAB 133/6
    CAB 133/87
    CAB 133/89
    CAB 133/91
    CAB 134/117
    CAB 134/118
    CAB 134/119
    CAB 134/1468
    CAB 134/1469

CAB 134/2460
CAB 134/2637
CAB 134/2639

(2) Colonial Office
    CO 537/1910
    CO 852/555/4
    CO 1006/1
    CO 1032/197

(3) Defence Ministry
    DEFE 4/8
    DEFE 4/20

(4) Dominion Office
    DO 34/807/7
    DO 35/104/2
    DO 35/106/4
    DO 35/111/3
    DO 35/1159/P201/19
    DO 168/47
    DO 168/48
    DO 175/92
    DO 176/2

(5) Foreign Office
    FO 5/1356
    FO 371/50912
    FO 372/5011
    FO 800/444
    FCO 30/780

(6) Home Office
    HO 45/10063/B2840
    HO 213/200
    HO 213/202
    HO 213/2331
    HO 344/14.

(7) Labour Ministry
    LAB 8/2701
    LAB 8/2704

LAB 26/226

(8) Prime Minister's Office
PREM 4/46/12
PREM 8/726
PREM 8/851
PREM 8/1008
PREM 13/1572

2. Reports and Government Documents

Report from the Select Committee on the Laws Affecting Aliens Together with the Minutes of Evidence and Index, HC. 307, 1843.

Report of the Royal Commissioners for the Inquiring into the Laws of Naturalization and Allegiance, No. 4109, 1869.

Report of the Inter-Departmental Committee Appointed by the Secretary of State for the Home Department to Consider the Doubts and Difficulties which Have Arisen in Connexion with the Interpretation and Administration of the Acts Relating to Naturalization, Cmd 723, 1901.

Colonial Conference 1902. Papers Relating to a Conference between the Secretary of State for the Colonies and the Prime Ministers of Self-Governing Colonies, Cmd 1299, 1902.

Papers Relative to the Laws and Regulations in Force in the Colonies under Responsible Government Respecting the Admission of Immigrants, Cmd 2105, 1904.

Colonial Conference 1907. Minutes of Proceedings, Cmd 3523, 1907.

Dominions No. 4. Further Correspondence Relating to the Imperial Conference, Cmd 5273, 1910.

Imperial Conference 1911. Precis of the Proceedings, Cmd 5741, 1911.

Imperial Conference 1911. Dominions No. 7. Minutes of Proceedings of the Imperial Conference 1911, Cmd 5745, 1911.

Imperial War Conference 1917. Extracts from Minutes of Proceedings and Papers laid before the Conference, Cmd 8566, 1917.

Imperial Conference 1926. Summary of Proceedings, Cmd 2768, 1926.

Report of the Conference on the Operation of Dominion Legislation and Merchant Shipping Legislation, Cmd 3479, 1929/30.

Imperial Conference 1930. Summary of Proceedings, Cmd 3717, 1930.

Central Organization for Defence, Cmd 6923, 1946.

Immigration from the Commonwealth, Cmd 2739, 1965.

The United Kingdom and the European Communities, Cmd 4715, 1971.

Treaty concerning the Accession of the Kingdom of Denmark, Ireland, the Kingdom of Norway and the United Kingdom of Great Britain and North

Ireland to the EEC and the European Atomic Energy Community (with Final Act) Decision of the Council of the European Communities Concerning the Accession of the Said States to the European Coal and Steel Community, Cmd 4682 - I, 1972.
Statement of Immigration Rules for Control on Entry: Commonwealth Citizens, HC. 79, 1973.
British Nationality Law: Discussion of Possible Changes, Cmd 6795, 1977.
British Nationality Law: Outline of Proposed Legislation, Cmd 7987, 1980.
Partnership for Progress and Prosperity: Britain and the Overseas Territories, Cmd 4264, 1999.

3. Legislation

United Kingdom
1350–51 25 Edw. 3, St. I (De natis ultra mare)
1634   10 Car. I., c. 4
1663   15 Car. II., c. 15
1696   7 & 8 Will. III., c. 22
1700   12 & 13 Will. III., c. 2 (Act of Settlement)
1707   6 Anne., c. 14 (Act of Union)
1708   7 Anne., c. 5 (Foreign Protestants Naturalization)
1711   10 Anne., c. 5
1714   1 Geo., I, c. 4 (Naturalization)
1731   4 Geo. II., c. 21 (British Nationality)
1740   13 Geo. II., c. 3
1740   13 Geo. II., c. 7 (Plantation)
1749   22 Geo. II., c. 45
1773   13 Geo. III., c. 21 (British Nationality)
1793   33 Geo. III., c. 4 (Aliens)
1800   40 Geo. III., c. 67 (Act of Union)
1826   7 Geo. IV., c. 54 (Registration of Aliens)
1844   7 & 8 Vict., c. 66 (Aliens)
1847   10 & 11 Vict., c. 83 (Naturalization of Aliens)
1848   11 & 12 Vict., c. 20 (Aliens)
1865   28 & 29 Vict., c. 93 (Colonial Laws Validity Act)
1870   33 & 34 Vict., c. 14 (Naturalization)
1905   5 Edw. VII., c. 14 (Aliens Act)
1914   4 & 5 Geo. V., c. 12 (Aliens Restriction Act)
1914   4 & 5 Geo. V., c. 17 (British Nationality and Status of Aliens Act)
1918   8 & 9 Geo. V., c. 38 (British Nationality and Status of Aliens Act)

1919	9 & 10 Geo. V., c. 92 (Aliens Restriction (Amendment) Act)
1922	12 & 13 Geo. V., c. 42 (British Nationality and Status of Aliens Act)
1931	22 Geo. V., c. 4 (Statute of Westminster)
1943	6 & 7 Geo. VI., c. 14 (British Nationality and Status of Aliens Act)
1948	11 & 12 Geo. VI., c. 56 (British Nationality Act)
1949	12 & 13 Geo. VI., c. 41 (Ireland Act)
1962	10 & 12 Eliz. II., c. 21 (Commonwealth Immigrants Act)
1964	c. 54 (British Nationality Act (No. 1))
1968	c. 9 (Commonwealth Immigrants Act)
1971	c. 77 (Immigration Act)
1981	c. 61 (British Nationality Act)
2002	c. 8 (British Overseas Territories Act)

Canada
1909	7 & 8 Edw. VII., c. 19 (Canadian Naturalization Amendment Act)
1910	9 & 10 Edw. VII., c. 27 (Canadian Immigration Act)
1921	11 & 12 Geo. V., c. 4 (Canadian Nationals Act)
1946	10 Geo. VI., c. 15 (Canadian Citizenship Act)

Australia
1864	no. 5 (South Australia)
1888	no. 4 (NSW)
1903	no. 11
1935	no. 62
1946	no. 9

Ireland
1935	no. 13 (Irish Nationality and Citizenship Act)
1948	no. 22 (Republic of Ireland Act)
1949	S. 1 no. 1 (Citizens of United Kingdom and Colonies (Irish Citizenship Rights) Orders)

Kenya
| 1967 | no. 25 (Immigration Act) |
| 1967 | no. 33 (Trade Licensing Act) |

New Zealand
| 1880 | 44 Vict., no. 10 |
| 1896 | 60 Vict., no. 64 |

1934–35   25 Geo. V., no. 38 (British Nationality and Status of Aliens
          (in NZ) Amendment Act)
1946   10 Geo. VI., no. 20 (British Nationality and Status of Aliens
          (in NZ) Amendment Act)

Trinidad
  1868   no. 26

Union of South Africa
  1883   no. 2 (Cape of Good Hope)
  1905   no. 18 (Natal)
  1926   no. 18 (Naturalization and Status of Aliens Act)
  1927   no. 40 (Union Nationality and Flags Act)

4. Parliamentary Debates

United Kingdom
  HOUSE OF COMMONS
  vol. 66   20 February 1843
  vol. 67   8 March 1843
  vol. 112   25 June 1850
  vol. 190   20 March 1868
  vol. 311   10 March 1887
  vol. 62   13 May 1914
  vol. 65   5 August 1914
  vol. 158   31 October 1917
  vol. 159   19 November 1917
              27 November 1917
  vol. 108   12 July 1918
  vol. 156   5 July 1922
  vol. 374   9 September 1941
  vol. 443   5 November 1947
  vol. 451   8 June 1948
  vol. 453   7 July 1948
              13 July 1948
  vol. 464   28 April 1949
  vol. 649   16 November 1961
              26 November 1961
  vol. 650   5 December 1961
  vol. 654   22 February 1962
  vol. 751   28 July 1967
  vol. 759   27 February 1968

vol. 813	8 March 1971
vol. 819	17 June 1919
vol. 843	23 October 1972
vol. 847	7 December 1972
vol. 997	28 January 1981
vol. 5	2 June 1981
	3 June 1981

HOUSE OF LORDS

| vol. 155 | 11 May 1948 |
| vol. 238 | 12 March 1962 |

Canada

HOUSE OF COMMONS

2nd Session 1945, vol. II	22 October 1945
1st Session 1946, vol I	2 April 1946
	5 April 1946
	29 April 1946

5. Papers of Other Organizations

(1) Conservative Party Papers (Bodleian Library, Oxford)
ACP 73/78
CRD 3/16/3
CRD 3/16/4
CRD 4/9/34
CRD 57

Conservative Party, *The Right Approach: A Statement of Conservative Aims*, Conservative Central Office, London, 1976.

(2) Labour Party Archives (National Museum of Labour History, Manchester)
LPA, *Citizenship, Immigration and Integration: A Policy for the Seventies*, 1972.

II. SECONDARY SOURCES

Albert, Mathias, David Jacobson and Yosef Lapid (eds), *Identities, Borders, Orders: Rethinking International Theory*, University of Minnesota Press, London, 2001.

Anwar, Muhammad, Patrick Roach and Ranjit Sodhi (eds), *From Legislation to Integration? Race Relations in Britain*, Macmillan, London, 2000.

Arendt, Hannah, *The Origins of Totalitarianism*, Harcourt Brace, London, 1973 [1948].

Aristotle, 'The Theory of Citizenship and Constitution', in *The Politics of Aristotle*, trans. Ernest Barker, Clarendon Press, Oxford, 1948 [1946].

Aron, Raymond, 'Is Multinational Citizenship Possible?', *Social Research*, 41, 4 (1971).

Bauböck, Rainer, *Transnational Citizenship: Membership and Rights in International Migration*, Edward Elgar, Aldershot, 1994.

Bendix, Reinhard, *Nation-Building and Citizenship: Studies of Our Changing Social Order*, University of California Press, Berkeley, CA, 1977 [1964].

Bird, J. C., *Control of Enemy Alien Civilians in Great Britain 1914–1918*, Garland, New York and London, 1986.

Blackstone, Tessa, Bhikhu Parekh and Peter Sanders (eds), *Race Relations in Britain: A Developing Agenda*, Routledge, London, 1998.

Blackstone, William, *Commentaries on the Laws of England*, in *A Facsimile of the First Edition of 1765–1769: of the Rights of Persons Published in 1765*, ed. Stanley N. Katz, University of Chicago Press, London, 1979.

Böhning, W. R., *The Migration of Workers in the United Kingdom and the European Community*, Oxford University Press, London, 1972.

Boyle, T., 'The Liberal Imperialist, 1892–1906', *Bulletin of the Institute of Historical Research*, 52, 125 (1979).

Brecher, Michael, 'India's Decision to Remain in the Commonwealth', *Journal of Commonwealth and Comparative Politics*, 12 (1975).

Brochmann, Grete and Tomas Hammer (eds), *Mechanisms of Immigration Control: A Comparative Analysis of European Regulation Policies*, Berg, Oxford, 1999.

Brubaker, Rogers (ed.), *Immigration and the Politics of Citizenship in Europe and North America*, University Press of America, London, 1989.

—— *Citizenship and Nationhood in France and Germany*, Harvard University Press, London, 1994.

Burke, Catherine L., 'The Great Debate: The Decolonization Issue at the United Nations, 1945–1980', D.Phil. thesis, Oxford University, 1986.

Butler, R. A., *The Art of the Possible*, Hamish Hamilton, London, 1971.

Callaghan, James, *Time and Change*, Collins, London, 1987.

Campbell-Johnson, Alan, *Mission with Mountbatten*, Robert Hale, London, 1951.

Cannadine, David, 'The Context, Performance and Meaning of Ritual:

The British Monarchy and the "Invention of Tradition", c. 1820–1977', in Eric Hobsbawm and Terence Ranger (eds), *The Invention of Tradition*, Cambridge University Press, Cambridge, 1994 [1983].

Canovan, Margaret, 'Patriotism is not Enough', *British Journal of Political Science*, 30, 3 (2000).

Carrier, N. H., and J. R. Jeffery, *External Migration: A Study of the Available Statistics*, HMSO, London, 1953.

Castells, M., 'Immigrant Workers and Class Struggles in Advanced Capitalism: The Western European Experience', *Politics and Society*, 5, 1 (1975).

Chalmers, George, *Opinion of Eminent Lawyers on Various Points of English Jurisprudence*, Reed & Hunter, London, 1814.

Chesterman, John, and Brian Galligan, *Citizens without Rights: Aborigines and Australian Citizenship*, Cambridge University Press, Cambridge, 1997.

Chou, Wan-yao, 'The Kominka Movement in Taiwan and Korea: Comparison and Interpretation', in Peter Duus, Ramon H. Myers and Mark R. Peattie (eds), *The Japanese Wartime Empire, 1931–1945*, Princeton University Press, Princeton, NJ, 1996.

Çinar, Dilek, 'From Aliens to Citizens: A Comparative Analysis of Rules of Transition', in Rainer Bauböck (ed.), *From Aliens to Citizens: Redefining the Status of Immigrants in Europe*, Avebury, Aldershot, 1994.

Close, Paul, *Citizenship, Europe and Change*, Macmillan, London, 1995.

Cobban, Alfred, *The Nation-State and National Self-Determination*, Collins, London, 1969 [1945].

Cockburn, Alexander, *Nationality: The Law Relating to Subjects and Aliens Considered with a View to Future Legislation*, William Ridgeway, London, 1869.

Cohen, Robin, *Frontiers of Identity: The British and the Others*, Longman, London, 1994.

Colley, Linda, *Britons: Forging the Nation 1707–1837*, Yale University Press, New Haven, CT, 1992.

Commission on the Future of the Multi-Ethnic Britain, *The Future of Multi-Ethnic Britain*, Profile Books, London, 2000.

Committee of the Society of Conservative Lawyers, *Toward a New Citizenship*, Conservative Political Centre, London, 1975.

Community Relations Commission, *The Participation of Ethnic Minorities in the General Election, October 1974*, Community Relations Commission, London, 1975.

Craig, F. W. S. (ed.), *British General Election Manifestos, 1900–1974*,

Macmillan, London, 1975.

—— *Conservative and Labour Party Conference Decisions 1945–1981*, Parliamentary Research Service, Chichester, 1982.

Crocker, W. R., *On Governing Colonies*, George Allen & Unwin, London, 1947.

Cunningham, W., *Alien Immigrants to England*, Frank Cass, London, 1969 [1897].

Dale, Iain (ed.), *Conservative Party: General Election Manifestos, 1900–1997*, Routledge, London, 2000.

Darwin, John, 'Imperialism in Decline?', *Historical Journal*, 23, 3 (1980).

—— *Britain and Decolonisation: The Retreat from Empire in the Post-War World*, Macmillan, London, 1988.

Davies, W. E., *The English Law Relating to Aliens*, Stevens & Sons, London, 1931.

Dawson, R. M., *The Development of Dominion Status, 1900–1936*, Oxford University Press, London, 1937.

Deakin, Nicholas *et al.*, *Colour, Citizenship and British Society*, Panther Books, London, 1970.

De Hart, E. L., 'The English Law of Nationality and Naturalization', *Journal of the Society of Comparative Legislation*, 2 (1900).

—— 'The Colonial Conference and Naturalization', *Journal of the Society of Comparative Legislation*, 8 (1907).

Dicey, A. V., 'A Common Citizenship for the English Race', *Contemporary Review*, 71 (1897).

Dilke, C. W., *Greater Britain*, Macmillan, London, 1869.

Doyle, Michael W., *Empires*, Cornell University Press, London, 1986.

Dowty, Alan, *Closed Borders*, Yale University Press, New Haven, CT, 1987.

Dummett, Ann, 'The Acquisition of British Citizenship: From Imperial Traditions to National Definitions', in Rainer Bauböck (ed.), *From Aliens to Citizens: Redefining the Status of Immigrants in Europe*, Avebury, Aldershot, 1994.

—— and Andrew Nicol, *Subjects, Citizens, Aliens and Others: Nationality and Immigration Law*, Weidenfeld & Nicoloson, London, 1990.

Edwardes, Michael, *The Last Years of British India*, Cassell, London, 1963.

Emerson, R., *From Empire to Nation*, Harvard University Press, Cambridge, MA, 1967.

Esman, Milton J. (ed.), *Ethnic Conflict in the Western World*, Cornell University Press, Ithaca, NY, 1977.

Falk, Richard, 'The Making of Global Citizenship', in Bart van Steenbergen (ed.), *The Condition of Citizenship*, Sage, London, 1994.

Faulks, Keith, *Citizenship in Modern Britain*, Edinburgh University Press, Edinburgh, 1998.

Favell, Adrian, *Philosophies of Integration: Immigration and the Idea of Citizenship in France and Britain*, Macmillan, London, 1998.

Fieldhouse, D. K., *The Colonial Empires: A Comparative Survey from the Eighteenth Century*, Macmillan, London, 1982 [1966].

Finlayson, Geoffrey, *Citizen, State, and Social Welfare in Britain 1830–1990*, Clarendon Press, Oxford, 1994.

Foot, Paul, *Immigration and Race in British Politics*, Penguin, Harmondsworth, 1965.

—— *The Rise of Enoch Powell: An Examination of Enoch Powell's Attitude to Immigration and Race*, Penguin, Harmondsworth, 1969.

Forsyth, William, *Cases and Opinions on Constitutional Law*, Stevens & Haynes, London, 1869.

Fransman, Laurie, *Fransman's British Nationality Law*, Fourmat Publishing, London, 1989.

Fraser, C. F., *Control of Aliens in the British Commonwealth of Nations*, Hogarth Press, London, 1940.

Freeman, Gary P., 'Can Liberal States Control Unwanted Migration?', *Annals of the American Academy of Political and Social Science*, 534 (July 1994).

Gainer, Bernard, *The Alien Invasion: The Origins of the Aliens Act 1905*, Heinemann Educational Books, London, 1972.

Gardner, J. P. (ed.), *Citizenship: the White Paper*, British Institute of International and Comparative Law, London, 1998.

Garrard, John A., *The English and Immigration 1880–1910*, Oxford University Press, London, 1971.

Gellner, E., *Nations and Nationalism*, Basil Blackwell, Oxford, 1994 [1983].

George, Stephen, *An Awkward Partner: Britain in the European Community*, Oxford University Press, Oxford, 1998 [1990].

Giddens, Anthony, *The Nation-State and Violence*, Polity Press, Cambridge, 1985.

Gordon, Charles, *et al.*, *Immigration Law and Procedure*, Matthew Bender, New York, 1998.

Gordon Walker, Patrick, *The Commonwealth*, Secker & Warburg, London, 1962.

Gregory, Robert G., *India and East Africa: A History of Race Relations within the British Empire 1890–1939*, Clarendon Press, Oxford, 1971.

Hammar, Tomas, *Democracy and the Nation State: Aliens, Denizens and Citizens in a World of International Migration*, Avebury, Aldershot, 1990.

Hancock, W. K., *Survey of British Commonwealth Affairs: Problems of Nationality 1918–1936*, Oxford University Press, London, 1937.

Hansen, Randall, *Citizenship and Immigration in Post-War Britain*, Oxford University Press, Oxford, 2000.

—— and Patrick Weil (eds), *Towards a European Nationality: Citizenship, Immigration and Nationality Law in the EU*, Palgrave, Houndmills, 2001.

Harris, José, *Private Lives, Public Spirit: Britain 1870–1914*, Penguin, Harmondsworth, 1994.

Heater, Derek, *Citizenship: The Civic Ideal in World History, Politics and Education*, Longman, London, 1990.

Held, David, *Democracy and the Global Order: From the Modern State to Cosmopolitan Governance*, Polity, Cambridge, 1995.

Heuston, R. F. V., 'British Nationality and Irish Citizenship', *International Affairs*, 26, 1 (November 1949).

Hobsbawm, E. J., *Industry and Empire*, Penguin, Harmondsworth, 1990 [1968].

—— *Nations and Nationalism since 1780: Programme, Myth, Reality*, Cambridge University Press, Cambridge, 1995 [1990].

Holland, R. F., *Britain and the Commonwealth Alliance 1918–1939*, Macmillan, London, 1981.

—— *European Decolonization 1918–1981: An Introductory Survey*, Macmillan, London, 1985.

Hoyt, Edward A., 'Naturalization under the American Colonies: Signs of a New Community', *Political Science Quarterly*, 2 (1952).

Huttenback, R. A., *Racism and Empire*, Cornell University Press, London, 1976.

Jackson, J. A., *The Irish in Britain*, Routledge, London, 1963.

Jones, J. Mervyn, *British Nationality Law*, Clarendon Press, Oxford, 1956 [1947].

Joppke, Christian, *Challenge to the Nation-State: Immigration in Western Europe and the United States*, Oxford University Press, Oxford, 1998.

Judd, Denis, *Empire: The British Imperial Experience from 1765 to the Present*, HarperCollins, London, 1996.

Juss, Satvinder S., *Immigration, Nationality and Citizenship*, Mansell, London, 1993.

Justice, *Going Abroad: A Report on Passports*, Barry Rose, London, 1974.

Keith, A. Berriedale, *The Sovereignty of the British Commonwealth*, Macmillan, London, 1929.

—— *The Constitution Law of the British Dominions*, Macmillan, London, 1933.

Kendle, John Edward, *The Colonial and Imperial Conferences: A Study in Imperial Organizations*, Longman, London, 1967.

Kent, James, *Commentaries on American Law*, Little Brown, Boston, 1866.

Kettner, James H., 'Subjects or Citizens? A Note on British Views Respecting the Legal Effects of American Independence', *Virginia Law Review*, 62, 873 (1976).

—— *The Development of American Citizenship 1608–1870*, University of North Carolina Press, Chapel Hill, NC, 1978.

Kindleberger, Charles, *Europe's Postwar Growth: The Role of Labour Supply*, Oxford University Press, London, 1967.

Koessler, Maximilian, '"Subject," "Citizen," "National," and "Permanent Allegiance"', *Yale Law Journal*, 56 (1946–47).

Kyle, Keith, *The Politics of the Independence of Kenya*, Macmillan, London, 1999.

Kymlicka, Will, and Wayne Norman, 'Return of the Citizen: A Survey of Recent Work on Citizenship Theory', in Ronald Beiner (ed.), *Theorizing Citizenship*, State University of New York Press, Albany, NY, 1995.

Landa, M. H., *The Alien Problem and its Remedy*, P. S. King & Sons., London, 1911.

Latham, R. T. E., 'The Law and the Commonwealth', in W. K. Hancock (ed.), *Survey of British Commonwealth Affairs: Problems of Nationality 1918–1936*, Oxford University Press, London, 1937.

Layton-Henry, Zig, *The Politics of Race in Britain*, Allen & Unwin, London, 1984.

—— 'The State and New Commonwealth Immigration: 1951–56', *New Community*, 14, 1/2 (Autumn 1987).

—— *The Politics of Immigration: Immigration, 'Race' and 'Race' Relations in Post-War Britain*, Blackwell, Oxford, 1992.

—— and P. Rich (eds), *Race, Government and Politics in Britain*, Macmillan, London, 1986.

Linklater, Andrew, *The Transformation of Political Community: Ethical Foundations of the Post-Westphalian Era*, Polity Press, Cambridge, 1998.

Louis, William Roger, *Imperialism at Bay: The United States and the Decolonisation of the British Empire, 1941–1945*, Clarendon Press, Oxford, 1977.

—— 'The Era of the Mandates System and the Non-European World', in Hedley Bull and Adam Watson (eds), *The Expansion of International Society*, Clarendon Press, Oxford, 1984.

—— and Hedley Bull (eds), *The 'Special Relationship': Anglo-American Relations since 1945*, Clarendon Press, Oxford, 1986.

Low, Eugenia, 'The Concept of Citizenship in Twentieth-Century Britain: Analysing Contexts of Development', in Peter Catterall,

Wolfram Kaiser and Ulrike Walton-Jordan (eds), *Reforming the Constitution: Debates in Twentieth-Century Britain*, Frank Cass, London, 2000.

Lynch, Philip, *The Politics of Nationhood: Sovereignty, Britishness and Conservative Politics*, Macmillan, London, 1999.

Lyons, F. S. L., *Ireland since the Famine*, Weidenfeld & Nicolson, London, 1971.

Macdonald, I., and N. Blake, *Immigration Law and Practice in the United Kingdom*, 4th edn, Butterworths, London, 1995.

Madden, A. F., 'Constitution-Making and Nationhood: The British Experience – An Overview', *Journal of Commonwealth & Comparative Politics*, 26, 2 (July 1988).

Mangat, J. S., *A History of the Asians in East Africa, 1886 to 1945*, Clarendon Press, Oxford, 1969.

Mann, Michael, 'Ruling Class Strategies and Citizenship', *Sociology*, 21, 3 (1987).

Mansergh, Nicholas, *Survey of British Commonwealth Affairs: Problems of Wartime Co-operation and Post-War Change 1939–1952*, Oxford University Press, London, 1958.

—— *The Commonwealth Experience*, Weidenfeld & Nicolson, London, 1969.

—— and Penderel Moon *et al.* (eds), *Constitutional Relations between Britain and India: The Transfer of Power 1942–7*, HMSO, London, 1981.

Marshall, T. H., *Class, Citizenship and Social Development*, Anchor, New York, 1965.

—— 'Citizenship and Social Class', in T. H. Marshall and Tom Bottomore, *Citizenship and Social Class*, Pluto Press, London, 1992.

Maxon, Robert M., 'Social and Cultural Changes', in B. A. Ogot and W. R. Ochieng (eds), *Decolonization and Independence in Kenya 1940–93*, James Currey, London, 1995.

Mead, Lawrence, *Beyond Entitlement: The Social Obligations of Citizenship*, Free Press, New York, 1986.

Meehan, Elizabeth, *Citizenship and the European Community*, Sage, London, 1993.

Miles, Robert, *Racism*, Routledge, London, 1995 [1989].

Miller, J. D. B., *Survey of Commonwealth Affairs: Problem of Expansion and Attrition 1953–69*, Oxford University Press, London, 1974.

Miller, W. L., 'What was the Profit in Following the Crowd? Aspects of Conservative and Labour Strategy since 1970', *British Journal of Political Science*, 10 (1980).

Minty, Leonard Le Marchant, *Constitutional Laws of the British Empire*, Sweet & Maxwell, London, 1928.

Monroe, Elizabeth, *Britain's Moment in the Middle East: 1914–1956*,

Chatto & Windus, London, 1963.

Moore, R. J., *Making the New Commonwealth*, Clarendon Press, Oxford, 1987.

Morrow, Rising Lake, 'The Early American Attitude toward the Doctrine of Expatriation', *American Journal of International Law*, 26 (1932).

Murray, James N., *The United Nations Trusteeship System*, University of Illinois Press, Urbana, IL, 1957.

Naoroji, Dadabhai, *Poverty and Un-British Rule in India*, Ministry of Information and Broadcasting, Government of India, Publication Division, 1962 [1901].

Nathan, Manfred, *Empire Government: An Outline of the System Prevailing in the British Commonwealth of Nations*, Harvard University Press, Cambridge, MA, 1930.

Norton, Philip, 'Intra-Party Dissent in the House of Commons: A Case Study. The Immigration Rules 1972', *Parliamentary Affairs*, 29 (1976).

Oldfield, Adrian, *Citizenship and Community: Civic Republicanism and the Modern World*, Routledge, London, 1990.

Oliver, Dawn, and Derek Heater, *The Foundation of Citizenship*, Harvester Wheatsheaf, London, 1994.

Ollivier, Maurice (ed.), *The Colonial and Imperial Conferences from 1887 to 1937*, 3 vols, E. Cloutier, Ottawa, 1954.

Oppenheim, L. F. L., and H. Lauterpacht, *International Law*, I, Longman Green, London, 1955 [1905].

Parekh, Bhikhu, 'Integrating Minorities', in Tessa Blackstone, Bhikhu Parekh and Peter Sanders (eds), *Race Relations in Britain: A Developing Agenda*, Routledge, London, 1998.

Patterson, Sheila, *Immigration and Race Relations in Britain 1960–1967*, Oxford University Press, London, 1969.

Parry, Clive, *Nationality and Citizenship Laws of the Commonwealth and of the Republic of Ireland*, Stevens & Sons, London, 1957.

Paul, Kathleen, *Whitewashing Britain: Race and Citizenship in the Postwar Era*, Cornell University Press, London, 1997.

Peach, Ceri, *West Indian Migration to Britain*, Oxford University Press, London, 1968.

Plender, Richard, *International Migration Law*, 2nd rev. edn, Martinus Nijhoff, London, 1988.

Porter, Bernard, *The Refugee Question in Mid-Victorian Politics*, Cambridge University Press, Cambridge, 1979.

Proctor, Harvey, and John Pinniger, *Immigration, Repatriation and the Commission for Racial Equality*, Monday Club, London, 1981.

Rau, B. N. (ed.), *India's Constitution in the Making*, Orient Longman,

Bombay, 1960.

Reynolds, David, *Britannia Overruled: British Policy and World Power in the 20th Century*, Longman, London, 1991.

Reynolds, Susan, *Kingdoms and Communities in Western Europe 900–1300*, Clarendon Press, Oxford, 1984.

Ridley, Jasper, *Lord Palmerston*, Constable, London, 1970.

Roberts, Adam, 'Beyond the Flawed Principle of National Self-Determination', in Edward Mortimer and Robert Fine (eds), *People, Nation and State: The Meaning of Ethnicity and Nationalism*, I. B. Tauris, London, 1999.

Roche, Maurice, *Rethinking Citizenship: Welfare, Ideology and Change in Modern Society*, Polity Press, Cambridge, 1992.

Rose, E. J. B., *et al.*, *Colour and Citizenship*, Oxford University Press, London, 1969.

Rose, Hannan, 'The Immigration Act 1971: A Case Study in the Work of Parliament', *Parliamentary Affairs*, 26 (1973).

Ross, J. M., 'English Nationality Law: *Soli* or *Sanguinis*?', *Grotian Society Papers*, Martihus Nijhoff, The Hague, 1972.

Rothchild, Donald, 'Citizenship and National Integration: The Non-African Crisis in Kenya', *Studies in Race and Nations*, Centre of International Race Relations, Graduate School of International Studies, University of Denver, 1, 3 (1970).

—— *Racial Bargaining in Independent Kenya: A Study of Minorities and Decolonization*, Oxford University Press, London, 1973.

Salmond, John W., 'Citizenship and Allegiance', *Law Quarterly*, 18, 69 (1902).

Sanders, David, *Losing an Empire, Finding a Role: British Foreign Policy since 1945*, Macmillan, London, 1990.

Shaw, W. A., *Letter of Denization and Acts of Naturalization for Aliens in England and Ireland*, Publications of the Huguenot Society of London, London, 18 (1911).

Shills, Edward, 'Primordial, Personal, Sacred and Civil Ties', *British Journal of Sociology*, 7 (1951).

Shimazu, Naoko, *Japan, Race and Equality: The Racial Equality Proposal of 1919*, Routledge, London, 1998.

Shutter, Sue, *Immigration & Nationality Law Handbook*, Joint Council for the Welfare of Immigrants, London, 1995.

Singh, Anita Inder, 'Imperial Defence and the Transfer of Power in India', *International History Review*, 4 (November 1982).

Smith, Anthony D., *The Ethnic Origins of Nations*, Basil Blackwell, Oxford, 1986.

—— *National Identity*, Penguin, Harmondsworth, 1991.

Smithies, Bill, and Peter Fiddick, *Enoch Powell on Immigration*, Sphere, London, 1969.

Sørensen, Jens Magleby, *The Exclusive European Citizenship: The Case for Refugees and Immigrants in the European Union*, Avebury, Aldershot, 1996.

Soysal, Yasemin Nuhoğlu, *Limits of Citizenship: Migrants and Postnational Membership in Europe*, University of Chicago Press, Chicago, IL, 1994.

Spencer, I. R. G., *British Immigration Policy since 1939: The Making of Multi-Racial Britain*, Routledge, London, 1997.

Stein, Rokkan, and Derek Urwin (eds), *The Politics of Territorial Identity: Studies in European Regions*, Sage, London, 1982.

Studlar, D. T., 'Policy Voting in Britain: The Coloured Immigration Issue in the 1964, 1966 and 1970 General Elections', *American Political Science Review*, 72 (1978).

Tanaka, Hiroshi, 'Nihon no Taiwan, Chosen Shihai to Kokuseki Mondai' (Japanese Imperial Rule over Formosa and Korea and the Issue of Nationality), *Horitsu Jiho*, 47, 4 (1975).

Tannahill, J. A., *European Volunteer Workers in Britain*, Manchester University Press, Manchester, 1958.

Tarring, Sir Charles James, *Chapters on the Law Relating to the Colonies to which are Appended Topical Indexes of Cases Decided in the Privy Council on Appeal from the Colonies, Channel Islands and the Isle of Man and of Cases Relating to the Colonies Decided in the English Court otherwise than on Appeal therefrom*, Stevens & Haynes, London, 1913 [1893].

Thatcher, Margaret, *The Path to Power*, HarperCollins, London, 1995.

Tinker, Hugh, *Separate and Unequal: India and the Indians in the British Commonwealth 1920–1950*, C. Hurst, London, 1976.

Torpey, John, *The Invention of the Passport: Surveillance, Citizenship and the State*, Cambridge University Press, Cambridge, 2000.

Turner, Bryan S., 'Outline of a Theory of Citizenship', *Sociology*, 24, 2 (1990).

Unit for Manpower Studies, *The Role of Immigrants in the Labour Market*, Unit for Manpower Studies, London, 1977.

van den Heever, C. M., *General J. B. M. Hertzog*, A. P. B. Bookstore, Johannesburg, 1946.

Vaughan, Bevan, *The Development of British Immigration Law*, Croom Helm, London, 1986.

Vincenzi, Christopher, *Crown Powers, Subjects and Citizens*, Pinter, London, 1998.

Walters, F. P., *A History of the League of Nations*, Oxford University Press, London, 1952.

Walzer, Michael, 'The Civil Society Argument', in Chantal Mouffe (ed.), *Dimensions of Radical Democracy: Pluralism, Citizenship, Community*, Verso, London, 1992.

Wambu, O., *Empire Windrush*, Gollancz, London, 1998.

Ward, John Manning, *Colonial Self-Government: The British Experience 1759–1856*, Macmillan, London, 1976.

Wasserstein, Bernard, *Britain and the Jews of Europe: 1939–1945*, Clarendon Press, Oxford, 1979.

Weis, Paul, *Nationality and Statelessness in International Law*, Sijthoff & Noordhoff, Alphen aan den Rijn, 1979 [1956].

Wendt, Alexander, 'Constructing International Politics', *International Security*, 20, 1 (Summer 1995).

Wheare, K. C., *The Constitutional Structure of the Commonwealth*, Clarendon Press, Oxford, 1960.

White, Robin M., 'Hong Kong: Nationality, Immigration and the Agreement with China', *International and Comparative Law Quarterly*, 36, 3 (July 1987).

Wigley, Philip G., *Canada and the Transition to Commonwealth, British–Canadian Relations 1917–1926*, Cambridge University Press, Cambridge, 1977.

Wilson, D. H., 'King James and Anglo-Scottish Unity', in W. A. Aiken and B. D. Henning (eds), *Conflict in Stuart England*, Jonathan Cape, London, 1960.

Wilson, Harold, *The Labour Government, 1964–1970: A Personal Record*, Weidenfeld & Nicolson, London, 1971.

Zebel, Sydney H., 'Fair Trade: An English Reaction to the Breakdown of the Cobden Treaty System', *Journal of Modern History*, 12, 2 (1940).

—— 'Joseph Chamberlain and the Genesis of Tariff Reform', *Journal of British Studies*, 7, 1 (1967).

Index